JUSTICE AND HUMANITY

JUSTICE
AND
HUMANITY

Edward F. Dunne, Illinois Progressive

Richard Allen Morton

SOUTHERN ILLINOIS UNIVERSITY PRESS
Carbondale and Edwardsville

00   99   98   97   4   3   2   1

Frontispiece: Edward F. Dunne, ca. 1905. Courtesy of the Illinois State Historical Library.

Publication of this work was made possible in part through a grant from the Oliver M. Dickerson Fund of the Department of History, University of Illinois at Urbana-Champaign.

Library of Congress Cataloging-in-Publication Data

Morton, Richard Allen, 1951–
    Justice and humanity : Edward F. Dunne, Illinois progressive / Richard
Allen Morton.
        p.   cm.
    Includes bibliographical references and index.
    1. Dunne, Edward F., 1853–1937. 2. Illinois—Politics and
government—1865–1950. 3. Chicago (Ill.)—Politics and government—
To 1950. 4. Progressivism (United States politics) 5. Governors—
Illinois—Biography. 6. Mayors—Illinois—Chicago—Biography.
I. Title.
F546.D92M67   1997
977.3' 1104' 092—dc20
[B]   96-20415
ISBN 0-8093-2095-9 (alk. paper)   CIP

CONTENTS

PREFACE

At the death of Edward Fitzsimons Dunne, a political insider said that he had been "to Illinois what Woodrow Wilson had been to the nation . . . far and away the most Progressive state executive Illinois ever had."[1] An Irish Catholic Democrat from Chicago, Dunne was the only person to have served as both mayor of that city and governor of the state. He was also one of the most consistent champions of the humane liberalism that dominated politics between the 1890s and the 1920s known as progressivism.

As chief executive of the state from 1913 to 1917, he supported a variety of progressive reforms with far-reaching effects: he championed woman suffrage, expanded state responsibility for overseeing workmen's compensation and teachers' pensions, oversaw the beginning of large-scale improvements of the state's roads, and created several regulatory boards and commissions, including the Public Utility Commission, the Efficiency and Economy Commission, and the Legislative Reference Bureau. More or less independently of the legislature, he encouraged major reforms in the operation of state prisons and juvenile facilities. Sadly, his most dearly sought goal—the addition of the initiative and referendum to the state constitution—was denied to him and to Illinois by a single vote in the House of Representatives.

He was not, of course, the only governor to support progressive reform. Certainly both his immediate predecessor and successor, Charles S. Deneen and Frank O. Lowden, were also supportive of legislation that may be defined as progressive. Yet, it can be convincingly argued that during the six months of the Forty-eighth General Assembly in 1913, the only time that he held the initiative, he was at least as effective in addressing the progressive agenda as Deneen was in his eight years as the state's executive or Lowden was in his four.

Moreover, he was the only one of the three men who was a "progressive at heart."[2] Deneen, although always a moderate and enlightened leader, remained throughout his career a politician of the old school. By the same token, Lowden, who was his own man as governor, had supported and had been supported by some of the state's most notorious and distinctively unprogressive figures, including Chicago's infamous mayor William Hale Thompson.

Further, Edward F. Dunne's contribution to progressivism in Illinois was not limited to his term as governor. In a public career that began with his election as a Cook County Circuit Court judge in 1892, and that found its first climax in a stint between 1905 and 1907 as Chicago's "first truly reformist mayor," he was always an advocate of progressive change. Even after leaving office, he remained a steadying political voice until as late as 1932 when he was seventy-nine years of age.[3]

His services as a reform governor and mayor would in themselves justify a biography, but such a study also offers important insights into the political dynamics of progressive Illinois. It was his unique role as an elected public official to bring into government the direct influence of Chicago's circles of social activists for the only significant time during this period. As mayor, he was the creature of one set of those circles, and as governor, he openly used their support and ideas in the conception and pursuit of his program.

With both impeccable reformist and party credentials, he was singularly qualified to play this role. All of which is not to say that he was anything like a universal reform leader; one of the ironies of his term as mayor was that his opposition came not so much from conservatives as from other reformers who did not share his goal of expanded government. Nor was he seen as "one of the boys" by the professional politicians who ran both major parties; he was genuinely a little too idealistic for that. Rather, this is to say that when, as in 1905 and 1912, the political order was eclipsed by demands for reform, Edward F. Dunne was the one person acceptable to reformers and politicians alike.

Not the least important factor in his success in becoming the state's most visible symbol of reform during this era was his personality. Repeatedly characterized as "optimistic," he was a humble man without the messianic or demagogic tendencies of many reformist leaders of the period, and his honesty and dedication to the public service were never seriously questioned. Those qualities were especially crucial in his dealing with the professional politicians, who never suspected him of having ulterior motives or of being a major threat to their entrenched power. Such was the mildness of his temperament that he was accused by some of not being ruthless enough. Indeed, his failures (like his successes) can in large part be explained in terms of his unwillingness to engage in arm twisting.

This study also speaks to some of the larger interpretative issues of urban progressivism, and it strongly buttresses a thesis proposed by Melvin Holli.

In his biography of Mayor Hazen Pingree of Detroit, Holli finds two types of urban progressives: (1) "structural reformers" (who were generally of native stock and upper middle class), who sought to restructure government to make it smaller, more efficient, as well as honest, and (2) "social reformers" (who drew their support from labor and the ethnic communities), who wished to expand government as the agency of public welfare while making it more accessible and democratic.

In his associations and aims, Edward F. Dunne was clearly and consciously a social reformer. For one thing, he counted among his friends and allies such prominent advocates of broader governmental responsibility as Henry Demarest Lloyd, Clarence Darrow, Jane Addams, Raymond Robins, and Louis Post. For another, his programs as mayor and governor, and especially his advocacy of the municipal ownership of public utilities (during the pursuit of which as mayor he functioned as the disciple of Cleveland's Mayor Tom L. Johnson, who had earlier counted Pingree as his mentor), were archetypally social reformist in character. In addition, those who resisted him were found among groups that neatly fit Holli's definition of structural reformers.[4]

Despite its obvious significance, his career has been largely overlooked. It was not until 1968 that the first survey of his administrations appeared in an article by John D. Buenker, who interpreted him primarily in reference to his urban ethnic origins—something that this study tends to deemphasize. Three years later, a dissertation by Richard D. Becker that focused on the mayoral years was completed at the University of Chicago, and from that point, only short biographical sketches have appeared.[5]

That may have been due to the fact that Dunne's role in progressive Illinois has been overshadowed by that of Governor Frank O. Lowden, thanks to an excellent biography by William T. Hutchinson that was published in 1957. It also may be a result of the sparsity of primary resource material concerning Dunne; his private papers were destroyed by fire in the late 1930s, and the state archives are shockingly incomplete. It has proven possible, however, through the extensive use of newspapers and the manuscript collections of some of his contemporaries to compile a fairly complete account. One pleasant surprise during the research for this effort was the discovery of his personal scrapbooks that besides containing the random letter included the kinds of memorabilia that can be priceless. Also extremely helpful was the information provided by the late Edward Dunne Corboy, the governor's grandson, who was old enough to remember his grandfather well and whose family stories are most useful.[6]

In part because of the nature of the sources, but also because the daily operation of politics is often as significant as the results, this study seeks to provide a close, chronological account. It also deliberately emphasizes the importance of leadership in the shaping of events and public policy. Similarly, it consciously eschews any efforts to portray Dunne and his contemporaries as abstractions or as pawns of irresistible social and political trends. Thus, the reader will come away with an understanding of a very real person (and his political world) who made an enduring contribution to his time and state through his vision of justice and humanity.

A project such as this is never a solitary effort. At the top of the list of the myriad people to whom I owe a debt of gratitude must go J. Leonard Bates, professor emeritus of the Department of History at the University of Illinois. Not only did Professor Bates direct me to this subject, but he has been a consistent source of direction and encouragement. Similarly, Robert Sutton, also professor emeritus at Illinois, has always been a friend and mentor. Not inconsequential either has been the financial support provided for this book by Professor Charles Stewart and the faculty of the Department of History of the University of Illinois through the agency of the Oliver M. Dickerson Fund.

John Hoffman, director of the Illinois Historical Survey at the Library of the University of Illinois and a man who has perhaps the greatest historiographical knowledge of Illinois of anyone alive, deserves my sincere thanks for innumerable favors. Helping with their advice and criticism have been my colleagues at Clark Atlanta University—Professor Alma Williams, Professor Janice Sumler-Edmond, Professor Thandekile Mvusi, and Claudia Combes—as well as my former colleagues Norman C. Camp III, Hooshang Fourodastan, Cynthia Martin, Lisa Broehl, and Tamara Botkin. Important, too, have been the patience and enthusiasm of James Simmons and the staff of the Southern Illinois University Press. Most directly assisting with the preparation of this book has been my sister, the lovely and talented Rebecca Blosser. Finally, I must thank my wife, Sharon, for her belief and emotional buttressing.

Justice and Humanity

1

ORIGINS OF A SOCIAL REFORMER

The roots of the politics of Edward F. Dunne lie ultimately in the soil of Ireland, not the Emerald Isle of leprechauns and fairy tales, but the Ireland of hunger, poverty, and centuries of British exploitation. It was this Ireland that fomented the ill-fated revolt of 1848 that brought about the forced immigration to the United States of such prominent Irish leaders as Michael Doheny, Thomas D'Arcy McGee, and Richard O'Gorman. Less well known was another political refugee from this uprising, a young man of sixteen years from Tullamore, King's County (now Offaly County) named Patrick William Dunne. "P. W.," as he was commonly known, became an American citizen but retained an active, if shadowy, role in the cause of Irish independence. Moreover, he inspired his family, including the future mayor of Chicago and governor of Illinois, with not only a pride in their Irish heritage but also with an instinctive sympathy for the oppressed and downtrodden.[1]

When he arrived in America in 1849, P. W. was fired with the flames of both revolution and love. He soon arranged for the passage of his fiancée, Mary Lawlor. Mary came from a "well-to-do" family of contractors "who built docks on Galway Bay," and she arrived with her own lady's maid. The couple quickly married and settled in Waterville, Connecticut, where Mary gave birth to their first child, a son whom they named Edward Fitzsimons.[2]

Sometime in 1855, P. W. moved his family to Peoria, Illinois. Attracted to the growing local transportation and light manufacturing center by the opportunities offered in railroad construction, P. W. prospered in a number of enterprises, including a contracting firm, a boiler works, a flour mill, and eventually a brewery. He also achieved a measure of local prominence. He was the captain and organizer of the Emmett Guards, an Irish militia unit, and during the Civil War he served on the Peoria City Council.[3]

The home environment of the Dunne family, which grew to include four children—Edward, Mary, Patrick Sarsfield, and Francis—was one of stability and love. It was also one greatly influenced by P. W.'s continued devotion to the Irish cause. He frequently entertained visiting Irish leaders in his home, and his decision to send his children to the local public schools, instead of the readily available Catholic academy, was possibly his response to the Church's disapproval of the Fenians, of which he was likely a member.[4]

Thus it was that "Eddy" Dunne graduated from the Peoria Public High School on 30 June 1870. As was the custom of the time, each of the sixteen graduates presented a short speech, Eddy's being "Liberty, Its Martyrs and Champions." Already a promising orator, his speech was singled out by a local newspaper as "one of the best school orations that it has been our privilege to hear for many years."[5]

It was decided that for his higher education Edward should attend Trinity College in Dublin, Ireland. This decision, too, was affected by P. W.'s Irish nationalism. In Edward's words of sixty-four years later: "My father believed because Robert Emmett [an Irish revolutionary] was a student there when he was executed, and because they had statues of Oliver Goldsmith and Edmund Burke in front of it, that it must be a good school so I was sent there."[6]

He began his studies at Trinity on 10 October 1871. Among his classmates was Oscar Wilde, of future literary fame, whom he "knew quite well" but found "unsociable." Wilde and Dunne were in fact rivals for scholastic honors. At the end of his freshman year, Dunne was third in the "First Rank" in "Logics" and fourth in metaphysics in a total class of seventy-seven. After his second, or "sophister," year, he had risen to be second in metaphysics.[7]

In 1874, he was unable to return to Trinity to complete his final year. He always explained this as being a result of his father "going broke." The Dunne family legend adds some detail by suggesting that P. W. had suffered financial reverses because of his heavy contributions to the Irish cause; he was said to have given more than one hundred thousand dollars by his death in 1921. Edward remained in Peoria and helped recoup the family fortune in the brewery business. Apparently things went well, for in 1876 P. W. was elected to a term as an "independent democrat" to the Illinois House of Representatives. Here he gained some attention by opposing a bill legalizing certain types of tenant farmership similar to those found in Ireland.[8]

In 1877, the family moved to Chicago, where P. W. began a new career in the heating oil business. It was here "sometime in the 1880s" that Mary Lawlor Dunne died as a result of a street accident. For Edward, the move meant he could continue his higher education through attendance at the Union College of Law while also studying in the office of a local attorney.[9]

He graduated in 1878 and set up a practice of family and business law with William J. Hynes, a former Arkansas congressman and officer of the

Cook County Treasury. A third partner, former Judge Walter B. Scates, briefly joined the firm, but he was replaced by William J. English. By 1890, Dunne was practicing alone, but he soon began another firm with Francis McKeever, who remained his partner until at least 1913.[10]

Three years after beginning his legal career, Edward, now aged twenty-seven, moved out of the family home to marry. His bride was Elizabeth F. Kelly, the daughter of a local businessman, Edward F. Kelly, and his wife, Kitty Howe Kelly. The couple were married on 16 August 1881, and it was truly a love match. His wife and children were to remain the enduring centers of Dunne's life. In all, they had thirteen children, nine of whom lived until adulthood.[11]

Now established as a reasonably successful lawyer and family man, Edward began showing a "fairly active interest in the various public questions being agitated at the time."[12] This interest did not apparently express itself in much direct participation, as it is certain that he did not become involved in the city's partisan politics. He may have been one of the young lawyers who agitated for pardons for the anarchists convicted after the Haymarket Riot in 1886, but the evidence, or lack of it, suggests that his interest was in fact rather passive.[13]

That was to change when he was chosen by the unruly Democratic county convention in 1892 to run to fill a vacancy on the Circuit Court of Cook County left by the death of Judge George Driggs. Dunne, himself, had little to do with securing his own nomination. Rather, it was achieved by the direct action of two powerful sponsors, Judges Richard Pendergast and Murray Tuley.[14]

Prendergast and Tuley headed a loose faction that had included Driggs and that was centered in the Cook County judicial machinery. They were also popular leaders among Chicago's middle-class, or "lace curtain," Irish. Pendergast, "the white-headed eagle of drainage reform," had been born in Ireland, and he had been elected judge in 1882. Murray Tuley had been born in Louisville, Kentucky, in 1827, and he had fought in the Mexican War. More recently, he had served as the city's corporation counsel (an appointive position with a status second only to that of the mayor), before winning election in 1887 as a circuit judge.[15]

It was Tuley who was to be the most important single influence upon Dunne's early public career. He became his "political father"; it was he who not only sponsored Dunne among the leadership of the Democratic Party but also provided him with an entry into Chicago's reformist political circles. Something of the aspirations he held for his young protégé was revealed when, soon after they met, he sent him a multivolume biography of Thomas Jefferson. With the gift came the advice: "Be like him!" Years later Dunne freely admitted that Tuley was "the man who made me mayor."[16]

It is uncertain under what circumstances Dunne met Tuley and Prendergast. It is possible that as a bright and charismatic young man, who was moreover Irish, he attracted them solely on his own merits. It is tempting, however, to see in all of this the hand of P. W. Dunne. P. W. was active among the city's Irish, and there are indications that he had retained some political prestige. He may well have arranged the sponsorship of his eldest son and brightest hope. Regardless, 1892 was a year that saw Democratic victories in the national, state, and county elections, and Edward F. Dunne was easily elected with almost no effort on his part.[17]

As judge, he rose to a position of prominence and respect within his party and city. He became known for his common sense in dealing with ordinary people caught up in the maze of the law. In situations where poverty was a mitigating factor, he regularly returned light or suspended sentences. That practice was not just a reflection of his genuinely kind heart, it was also a result of his recognition of the role of environment in promoting crime. In his words, "the policy and tendency of all intelligent governments is to prevent crime, not by increase of penalties as a deterrent, but by ameliorating the conditions which provoke or tempt to crime."[18]

In addition, he showed a concern for maintaining constitutional liberties. In the so-called free speech case of 1901, he made his reputation in this regard. It all began when Judge Elbridge Hanecy cited the editor and a reporter of the *Chicago American* for contempt. It seemed that the newspaper had scathingly criticized Hanecy for allowing the consolidation of the city's ten largest gas companies. Although the criticism had occurred after the case had been settled, the judge had sentenced the two men to jail terms for conduct "prejudicial to the public welfare." Dunne received the case on a writ of habeas corpus. After listening to impressive arguments from a defense team that included Clarence Darrow and former Governor John Altgeld, he not only dismissed the sentences but also established a precedent by declaring that criticism, fair or not, was "one of the incidents and burdens of public life" and that any legal effort to stifle it would be unconstitutional.[19]

While on the bench, Edward Dunne also carefully cultivated his standing among his fellow Irish. He was always good for a strong speech against British oppression in Ireland, and while never apparently directly involved in the American end of the Irish revolutionary movement, he was active in the various Irish fraternal organizations in the city. As early as 1897, he was recognized by the *Irish-American*, a newspaper published in New York City, as being both "the son of our esteemed friend, 'P.W.' Dunne" and "well and honorably known in connection with Irish national affairs," in his own right.

It was no accident, then, that when the Chicago Knights of the Red Branch reorganized in 1903 as the Irish Fellowship Club, it was Edward F. Dunne who was elected their first president.[20]

During this same period, he was known as "an intense believer in the principles of the Democratic party," which after 1896 meant for him the principles of William Jennings Bryan.[21] He was in the hall during the Democratic National Convention when "the Great Commoner" gave his famous "Cross of Gold" speech, and like most of those present, he was instantly converted. Bryan's stands on the silver issue, American overseas imperialism, which Dunne saw as similar to the British occupation of Ireland, and other issues closely mirrored his own.

It was on Bryan's behalf that he led, in February 1898, a contingent out of the Iroquois Club, the organization of the local Democratic leadership. At issue was the club's condemnation of the free coinage of silver. Joining with him in his exodus were Tuley, Altgeld, Clarence Darrow, and others. Together they formed the Monticello as a rival club, with Dunne as president. In November 1899, the Iroquois surrendered as the two groups reunited. Dunne became the Iroquois's new president, and Bryan became his permanent ally.[22]

In 1899, the Illinois Democratic Party published a volume of biographies of its more notable members. Edward F. Dunne was among those specially featured. He was praised for being a conscience of the party, for his honesty, and, not the least, for having been overwhelmingly reelected in 1897 (as he was to be in 1903). Yet, he was also accurately described as "not taking an active part in party politics"; the secession from the Iroquois had little directly to do with the party's real factional battles.[23] For all of his success on the bench, for all his popularity, he remained on the outskirts of the circles of power. He did not have a personal organization, and he did not control anything like the patronage that was necessary to build one. Nonetheless, in what was in terms of Chicago's political history an unprecedented miracle, he was to rise in six short years to become mayor of the city.

The magnitude of this achievement becomes clear in light of the almost Byzantine complexity of Chicago's political culture. One source for that was the very fact of the city's tremendous growth in successive ethnic waves. First, there were the Irish, by far the most politically active, followed by Germans, Swedes, Norwegians, Poles, Bohemians, Italians, and others. Each of those groups created a new political constituency, with their own leaders and special interests.[24]

Many of these immigrants, moreover, contributed politically through their involvement in Chicago's vigorous labor tradition; the Chicago Federation of Labor was always an active player in the Democratic Party and city politics.

Others brought a more radically defined working-class consciousness, and it was no accident that Chicago became the headquarters of the Socialist Party of America and the considerably more extreme Industrial Workers of the World.

Another source of the complicated nature of Chicago's politics was the city's governmental structure. A bureaucratic nightmare of ill-defined and overlapping authority, it provided for literally hundreds of niches for patronage and personal political power. Besides the mayor and the seventy (in 1905) members of the city council, there were a multitude of independently elected offices, including the city clerk, the city treasurer, the Metropolitan Sanitary Board, the Board of Review (a taxing authority), the commissioners of Cook County, the county sheriff, the county treasurer, and most of the judiciary. Moreover, several of the boards that were chosen by the mayor, such as the Board of Education and the Public Library Board, in fact functioned independently and were protected by a tradition of noninterference. The largest sources of patronage were the three park boards, and those, too, were independent of the mayor and city council. The West and North Park District Boards were appointed by the governor of Illinois, while the South Park Board was selected under a curious 1869 law by the twenty Cook County circuit judges. Added to this were the county's ten United States congressmen, nineteen state senators, fifty-seven state representatives, and the federal postmaster, all of whom exercised a degree of political power.[25]

The end result was a political culture frequently described as "feudal." While the city's politics with its bosses of all sizes and kaleidoscopic panorama of shifting alliances and rivalries did resemble those of the Middle Ages, Chicago at the turn of the century (unlike medieval Europe), as yet had no kings. It did, however, have some grand dukes who through personal charisma and skill were able to amass ongoing power.

Among the city's Republicans, there were three main leaders and rivals for control of the party. In the North End, there was Fred Busse, who served as state treasurer, Chicago's postmaster, and mayor. The South Side was the territory of Charles S. Deneen. He became governor of Illinois and eventually a United States senator. William Lorimer was the boss of the West End, and he used his power to become both a United States congressman and senator. It was Lorimer's organization that was later to provide the basis for that of William Hale Thompson, the city's most notorious mayor and politician.[26]

The most prominent Democrat at this point was Carter Harrison II. He was the son and namesake of a martyred, five-term mayor who had been assassinated in 1893. At his father's death, he had inherited a powerful organization propelling him into the mayor's office in 1897 for the first of five terms of his own. Although native-born, and upper middle class, Harrison enjoyed a wide appeal among Chicago's working people. A self-described "conservative liberal," Harrison oversaw a loose faction that ranged from Michael "Hinky Dink" Kenna and "Bathhouse John" Coughlin, the infamous aldermen of the First Ward, to some of the city's most honest and civic-minded citizens.[27]

Directly opposing the Harrison faction in the Democratic Party was the growing machine of Roger Sullivan and former Mayor John Hopkins. Where the Harrison forces were essentially a personality cult, the Sullivan/Hopkins group was almost a shadow government. Sullivan, who was a political genius and the increasingly dominant partner, organized his followers into a tightly disciplined and highly effective chain of command. With little interest in issues other than those of power, he became for many the living symbol of politics at its worst. One reformer was to later characterize him as the chief of the "black horse cavalry of Illinois that has raided every legislative body in the interest of corporate wealth."[28] Nonetheless, after battling Harrison for more than twenty years, he was to emerge as almost absolute ruler of the city and state party. It was his organization that was to be the direct ancestor of the famous Democratic machine that came into full bloom under Mayor Richard J. Daley.

The engine of Chicago's politics was not, however, solely fueled by patronage, profit, and power. In this period reform was becoming in the Windy City, as in many American urban centers, an increasingly potent force. In Chicago, reformers closely followed the pattern discovered and outlined by Melvin G. Holli in his study of Detroit.[29]

First, there were the "structural reformers." Mostly Republican, native-born, and middle class, these "good government" people, or "goos goos," sought "efficiency" in government through the rooting out of corruption. Firm believers in private enterprise and individual effort, they worked for a limited municipal authority that freed of graft would theoretically guarantee lower taxes as well as the enforcement of public order and private morality. Many went further and called for a "restructuring" of city government by either the introduction of a professional city manager or the replacement of the traditional mayor and city council with elected commissioners.

Highly organizational, these structural reformers were the force behind such groups as the Citizens Association, the Civic Federation, and the Chicago Bureau of Public Efficiency. They found their greatest success in the formation of the Municipal Voters League in 1896, which by 1905 had gone far toward removing the "Gray Wolves," or aldermen thought to be corrupt, from the city council. Prominent among the structural reformers in Chicago were Kent E. Keller, George Cole, and Walter Fisher.[30]

"Social reformers," on the other hand, were less concerned with bringing businesslike efficiency into government than they were dedicated to transforming municipal power into an agency of the people's will and welfare. Accordingly, they supported the initiative and referendum as a means of making government more democratic, expanding its role to include city ownership and operation of the public utilities and public baths while guaranteeing decent employment and living conditions for working men and women. As a rule, they also exhibited an almost paranoiac antipathy toward the "interests" of corporate wealth, which they saw as the corruptors of society. At the same time, they showed far less concern for issues of private morality. In part, this was due to concerns for individual liberty, but it followed, too, from their belief that private "immorality," such as overindulgence in alcohol consumption by the working class, was the result of an oppressive environment.

The social reformers in Chicago included a wide span of people, including liberal judges, most of the leadership of the unions, and middle-class social activists. They also tended to congregate in the Democratic Party. Included among their leaders were Judge Murray Tuley, Clarence Darrow, Henry Demarest Lloyd, Jane Addams, and Louis Post. Moreover, they were very conscious of being part of a national movement, and they were in close contact with Cleveland's Mayor Tom L. Johnson, Toledo's Mayor Samuel M. Jones, and others. In addition, William Jennings Bryan, who always treated Chicago and Illinois as special concerns, was highly influential among them. Newspaper support was provided by William Randolph Hearst, who used his publications throughout the United Sates, including the *Chicago American* and the *Chicago Examiner*, to further his own political ambitions through the promotion of social reformist causes.

It is highly likely that Edward F. Dunne had at least the beginnings of a social reformist outlook well before he became judge. It is difficult to imagine that the son of P. W. Dunne, that ardent Irish nationalist and liberal Democrat, could have had much sympathy for corporate power, or by the same token, that he could have been apathetic toward the plight of the industrial working class. After his election as judge, his speeches, which he gave with increasing frequency around the city, showed an unmistakable social reformist stamp. In one address, for instance, he made the direction of his sympathies clear when he stated: "We who believe in the democratic gospel of equal rights to all and special privileges to none, we who think the Government [sic] was organized and should be conducted so as to secure the greatest good to the greatest number, have noted with amazement and alarm that . . . the interests and welfare of the common people were being openly violated and ruthlessly trampled on in the interest of monopoly and an overgorged plutocracy."[31]

For all his verbal ardor, however, he did little else at this point of his career to promote any particular social reformist cause. After 1900, this began to change as he embraced with both arms what was not only the primary goal of Chicago's social reformers but also the single most important municipal issue in the city—the question of the public ownership and operation of the street railways. It was to be his road to the mayor's office.

Public transportation was a problem that virtually all the urban centers of the United States struggled with in this period as they sought to cope with their own unprecedented growth. In Chicago, the issue assumed a special urgency. That was so not only because there was a consensus of opinion that the city had the worst street railway system in the country but also because a combination of the machinations of the traction companies, which seemed to exemplify predatory capitalism at its worst, and a series of unfortunate laws and concessions made any simple solution appear impossible.[32]

Chicago's first misfortune was to be divided for franchise purposes by the state legislature in 1853 into three divisions based upon the two branches of the Chicago River. That led to the creation of a number of companies to serve the public's need for inexpensive transportation. Service was, therefore, uncoordinated, and as each company possessed a separate charter, the city was unable to easily force broad improvements.[33]

In 1865, the state legislature further complicated matters by enacting the infamous Ninety-nine Year Act. Passed as an amendment to the charters of the city's three largest traction companies, the law extended these franchises from the original twenty years to ninety-nine years. The situation became confused when a new state constitution was written in 1870 that withheld from the legislature the right to grant street franchises without a municipality's permission. Since the Chicago City Council had never approved the Ninety-nine Year Act, it now appeared to be invalid. In its charter of 1875, the city was careful to limit street franchises to twenty years, and three years later, the traction companies were even compelled to begin paying the city for the use of the streets.[34]

In 1883, the issue reappeared when two of the companies' franchises expired, and the sitting corporation counsel, Francis Addams, ruled that the Ninety-nine Year Act was still valid. Not wishing to recognize this claim, but hoping to avoid a legal battle, the city council extended the charters for another twenty years, and this became their regular practice as the other franchises expired.[35]

By the 1890s, the traction companies had become big business in Chicago; in 1900 more than a million and a quarter passengers were riding streetcars provided by ten surface railway companies, two of which grossed more than a million dollars annually.[36] The growing economic power of these companies began creating apprehensions about their political influence. These fears appeared to be realized in the activities of Charles Yerkes, the controlling officer of the West Chicago Company and the North Chicago Railway Company. It was he who was behind the Humphrey bill of 1897. Had it not been narrowly defeated in the Illinois House of Representatives, it would have allowed the extension of the charters of the traction companies to a fifty-year term. He followed this defeat by successfully lobbying the legislature to pass in 1898, the Allen law, which gave the city the choice of either disadvantageous fifty- or twenty-year charters. Such was the power of the companies with the Chicago City Council, that an ordinance extending all franchises to fifty years was soon enacted. Mayor Carter Harrison vetoed the measure, and a mob formed outside city hall that threatened to lynch any alderman who did not sustain the mayor's action—the mayor's action was sustained. Yerkes, seeing the writing on the wall, consolidated his holdings into two new companies, the Union Traction Company, with 303.7 miles of track the city's largest, and the Chicago Consolidated Traction Company. He then left for England, where he gained fame and fortune by building the London subway.[37]

Such was the background of suspicion and anger that formed the seedbed in which the growing public demand for municipal ownership germinated. By 1900, both major parties had come to routinely endorse the notion, and in 1899, former Governor John Altgeld ran on an independent municipal ownership ticket for mayor against his enemy Carter Harrison. He was unsuccessful, but in 1902, the enfranchised citizenry made its will known when it voted by a margin of 142,826 to 27,998 for public ownership in an advisory referendum.[38]

Although the notion enjoyed wide support, there was a sizable number among Chicago's leadership who had their doubts. Many structural reformers were cynical about the city's ability to run the multimillion-dollar traction industry efficiently and without corruption. Others, while attracted to the idea, balked at the tremendous costs and legal battles that municipal acquisition of the existing traction properties would entail.[39]

For the social reformers, municipal ownership was an ideological imperative. It fulfilled at once their vision of an expanded government providing essential services and their goal of using the governmental apparatus to protect the people from the "interests." They had no doubts about its practicality. Chicago, they liked to point out, had been running its own waterworks since 1857, and it had owned and operated a lighting plant since 1887. Moreover, they cited the fact that many European cities, such as Berlin and Glasgow, owned and ran their own traction systems. Closer to home, there were the examples of Cleveland, Toledo, and Detroit to be followed.

Edward F. Dunne spoke out on the traction issue as early as October 1898, when he called the Allen law "a stench in the nostrils of the people." In 1900, he visited Europe and toured various municipally owned systems, and in March 1902, he issued a public statement that argued that city ownership of the traction systems would bring greater service at a cheaper cost. In May of the same year, he was appointed by Mayor Harrison to a committee that included Andrew M. Lawrence, the local publisher of the Hearst papers, and Daniel L. Cruice, a social reformer and activist, as well as two aldermen to prepare sample bills that would provide for municipal ownership of not only the street railways but electrical and gas services as well. They were also charged with composing a bill that would bring direct primaries for candidates for city office. The committee made its report in December, and although it was not directly implemented, it was one source for the Mueller bill.[40] Introduced into the legislature in January 1904, by Senator Carl Mueller, this bill gave the city permission to "own, construct, acquire, purchase, maintain, and operate street railways," if three-fifths of the voters approved in a referendum. To finance this, the city could issue bonds if two-thirds of the voters so voted. Moreover, by a simple majority vote, any new franchises with the traction companies could be overturned.[41]

The Mueller bill attracted a wide support in Chicago. Even those who did not necessarily believe municipal ownership was practical saw in the bill a means to force concessions from the traction companies. To lobby for passage of the bill, Mayor Harrison appointed a committee with Judge Tuley and Dunne as its most prominent members. Because Tuley was unable to make the trip, it was Dunne who became de facto chairman when the group went to Springfield. Doubtlessly in part due to their efforts, the bill passed the legislature and was signed into law in May 1904.[42]

Where Dunne as yet had confidence in Mayor Harrison's ability and willingness to bring municipal ownership to Chicago, other social reformers did not. In May 1902, the Public Ownership Party was formed, with Clarence Darrow and Daniel L. Cruice on its executive committee. They fronted a slate of candidates in the November elections, and they succeeded in electing Darrow to the Illinois House of Representatives. After the election, a new organization was put together with strong support from the teamsters and boxmakers unions that called itself the United Labor Party. They immediately began to boom Darrow for mayor. It was Dunne who dissuaded Darrow from making the race, arguing that a Darrow candidacy would only throw the elections to the Republicans. The United Labor Party ran Cruice instead, who was considerably less well known than Darrow, and Harrison narrowly won reelection in the April 1903, elections.[43]

After the elections, a new entity appeared, the Municipal Ownership Delegate Convention. Among those participating were Darrow, Cruice, former Judge William Prentiss, Margaret Haley of the Chicago Federation of Teachers, John J. Fitzpatrick of the Chicago Federation of Labor, and Jane Addams of Hull House fame. Organized in June 1903, by Henry Demarest Lloyd, and led by him until his death in September, the purpose of the Delegate Convention was to pressure the city council and the mayor into implementing the Mueller law. Speeches and presentations were made, but the chief thrust of their efforts centered in obtaining signatures for a petition to place on the ballot in the April 1904 elections: an advisory referendum proposition that questioned whether under the Mueller law the city council "should proceed without delay to acquire" the street railways. Also to be asked was whether the traction companies should meanwhile be compelled "to give satisfactory service." Both propositions were approved when the elections were held by a better than two-to-one margin.[44]

Edward F. Dunne was not involved in the Delegate Convention's efforts, although he was clearly sympathetic to its aims. Moreover, he maintained close ties with its leadership. For instance, on 29 November 1903, he presided at Lloyd's memorial service, where he shared the platform with Darrow, Mayor Johnson, and Mayor Jones.[45]

His faith in Mayor Harrison was not, however, blind, and his patience was not infinite. When the city council's Committee on Local Transportation (created in 1901 to deal with the traction problem), at last, after a year and a half of tortuous negotiations, announced a settlement with the Union Traction Company and the Chicago City Railway Company, he was intensely disappointed. Despite the votes of the referenda of 1902 and 1904 and Mayor Harrison's publicly voiced commitment, the agreement did not point the way to immediate municipal ownership. Rather, it provided for twenty-year franchises, improved services, and the possibility that the city could begin buying traction property after thirteen years. It was a not entirely unreasonable effort, especially given the fact that federal Judge Peter Grosscup, in his role as overseer of the bankruptcy of the Union Traction Company, had ruled in May 1904, the Ninety-nine Year Act valid, but for Dunne and the social reformers this "tentative ordinance," as it became known, was a betrayal. The Municipal Ownership Delegate Convention immediately announced their plans to defeat the "tentative ordinance" on the ballot as provided for in the Mueller law, and Edward F. Dunne gave a speech.[46]

It was to be the single most important address he ever delivered. Appearing at a meeting of the Fortschrift Turner Society on 4 September 1904, he emotionally attacked the settlement and the mayor; he went so far as to accuse Harrison of selling out to the traction companies, and of breaking his word. Although William Prentiss and Daniel Cruice also spoke at the same meeting, it was Dunne's words that excited the city. Such were the passions that his address invoked that not long afterward he found himself, to his surprise, being given a standing ovation upon entering a public theater.[47]

Also excited by Dunne's words, although in a different way, was Carter Harrison, who suggested that the judge would be better served if he used his brains more than his lungs. In truth, Dunne's speech and the reaction it caused were the final fatal blows to any hopes the mayor may have had for his own renomination and reelection. He had just that summer lost control of the county and state party to the Sullivan/Hopkins faction, and even within his own organization, he was having to deal with disaffection. Always a realist when forced to be, Harrison let it be known in November that he would not seek another term.[48]

Even before Harrison's withdrawal, Dunne was being boomed for the mayor's office. He, however, repeatedly denied any interest in running. In part because of this reluctance, Judge Tuley issued on 15 January 1905 a public letter that insisted he enter the race as a matter of duty. Dunne shifted his position somewhat. He no longer asserted that he did not want to be mayor, but nor did he announce he was seeking the nomination. Instead, he let it be known that he would accept if chosen, but that "no one has been requested by me to raise a finger towards securing the nomination." Nonetheless, a "committee of 100" was soon organized and began working vigorously on his behalf.[49]

By early February 1905, it was certain that he would be nominated; the *Chicago Tribune* was reporting that 804 of 988 delegates to the upcoming city convention had declared for him. Somewhat ironically, among his earliest supporters was the Sullivan-Hopkins faction that, concerned about recent Democratic reverses at the polls, saw in him a sure "vote getter." Equally ironic was the fact that a number of social reformers, especially those associated with the labor unions, preferred former Judge William Prentiss, and Prentiss only reluctantly withdrew in face of the overwhelming momentum of the Dunne bandwagon. Last to fall into line was the Harrison organization. Dunne was careful to make some conciliatory statements about the mayor to the delegations from the various wards that were visiting him almost daily, and while Harrison remained "personally unfriendly," his supporters were not about to oppose a man who was so obviously headed for the nomination.[50]

It is not too difficult to understand why Edward F. Dunne was such an attractive candidate for the nomination in 1905. He possessed a series of qualities that in retrospect seem to have made him the ideal choice. Not the least of those was the fact that although he had solid social reformist credentials, he was also a good party man. By the same token, although a regular Democrat, he had never been involved in his party's factional wars, and he could be supported by all. He, in addition, enjoyed the very real advantage of being Irish, but although of an ethnic background, he also was known for his respectability and honesty, qualities likely to appeal to Chicago's native-born middle class.

On 11 February, he officially announced that while not seeking the office, he would accept the nomination, and on 25 February 1905, he was chosen unanimously by the city convention. The platform, which he composed, set out his proposed plan to bring municipal ownership to Chicago. First, the city was to cease all franchise negotiations and begin talks with the object of purchasing all traction property. Should these discussions fail, the city should begin condemnation proceedings, while temporarily licensing the companies until they were complete. After the properties were acquired, a referendum would be held to determine if the people still desired municipal ownership and operation. The platform, in addition, also called for city ownership of all gas and electrical services, while including the usual promises of better law enforcement and a more efficient government.[51]

The Republicans, too, in their nomination of John Maynard Harlan, reflected the public concern over the traction issue. A lawyer who had sought the nomination twice before, he had helped to negotiate the "tentative ordinance." He had originally been a supporter of immediate municipal ownership, but he had evolved to a position close to that held by Carter Harrison. He now favored short-term franchises with a thorough modernization of the systems, followed by municipal acquisition after a number of years.[52]

In the early weeks of the campaign, Harlan virtually had the field to himself. Dunne was still maintaining the posture that the office was seeking him, and he declined to actively campaign. Harlan, unable to counter the simple and compelling slogan of immediate municipal ownership, sought to impeach Dunne of guilt by association. First, the Republican candidate insisted that the real issue of the campaign actually centered around William Randolph Hearst, and then he hit upon the fact that Dunne was being supported by Michael "Hinky Dink" Kenna and others thought to be unsavory. These tactics had some effect. For instance, Raymond Robins, a well-known social activist and superintendent of the Municipal Lodging House, issued a statement of support for Harlan because "the masters of the underworld" were for Dunne.[53]

Finally, after the county committee of the Democratic Party passed a resolution urging him to do so, Dunne in mid-March began to campaign. Once committed, he showed an untiring vigor as he stumped the city at as many as four meetings a day with a campaign team that included Tuley, Darrow, Colonel J. Hamilton Lewis, Judge Samuel Alschuler, and Joseph Medill Patterson, maverick scion of the family that owned the *Chicago Tribune*. Generally not deigning to answer Harlan, Dunne, as a rule, tended to ignore the Republican candidate and concentrated his fire against the traction companies. That was less true of his supporters. The Hearst newspapers delighted in portraying Harlan as a tool of J. P. Morgan, and Darrow, especially, took to defining the Republican candidate's primary purpose as the delivery of "the streets to the New York-Wall Street syndicate."[54]

As the election approached, it became increasingly clear that Dunne was headed toward victory. A few days before the balloting, James O'Leary, "King of the Bookmakers," calculated that the Democratic candidate was a five-to-one favorite, while the Dunne camp confidently predicted victory by as many as 45,000 votes. Harlan, of course, disagreed, and he claimed the election would be his by 25,000 votes. In fact, when the votes were counted after the election on 4 April, Edward F. Dunne won with majorities in 22 of the 35 wards. By the final tally, Dunne received 161,189 votes to 138,671 given to Harlan. He did especially well in the traditionally Democratic working-class wards, and his margins in the German-Irish Twenty-ninth and Thirtieth Wards were overwhelming. Moreover, in the city's outskirts, middle class and usually Republican, he showed greater strength than any previous Democratic mayoral candidate.[55]

His triumph was more than merely personal. In the same election, the "tentative ordinance" was overturned by a margin of 153,323 to 30,279. Simultaneously, by a slightly smaller percentage, the voters approved a proposition that called for the municipal acquisition of the traction systems using bonds as authorized by the Mueller law.[56]

Edward F. Dunne's election as mayor was greeted with jubilation by social reformers throughout the nation. One sympathetic writer proclaimed him "a sincere prophet of a new municipal era," while William Randolph Hearst, who was even then preparing for his unsuccessful bid for the mayor's office of New York City, wired his congratulations for "Chicago's splendid service to the nation." At the annual Jefferson's Day banquet, held not long after his inauguration, he was praised by William Jennings Bryan and Mayor Tom L. Johnson as a dynamic new leader of the national movement for reform. To many of those present, including Darrow, Tuley, Prentiss, and Louis Post, it appeared certain that the millennium had come to Chicago at last. Or so it seemed.[57]

"I SHALL NOT RESIGN"

Edward F. Dunne was Chicago's "first truly reformist mayor," and indeed, with the possible exception of his friend William Dever (who served as the city's chief executive between 1923 and 1927), he was Chicago's only truly reformist mayor. His nomination and election transcended the existing political order and were genuinely revolutionary. Yet at the same time, his rise to power did not represent a true political "revolution." Although the darling of his party, his influence did not extend even so far as controlling the remainder of the city ticket, nor did his nomination reflect any meaningful change in the balance of power between the Harrison organization and the Sullivan/Hopkins machine. By the same token, the elections of April 1905 that swept him into the mayor's office did little to change the political complexion of the city council. As a result, Mayor Dunne's first year in office proved to be the most frustrating of his life as he confronted the reality that even in the most democratic of societies the openly expressed will of the people does not necessarily dictate the actions of their elected leadership.[1]

Things began pleasantly enough. The atmosphere was festive and relaxed when he was inaugurated in the council chambers on 11 April 1905. As many as fifteen hundred people, including a sizable delegation of his own family, were present to witness him taking the very simple oath of office on a platform that was a "bank of flowers and femininity." His inaugural address was equally succinct, as he acknowledged the achievements of his predecessor and rededicated himself to the difficult task of bringing municipal ownership to Chicago.[2]

As his primary assistant he chose Clarence Darrow, who was given the title of "special traction counsel to the mayor." Darrow was to be in charge of not only negotiating with the traction companies but also pursuing the city's ongoing legal fight against the Ninety-nine Year Act. Also directly and indirectly involved in the administration's traction policy was Dunne's corporation counsel, J. Hamilton Lewis. "Colonel" Lewis, as he was known for his rank in the Spanish-American War, had only come to Chicago in 1903 with a record of successful federal appointments and unsuccessful political campaigns. In Illinois he was to do much better, and he was Dunne's most loyal and powerful ally. With this team, Mayor Dunne expected to immediately attack the traction question. That, however, was not to be. Rather, he found his first challenge in coping with a massive teamsters strike that broke out in full force just days after his inauguration.[3]

The teamsters had struck before in Chicago, most recently in 1904, but never so violently, and the 1905 conflict threatened public order in a way that the city had not seen since the Pullman strike in 1892. It all began when the United Garment Workers struck against twenty-seven wholesale companies in November 1904. At issue was the closed shop that although guaranteed by existing contract had been threatened when Montgomery Ward and Company sent work to "unfair houses." Ward's nineteen resident garment workers walked out only to be replaced by nonunion men, and the strike was on. With the entry of the teamsters into the fray in the spring of 1905, the strike expanded from being a relatively minor dispute into what was called at the time "an advanced skirmish in the war which is to come between labor and capital the country over."[4]

It was in this spirit of class warfare that Montgomery Ward, together with the other major department stores—Marshall Field's; Farewell's; and Carson Pirie Scott— created through the agency of the Employers Association under the laws of West Virginia, the Employers Teaming Company to make nonunion deliveries. That, of course, made things worse, and the situation became truly dangerous when strikebreakers, including a large contingent of African Americans, were imported. The striking teamsters responded with fists, clubs, knives, "acid bombs," and bullets. On 29 April, the first strikebreaker was killed, and riot and anarchy became daily threats on the downtown streets.[5]

While Mayor Dunne was instinctively sympathetic to the cause of labor, he could hardly allow public chaos. After his first efforts at mediation were rebuffed by the employers, and after it became clear that he lacked sufficient moral force with the strikers to quell the violence, he met with Judge Murray Tuley and Jane Addams in later April, and together they decided that the best approach was to appoint a "blue-ribbon" panel to investigate the causes of the strike. Their apparent strategy being that the revelation of the true facts of the strike would cause the public to pressure the employers to be more reasonable. In fact, by the time the committee, which included Addams and a bevy of prominent citizens, issued its rather inconclusive report in mid-May, public opinion had swung decisively against the strikers. In part because of that, but also because of the growing specter of federal intervention, the mayor, on 10 May mobilized seventeen hundred extra policemen to guard the delivery wagons. The strike lingered on until July, when the strikers, unable to halt service and facing legal harassment, began piecemeal to return to work. The strike was unquestionably a political reversal for Mayor Dunne. It focused the city's attention away from the traction issue, thus robbing him of the momentum for municipal ownership his election had achieved, while his somewhat indecisive handling of the conflict left, in some circles, a lingering impression of weakness.[6]

Mayor Dunne had not, however, totally postponed his efforts to realize his traction program. Among his first acts in office was to accept the suggestion by Cleveland's Mayor Tom L. Johnson and to wire Glasgow, Scotland, for advice. Although somewhat bemused by the request, Glasgow governing council sent over James Dalrymple, the manager of their municipally owned traction system.[7] Dalrymple arrived in time to accompany Clarence Darrow and Louis Post, editor of *The Public* and fervent Dunne supporter, as well as the Marching Club of the Cook County Democracy, to Cleveland on 4 June for the annual Cuyahoga County Democratic picnic. A fine time was had by all, and on the instruction of their mayor (who was unable to attend because of the strike) Darrow and Post met with Mayor Tom L. Johnson; Antoine B. DuPont, Cleveland's traction engineer; Edward Bemis, a former University of Chicago professor and current head of the Ohio city's waterworks; and others to begin searching for a detailed solution to Chicago's traction question.[8]

Dalrymple was not, however, invited to take part in this conference. He had "keenly disappointed" Darrow with a speech that seemed to hedge on the feasibility of municipal ownership in Chicago. On 4 June, the Scottish expert left the Windy City for home, and his report, while not made public for nearly a year, was the source of harmful rumors that haunted Mayor Dunne in the months ahead.[9]

In late June, Johnson and Dupont twice traveled to Chicago to tour the traction systems and to confer further. In the course of these meetings, it was decided to forgo the Dunne campaign's condemnation plan as costly and full of legal obstacles and to introduce two new alternative schemes to achieve municipal ownership.[10]

The first, the "City Plan," provided for the immediate acquisition and operation of the street railways through the use of Mueller bonds. Predicated upon the eventual success of the city's efforts to overturn Judge Grosscup's ruling on the Ninety-nine Year Act, a prospect made more unlikely by a recent court affirmation of the Union Traction Company's subleases dating after 1875, the City Plan, as Dunne freely admitted, had important disadvantages. There was, of course, an inescapable problem of determining the true worth of the traction companies' property, but there was also the requirement under the Mueller law for a three-fifths majority in a public referendum if the city were to *operate* its own streetcar system. Simple municipal *ownership* needed only a simple majority vote.[11]

The mayor favored instead the "Contract Plan" as the alternative that satisfied at once the demand for municipal ownership and the need for "sound business principles" that were so dear to Chicago's structural reformers and others. That scheme called for the creation of a semipublic holding company, with the city council naming its incorporators. The company was to take over ownership and operation of the traction lines (beginning with the hundred or so miles available under Grosscup's 1904 ruling), rehabilitate them, and upon demand turn them over to the city for cost plus a reasonable rate of interest. It was not an irrational approach and, as an "Impartial Observer" in the *Review of the Reviews* noted, "highly creditable to the mayor's judgement."[12]

Despite the enthusiasm in some quarters for the plans, the city council greeted them upon their introduction on 5 July with something very much like indifference. They immediately sent the mayor's proposals to their Committee on Local Transportation, which sat on them for over a month.

Meanwhile, Mayor Dunne turned his attention to the city's street crime. Chicago, which General Ballington Booth of the altruistic Volunteers of America was soon calling "the wickedest of all cities," was suffering through a particularly vicious proliferation of muggings, assaults, and robberies. Even the mayor was not exempt, as he found when his own home was broken into in August. Accordingly, he appointed a tough new police chief named John C. Collins with instructions to attack the problem. The new chief created "flying squads" of detectives to make "lightning raids" upon saloons, pool halls, and other habitats of street criminals.[13]

Similarly, the mayor attempted to confine vice to Chicago's notorious Levee District. In this he received some criticism that he was legitimizing prostitution. He tried to explain: "I am afraid some of my friends . . . have got the wrong idea of my position," he stated, "my desire is to redistrict the territory into still narrower boundaries . . . that the evil should be confined."[14] In truth, Mayor Dunne, a man of great personal morality, recognized that there was as yet insufficient public support for an eradication of the vice district. Moreover, he realized that such a crusade might alienate some of the political support he needed to achieve municipal ownership.

If he were willing to tackle street crime and limit vice, he, like Tom L.

Johnson of Cleveland, Hazen Pingree of Detroit, and other social reformers, was unwilling to support unwarranted intrusions into the recreational activities of common people. He refused, for instance, to shut down the dance halls despite the fervent pleas of a reform group led by Mrs. Hannah G. Solomons. As Chief Collins put it, "people have to have some place for entertainment," and that it would be useless to try to "make a Sunday school out of Chicago."[15]

Not making a Sunday school out of Chicago also meant not enforcing the Sunday Closing Law for saloons. Long on the books, the law had been largely ignored by the government and police. Mayor Harrison had refused to implement it, and even Dunne's Republican opponent, John Harlan, had agreed it had no place in Chicago. In Dunne's words: "When an old and mildewed law has no public sentiment behind it, it is impossible of enforcement; it is repealed by the lack of public sentiment."[16] More generally, he simply felt it was unfair to take away from laboring men their chief center of recreation on the only full day that most of them had to themselves. Confident of the support of the majority of the citizenry, including a sizable group of German Americans to whom Sunday beer was a sacred institution, Dunne withstood months of tirades from Protestant pulpits, Woman's Christian Temperance Union meetings, and other such gatherings. As the months went by without a positive response from the mayor, those groups became more desperate in their tactics. First there were public prayer meetings, followed by demonstrations, and then an attempt to obtain an indictment of the mayor for failing to enforce the law. This last effort was thwarted when the state's attorney's office refused to become involved. Finally, Mayor Dunne quieted things a bit by offering to work for a public referendum on the issue.[17] Not daring to put the issue before the voters, the ministers and their allies allowed the issue, for the moment, to fade.

For all its holy passion, the Sunday closing crusade was, by mid-August, but a sideshow to the ongoing spectacle of the mayor and the city council locked in noisy combat over the Contract Plan. Following the submission of the mayor's plans and recommendations on 5 July, the council routinely referred them to the Committee on Local Transportation. Among neither the twelve members of the committee nor the seventy aldermen of the council did Dunne enjoy the support of the majority. In the council, there were three loose divisions on the traction question. The administration Democrats led by the Alderman William Dever numbered from twelve to thirty. At the other extreme were the "Gray Wolves." Almost by definition antireformist and rumored to be in the pay of the traction companies, the Gray Wolves were relics of Chicago's more wide-open past. Led by Alderman Edward "Sly Ed"

Cullerton, their number was calculated in 1905 by the Municipal Voters League at fourteen. In between were Republicans, Harrison and Sullivan Democrats, as well as others of varying shades of political opinion who, in general, had reservations about immediate municipal ownership and the Contract Plan. On the Committee on Local Transportation, the mayor could count on the unconditional support of only three of its twelve members.[18]

These numbers go far toward explaining why the committee sat on the traction issue until mid-August when it began hearings with representatives of the major traction companies. Although not officially "negotiations," the clear purpose was to seek some alternative settlement. Mayor Dunne, aware of this, sat in and dominated the proceedings. After hours of fruitless talks that spanned two days, he asked the companies' representatives to leave. He then embarked upon an emotional address in favor of his scheme. Pointing to the obstinacy and untrustworthiness of the companies, he promised that his plan would force a reasonable settlement—if it were only given a chance![19]

His appeal had little apparent impact. When the committee bothered to address the issue a month later, the objections to the Contract Plan swayed the day. Alderman F. I. Bennett, for instance, simply could not believe that adequate financing could be assured using Mueller bonds. Alderman William Maypole questioned whether the disruption of the "entire street railway system" that seemed promised by the mayor's plan "wouldn't make things worse than they are now." Dunne and his supporters attempted to answer these criticisms, but the committee, by a margin of eight to four, voted to defer further discussion of the traction question until the companies could make a counterproposal. This action was, in effect, a filibuster of the mayor's scheme. If the committee had simply voted down the Contract Plan, it would have gone to the full city council as a minority report. As things stood, however, the progress of the administration's program was halted without the political risk of the council being forced to commit themselves on the public record on the popular issue of municipal ownership.[20]

It was not as if the people of Chicago were unaware of the mayor's plan and the opposition it was meeting. Since Dunne had first announced the two proposals, a majority of Chicago's newspapers had engaged in a campaign to discredit them. Only Hearst's *American* and *Examiner* stood with the mayor, while the *Tribune*, the *Daily News*, the *Inter-Ocean*, and to some extent the Democratic *Journal*, all did their best to convince their readers of the impracticality of the mayor's ideas.

Cut off from an objective hearing in most of the press, Mayor Dunne took his case directly to the people in a series of speeches. In each of those talks he outlined the merits of his pet plan, attacked the traction companies as tools of outside capital, and chided the city council for opposing the will of the people. One speech, delivered on the night of 12 September, a few hours after the Committee on Local Transportation had shelved the Contract Plan, was especially fiery:

> You may ask why the administration has nothing thus far tangible to show for the months which it has been in power. I ask you to consider, first that the administration at its beginning faced the strike. I ask you also to remember the mayor is but one arm of the city government, the city council is the other arm. . . . One arm may be reaching out get this municipal ownership prize . . . but it will not be able to get it without the aid of the other arm. What if one arm does reach out, if the other remains prone by the side? What if one arm is paralyzed? What if the traction interests be hanging on to one arm? Can the city council and the committee afford to ignore the statement of the people?[21]

The implication that they were being "hung onto" by the traction companies angered many aldermen. One asked "what rule of ethics . . . made it immoral to disagree with the chief executive of a city."[22] Others were more charitable, blaming the passion of the moment for Dunne's heated remarks.

Now it was the turn of the traction companies to confound the mayor's hopes. In early September, the Chicago City Railway Company, in cooperation with the Union Traction Company, presented a proposal that was designed to undercut popular and council support for Dunne's versions of immediate municipal ownership. It called for a twenty-year lease, a waiver by the companies of all rights under the Grosscup ruling of 1904, and a generous sliding scale of compensation to the city for the use of the streets. Moreover, it also provided for such consumer needs as universal transfers, a five-cent fare, rehabilitation of the lines, and improved equipment. The most important clause for those who looked for some kind of municipal ownership was one that allowed the city to purchase the lines at any time based upon a mutually agreeable valuation of property and lease rights.[23]

Mayor Dunne opposed the proposal. Why, he asked, should the city create for the companies additional value by giving them a twenty year lease, and by what right did they seek to thwart the repeatedly expressed will of the people? He also found flaws in the city's proposed role in the assessment of the worth of the companies' property and rights.

To many who were concerned over the public transportation situation, but did not share the mayor's ideological commitment to immediate municipal ownership, it seemed he was quibbling, and he was clearly losing control of the situation. Even Clarence Darrow, his special traction counsel, was quoted as doubting the prospects of the Contract Plan, and such were the growing feelings of frustrations among his supporters that at one meeting of the Municipal Ownership League violence was openly threatened against the city council.[24]

To regain the initiative, he ordered the Committee on Local Transportation, in his capacity as presiding officer of the council, (1) to act upon the Contract Plan and (2) to cease all deliberation upon the traction companies' offer. This threw the issue to the entire city council, which either had to sustain or invalidate his action. On both counts he was overridden—on his first order by a margin of forty-three to twenty-one and on his second, by forty-five to eighteen. The mayor professed to be "satisfied" that at least the vote "cleared the air" and forced the council to commit itself on the public record. In that same spirit, he next ordered the committee to act upon the City Plan, but his directive was countermanded by a vote of thirty-seven to twenty-seven.[25]

As a final effort, he proposed that the traction issue be taken away from the Committee on Local Transportation and given to a special committee of thirteen to be appointed by him. Not surprisingly, the idea found little support as the council consigned it to oblivion by a vote of fifty-two to fourteen. To make matters worse, they also voted a resolution calling upon the mayor to release the Dalrymple report.[26]

Those council votes were perceived both locally and nationally as major, if not fatal, reverses for the cause of municipal ownership in Chicago. There were even suggestions that Mayor Dunne might resign. While he vigorously denied any such intention, the gloom that now covered his administration deepened still further when Clarence Darrow announced on 7 November that he was quitting as special traction counsel "in view of the present condition of the traction question." Darrow explained further that he had never enjoyed public office (he had been only an indifferent legislator), that he was "anxious" to avoid "the great deal of annoyance" that came with the job, and that he felt he could be "of no further use."[27]

It was widely rumored in Chicago, rumors later reported as fact by the contemporary writer Ida Tarbell, that Darrow had resigned because he was disillusioned with the mayor. Darrow himself called these rumors "rubbish," but he went on to allow that "Mayor Dunne may be too optimistic at times, but that is temperamental."[28] It is a fact, however, that the former special traction counsel did not campaign for Dunne in 1907, and the two men did not work closely together again until 1922. Dunne did not offer any meaningful comment on the resignation at the time, and he passed over the incident entirely in the autobiographical section of his *Illinois, the Heart of the Nation.*

Clarence Darrow, in his autobiography, completely ignores his tenure as Mayor Dunne's traction assistant.[29]

Clarence Darrow was not far off the mark in assessing his boss as having been overly optimistic. Mayor Dunne had been somewhat naive in assuming that his electoral mandate would be sufficient in itself to overcome the political complexities and obstacles of introducing municipal ownership. Moreover, he had grossly underestimated the determination of his opposition by allowing them time to organize during the teamsters strike; had the Contract Plan been composed and presented immediately after the inauguration, it may well have passed in the lingering afterglow of the election. Finally, he would have probably had greater success had he not been oblivious to the resentment engendered among many of Chicago's leadership by his reliance upon the advice of outside figures like Mayor Johnson in the construction of his traction policy.

Edward F. Dunne may have suffered from an overly strong faith in the ultimate goodness of humanity and in democracy, and he may have been apparently unaware of some of the harsher realities of Chicago's politics, but he was not a weak man nor one to be turned in the face of adversity. Indeed, following the effective defeat of his program in November 1905, he began to shed the role of the gifted political amateur and to assume a more dynamic, fighting stance. Nowhere was this more apparent than in the speeches he gave outside the city. Heretofore, in the aura of his newfound celebrity as the "prophet of a new municipal era," his addresses in such places as New York, Boston, Milwaukee, and Toledo had been relatively mild and confident. Now, he began to sound almost revolutionary. Speaking in Denver in January 1906, for instance, he attacked the "capitalists," whom he identified as the opposition newspapers, the country's leading financial circles, including most especially the House of Morgan, and the "swell clubs of the rich," whose "influence" had corrupted the people's representatives in Chicago.[30]

As radical as his rhetoric was becoming, however, when pressed, he was careful to explain that he was in fact "not a socialist" but that he believed "in what is called municipal socialism," where "public property should be utilized and operated by the public, and that no special privileges should be given to private persons in [the use of] public property." Obviously feeling that "public property" included public transportation on public streets, he therefore saw no contradiction between his traction program and his other belief that "private property should be exploited and utilized by private persons."[31]

Mayor Dunne was to find his renewed determination sorely tested in the months ahead as his policies continued to be a source of controversy. Almost immediately after the apparent demise of his traction plans, he submitted to the council (in response to a recent state law) a proposal to lower heating-and-light gas rates from the current 90 cents to 75 cents per one hundred cubic feet. He argued in his written communication that this was above or equal to the going rates in comparable cities, that the gas companies were already committed to this price by an agreement dating back to 1901, and that, moreover, the companies owed the city nearly $14 million in overcharges since that year. To publicize the issue, he attended the hearings of the gas committee of the council, and used these occasions to grill the executives of the gas companies, including the Democratic boss, Roger Sullivan, in his capacity as secretary of the Ogden Gas Company.[32]

The companies, almost needlessly to say, disagreed with the mayor's analysis. They claimed not only that there had been no overcharging but also that his calculation of production and distribution costs were completely unrealistic. Initially they insisted costs were 88.53 cents per one hundred cubic feet. Dunne and his corporate counsel, J. Hamilton Lewis, went to the other extreme and cited a letter from Edward Bemis, the head of Cleveland's municipally owned gasworks, which asserted that gas could be produced and distributed for as little as 45.45 cents.[33]

For all the passion and statistics of the administration's arguments, the city council remained unimpressed. When the gas corporations offered a compromise figure of 85 cents, they quickly accepted by a vote of fifty-eight to nine. Dunne vetoed the measure, and although he was "encouraged" that "the veto would be sustained," the council overwhelmingly overrode him.[34]

Even as he was seeking to lower gas prices, the mayor suffered a grievous personal loss in the death of Judge Murray Tuley on Christmas day, 1905. His seventy-eight-year-old mentor had become seriously ill in early December and had been removed to a sanitarium in Kenosha, Wisconsin. By Christmas Eve it became clear that Tuley would not survive, and Dunne's presence was urgently requested. He was reduced to tears as he bade his "political" father" good-bye, and the Judge took his hand and assured him, "You have not disappointed me, Edward." Tuley died the next day, and a memorial service was quickly arranged featuring Mayor Dunne and Jane Addams as the principal speakers."[35]

As genuinely grief-stricken as he was, Mayor Dunne was, if anything, made by his loss more determined to bring municipal ownership to the city. Speaking in Denver on 11 January 1906, he promised that this "movement . . . will win in the city of Chicago. It will win throughout the United States."[36] Less than a week after this speech, his optimism seemed to be realized as the city council unexpectedly on 18 January passed his City Plan.

Following the defeats of November, the mayor and his council support-

ers had continued more or less to routinely introduce variations of their traction schemes. Just as routinely, the city council had frustrated their efforts
and had even directed the Committee on Local Transportation to resume independent negotiations with the streetcar companies. It was therefore something of a shock to all concerned, Dunne called it a "flash of lightning," when
the Gray Wolves figuratively crossed the aisle to help ratify one of the mayor's
favorite traction plans. Consternation reigned even among the mayor's men.
William Dever, his floor leader, who was aware that Sly Ed and company had
changed their position to induce the traction companies to resume their subsi-
dies, was especially vocal in his insistence that the mayor renounce their support. Dunne was not worried about any possible taint upon the sacred cause,
and he brushed all such arguments aside.[37]

As encouraging as the council victory was, the City Plan under the provisions of the Mueller law still had to be approved by the voters in public referendum. Signatures were quickly gathered for three propositions to be placed
on the ballot in the upcoming April elections. The first asked the voters to
approve municipal ownership, the second concerned municipal operation, and
the third whether the city should refrain from negotiating franchises and instead proceed under the provisions of the Mueller law. Given the fact that in
the previous four years the people had voted for municipal ownership on three
occasions, things seemed very promising. Even as Mayor Dunne was beginning to campaign, however, a controversy emerged that threatened to divert
public attention and enthusiasm from municipal ownership, and it was one
that underscored the shifting nature of the alliances of urban progressivism.

It was a growing concern over street crime that was at the root of the
sudden popular demand for a higher license fee for saloons. The mayor, of
course, had been aware of the problem, and his police chief had initiated a
symbolic crackdown. Nonetheless, a series of violent and audacious crimes,
exemplified by the robbery and murder of a middle- class matron named Bessie
Hollister, led to mass meetings in February that demanded an increase in the
fee from the current five hundred dollars to one thousand dollars. Presiding
over these gatherings was a cross-section of the city's middle-class leadership, including prominent lawyers, ministers, and physicians. Not included
in their number, however, were the forces responsible for the clamor for Sunday closing—the issue was public order, not private morality. Indeed, the
local chapter of the Anti-Saloon League dismissed the movement as an effort
to merely raise liquor prices.[38]

It could not be denied that saloons were the meeting places of habitual
criminals and peddlers of vice; often the only difference between a saloon and
a brothel was the contents of a wallet. Nor could it be argued that there was

not an overabundance of drinking establishments. By a count made in 1903, there were in all 7,017 in the city, some of which boasted only a plank between two barrels as a bar. In contrast, there were but 398 schools and 2,875 policemen.[39]

On the other hand, for most urban workingmen the saloon was an established institution that together with a grueling job and an often overcrowded home, and sometimes a church, formed one of the centers of their lives. A saloon was just about the only place available where they could cash a check or stretch their earnings with the "free lunch" that came with a drink. More importantly perhaps, a saloon offered through the agents of drink and companionship a brief escape from the gray toil of existence.[40]

Recognizing this, the mayor at first opposed the proposed increase, while seeking to propitiate its proponents with a new set of police raids upon gambling joints and with police guards at dance halls. Those actions did little to muffle the outcry that came when a combination of administration forces and Gray Wolves voted to defeat the increase by a margin of thirty-five to thirty-two in mid-February. Dunne's support on this was very thin; not only did a motion to maintain the current fee fail by a vote, but even William Dever voted for the increase. Understanding that the issue could interfere with his hopes for traction reform, Dunne retreated to a position of neither endorsing nor supporting the saloon fee increase, and he declined to use his veto when the measure passed the council on 5 March by a vote of forty to twenty-eight.[41]

Not all of his supporters were pleased by this laissez-faire attitude. At one meeting of the Chicago Federation of Labor not long afterward, his name was hissed when mentioned, and "someone" engaged in a vituperative attack accusing him of closing "up the dance halls and saloons and everything just because he expected to get municipal ownership votes in return." This might be acceptable, "someone" implied, except that "he hasn't made any headway" toward solving the traction problem. Mayor Dunne called a meeting at Sherman House to explain, but the CFL, still miffed, declined to send a representative.[42] The mayor could afford to be somewhat complacent about this minor ripple of disaffection in the ranks. Just days later the United States Supreme Court at last announced its decision to overturn the Ninety-nine Year Act.

It had been a long battle through the judiciary with Clarence Darrow, who had remained head of the city's legal team after resigning as special traction counsel, arguing that not only did the state constitution of 1870 render the law void but that, in any case, it had been written to apply to only horse-powered streetcars. The Court accepted these arguments and finally ruled by a margin of six to three that the traction companies held no long-term rights to Chicago's streets. Chicago breathed a collective sigh of relief having been freed of the haunting specter of the traction companies holding a legal claim to the streets for an unimaginably long time. For the Dunne administration, the victory was especially sweet, and it went far toward countering an impression of ineffectiveness that was growing more general.[43]

Showing some political astuteness, the mayor chose the occasion of the announcement of the Court verdict to release the long-suppressed Dalrymple report. Despite the clamor of the opposition newspapers and the city council, Dunne had refused to allow it to be the subject of public scrutiny, claiming that since he had personally paid the expenses of the Scottish expert, the report was his private property. Still, the often exaggerated rumors of the report's contents were a continual source of embarrassment, and now seemed to be the best opportunity to dispose of it once and for all.[44]

It was not too difficult to understand his reluctance to have the report become public knowledge. Dalrymple indeed had observed that Chicago's traction situation was a mess and that basic improvements were needed. Also, he had recommended that municipal ownership should be introduced at some point. For all that, however, he advised that the city first should make every effort to work with the traction companies because "from my knowledge and experience of what it means to operate a municipal street railway system that the municipalities of the United States are not quite ready to successfully initiate this work."[45] The reason for that, the implication was clear, was the country's and especially Chicago's political structure.[45] This, of course, was exactly what many critics of municipal ownership had been saying all along.

Mayor Dunne, who had an infinite faith in the ultimate goodness of the nation's and Chicago's political system, had dismissed those objections out of hand, and even as the report was being publicized, he was continuing to do his best to use the political order to bring about his cherished municipal ownership. The campaign for the ratification by referendum of his traction scheme had been naturally boosted by the Supreme Court decision, and it seemed little affected by the Dalrymple report. With Alderman William Dever and Corporate Counsel J. Hamilton Lewis, the mayor hammered into the heads of the voters in meetings throughout the city the potential benefits of immediate municipal ownership: it would solve the traction tangle, he insisted, by bringing lower fares and more efficient service, and it would have the added advantage of raising the pay and lowering the hours of the traction workers.[46]

The administration forces were also using the campaign to secure a more friendly city council. With thirty-five of the seventy aldermanic seats up for election, and with the fact that they had won some victories in the February primaries, the Dunne camp was optimistic. Some of these contests inspired the mayor's direct intervention. Perhaps the most important of those was the race in the working-class and traditionally Democratic Nineteenth Ward, where the party had split on its choice to replace the retiring Fred Ryan. On one side, there were the "regular" Democrats, in this case pro-Dunne, who supported Simon O'Donnell, who had won the primary. On the other side were the "independent," or pro-Harrison, Democrats who were running J. B. Bowler as their candidate. Two of the administration's most vocal critics, the *Tribune* and the *Daily News*, although both Republican in affiliation, supported Bowler. Dunne, as well as Dever and Lewis, made frequent appearances in the ward on O'Donnell's behalf, and it was clear that the mayor was staking his prestige on the outcome. Given the fact that the Nineteenth had, in 1905, returned a strong Dunne majority, it seemed a good bet.[47]

The elections proved to be a disappointment. To be sure, the voters returned majorities on all three propositions. However, where a majority vote was sufficient for the city to begin municipal ownership, the margin of barely 50 percent for municipal operation and for financing this process by issuing bonds was far from the three-fifths majority as required by the Mueller law. Nor could the mayor have been encouraged by the council races. The Democrats did gain three seats, but none of the new aldermen proved to be especially friendly to the administration or its goals. Even in the Nineteenth Ward, which approved the three propositions by large votes, Dunne's candidate, O'Donnell, lost to Bowler. The hostile *Chicago Tribune* calculated under the headline "A Black Eye for the Mayor" that Dunne's council opposition had actually increased with only seventeen (eleven Democrats and six Republicans) aldermen now counted as being in his corner.[48]

The mayor and the proponents of immediate municipal ownership did their best to put on a good face. Dunne proclaimed the election as "a victory of great moment, a greater victory than many people now understand." The *Chicago American* heralded the returns as a "glorious victory." It went further into its accustomed realm of hyperbole and even announced an increase in the strength for municipal ownership on the city council. As events were to show, it was the *Tribune* that was the better prophet.[49]

During his first year as mayor, Edward F. Dunne had largely eschewed the usual practices of Chicago politics. He had treated his mission to achieve immediate municipal ownership as one that was above partisan considerations. Not only had he neglected to organize an enduring power base in his own party (his distribution of patronage had succeeded primarily in alienating both the Harrison and Sullivan factions), but also he had done little to cultivate further support for his program among the city's sitting leadership. His mandate, he believed, had come directly from the people, whose will in the end would prove to be irresistible. The elections of April 1906 were thus a sobering experience. It was clear that popular support for his version of traction reform still remained, but it was equally clear that a new approach was needed if he were ever to translate that will into results.

3

CHICAGO'S RADICAL MAYOR

As far as his critics were concerned, the administration of Edward F. Dunne had been fatally injured by the April elections. The *Chicago Tribune*, among the mayor's most consistent detractors, wrote within weeks his political obituary, declaring that "the next mayor, whether he be a republican [*sic*] or democrat [*sic*] will not be a man of one idea and that an impracticable one."[1] In truth, this assessment seemed well founded in reality. The mayor's power had been anchored in a nonpartisan popular demand for an immediate rectification of the traction situation, and as the elections underscored, this base had been severely eroded by the council battles and by the traction companies' efforts to torpedo what had appeared to be an irresistible movement for immediate municipal ownership.

Having lost his trump card—the certainty of overwhelming public backing at the polls—Mayor Dunne was forced to try to broaden his base of support. Showing a growing political skill, he now sought to draw the city's structural reformers to his side by first appointing Walter L. Fisher, one of their most influential leaders, as his new special traction counsel and then by publicly calling for consensus and compromise in the so-called Werno letter. Sadly, the not inconsiderable benefits of this effort were to be ultimately dashed upon the ideological rocks of social reformism.

Walter Lowrie Fisher had been prominent among Chicago's structural reformist circles for well over a decade. Born in Wheeling, Virginia (now West Virginia), on 23 March 1858 and educated at Hanover College in Pennsylvania, he had an "active interest in the foundation and work of the Municipal Voters' League," and he was a principal founder of the City Club and later, in 1910, of the Chicago Bureau of Efficiency. Moreover, like Dunne, he had established a reputation of expertise in traction matters. Between 1887 and 1888, he had served briefly as the equivalent of special traction counsel for Mayor John A. Roche, and in 1905, he was part of a commission appointed and financed by the National Civic Federation "to investigate public utilities in the United States and Europe." Politically he considered himself to be among "the so-called progressive movement of the republican [sic] party," an outlook that was to lead to his eventual appointment as secretary of interior by President William Howard Taft. Toward municipal ownership, he found himself "somewhat near the middle of the road, convinced that public ownership was theoretically sound as the ultimate solution, but practically undesirable and inexpedient under existing political conditions."[2] In 1905, he had supported Harlan.

By his own account, Fisher only took the job as special traction counsel to the mayor because Dunne came to his office and "insisted" he do so "in the public interest."[3] While this may have been, it was also true that he had become attached to the Dunne administration as early as December 1905, when he took a trip to Springfield with the mayor to help lobby for broader city powers to regulate gas rates, and that he had been ever since increasingly perceived as one of Mayor Dunne's leading advisers. Regardless of the relative level of his enthusiasm, his appointment was announced on 11 April 1906.[4]

The advent of Fisher was, on the whole, well received. The *Outlook* wrote approvingly, calling Fisher "capable," a sentiment echoed in nearly all of Chicago's newspapers with the notable, if somewhat puzzling, exception of the *Tribune*. Others, who were more attached to the social reformist doctrine, were less enthusiastic. Glen E. Plumb who had been Darrow's assistant, and who had temporarily taken over his job, resigned from the administration in protest, and it was reported that at a meeting of the Public Ownership League, Fisher's appointment occasioned a near riot.[5]

The fears of the social reformers proved to be not entirely unfounded when the new Dunne/Fisher traction program was presented in the form of an open letter to Charles Werno, the chairman of the council's Committee on Local Transportation. This "Werno letter," as it became known, outlined proposed conditions under which the city could begin a new round of negotiations with the traction companies. Strongly reflective of Fisher's influence, the new plan called for the companies to continue operations under the condition that they initiate improvements until the city could arrange purchase. The eventual cost to the city was to be based upon a negotiated valuation of all tangible property and intangible rights, including those few franchises that had survived the Supreme Court ruling on the Ninety-nine Year Act. In addition, the companies were, in the period before municipal purchase, to split evenly all profits with the city. The Werno letter also called for Chicago to begin litigation to test the constitutionality of the Mueller law.[6]

Reflecting the input of the mayor, the letter included a stern warning to the companies that should they refrain from negotiations in good faith, the city would immediately enact the Contract Plan and set up a semipublic company that would, through the device of condemnation, take over their property and operations. Dunne explained:

> I believe the companies should be fairly treated in these matters so long as they themselves act with fairness towards the city. I have no desire whatever to confiscate one dollar of their property, even if I could do so. They should be given all that they are legitimately entitled to receive under the decision of the Supreme Court. It must be obvious to them, however, that any attempt upon their part to obtain more than this, by dilatory tactics or obstruction, can result only to their serious disadvantage.[7]

The Werno letter was a success. The *Chicago Daily News* offered the hope that the council "will see its way clear to support this program." Alderman Milton Foreman, a major leader of the mayor's opposition on the council, called the plan "commendable," and the *Tribune* congratulated Dunne for having "abandoned the battle for immediate municipal ownership."[8] The city council as a whole was equally impressed and soon voted to begin negotiations with the very willing traction companies. For Mayor Dunne, the Werno letter was a bittersweet compromise with political reality. As shown by his threat to return to the Contract Plan, he retained his emotional attachment to his original program. For the mayor the letter represented a kind of municipal ownership "as-soon-as-possible."[9]

For a brief moment it seemed that "as-soon-as-possible" would be very soon indeed. Relations between the principal traction companies and the city were unprecedently cordial and cooperative. There was, in Dunne's words, "a get-together atmosphere."[10] Not only had the companies agreed to negotiate, but they also had agreed to the replacement of the remainder of Chicago's cable cars within ninety days and to the lowering of three tunnels that passed under the Chicago River, two issues that had long been a center of controversy.[11]

Predictably, this happy state of affairs was but short-lived. The city council soon reverted to their habit of questioning the administration's efforts to regulate daily traction matters, and, more importantly, by late June, after the companies had presented their proposed property valuation, the talks degenerated into a situation in which every minor point tended to become a major battle. For all that, the negotiations at least had the benefit of removing the traction issue from the front page, which doubtlessly gave the mayor the hope that he would be granted a few peaceful months. Unfortunately, any expectation in that direction was frustrated by the activities of his appointees to the Board of Education that provided yet another fertile source of ammunition for his critics.[12]

At the heart of the school board crisis of 1906 and 1907 were the aspirations of the Chicago Federation of Teachers. Founded on 16 March 1897, the CFT's influence grew to include at different times as many as 90 percent of the city's elementary and secondary instructors. The organization's stated purpose was "to raise the standard of the teaching profession by securing for teachers conditions essential to the best professional service."[13] That lofty goal was translated into two general areas of activity. The first concerned the material welfare of teachers, and it was expressed in such things as a burial organization and an ongoing push for higher salaries. Not content with just concerning itself with immediate benefits for its members, the teachers organization also sought a voice in determining school system policy through proposed "teachers councils." That area of activity proved to offer the best opportunities for direct positive action. In the face of recurring pleas of poverty by the school board, the CFT began to take an active interest in the school system's financial structure and, under the leadership of Margaret Haley and Catherine Goggin, the organization initiated a series of well-publicized lawsuits designed to recover overlooked sources of income. The first of those efforts was directed against seven companies, including the Union Traction Company, the Chicago City Railway, and the People's Gas and Electric Company, which were declining to pay school taxes on their franchises. Eventually, the teachers were able to obtain a ruling that put an additional $600,000 into the school board treasury. At the same time, an investigation was made into the leasing of lands given under the Ordinance of 1785 to the purpose of financing public education. It was found that much of that property was being leased for patently much less than it was worth. Although leasing rates were periodically reviewed, the power of the leasees was such that relatively little upward revision occurred. Among those leasing school lands were the *Chicago Daily News* and the *Chicago Tribune*, which built its headquarters on school lands. It is not too much to suggest that much of the antipathy shown by both papers toward the CFT and subsequently the "Dunne school board" had its source here. The lease conflict dragged on for years, and it was not resolved while Edward F. Dunne was mayor.[14]

As skilled as the CFT became in the difficult and controversial vocation of rooting out additional school income, it found less success in promoting its educational philosophy. By its constitution, the organization was dedicated to the professionalization of teachers, and it sought "democracy" through the device of teachers councils, which were to give them an equal policy voice with principals, the superintendent, and the Board of Education. Their educational philosophy and aspirations were closely reflective of the body of thought associated with the writings of such prominent educators as John Dewey, Charles W. Eliot, and others. Unfortunately for those aspirations, the sitting superintendent's approach to education, while progressive, was nonetheless contrary to that of the Chicago Federation of Teachers. That man was Edwin Cooley.[15]

Cooley brought to his position a solid, if undistinguished record. Educated at the University of Illinois and the University of Iowa, he had served as both a teacher and a principal in a number of school systems before rising to become superintendent of schools in Cresco, Iowa. It was from there that he came to Chicago. He soon established himself as an honest and able administrator. He was described as "a sane man without fads" and as devoted to whatever was "best for the benefit of the young."[16] Also described as an "apostle of efficiency," he was "unmoved by doctrinaire proposals regarding the democratization of education and the development of the personality of the teacher."[17]

The inevitable clash between Cooley and the CFT came with the superintendent's plan of 1902 for a new system of merit promotion. It called for examinations after every seven years of service based upon academic advancement gained in outside studies and a secret evaluation of each teacher's efficiency by his or her principal. For the teachers union this plan was both unfair and demeaning. While the emphasis upon outside academic work ignore experience gained in the classroom, making admission to the examinations contingent upon a secret rating left the door open to abuse and favoritism. It also, of course, completely shut out teachers from any voice in their own promotions.[18] Despite vigorous protest, the Board of Education approved the scheme.

As an active political figure, Edward F. Dunne was aware of the conflict in Chicago's school system. Moreover, as a proponent of both "democracy" and unionism he was sympathetic to the aims of the CFT. His knowledge of educational theory, however, was of the most general sort, and it was unlikely that he was ever fully conversant with the educational issues of his day. He had been made intimately acquainted with one important episode of the CFT's battle—in 1902, as a judge he had ordered the school board to surrender to the teachers in the form of salary increases the $600,000 the union had procured for the city in their most important lawsuit. The decision made him a hero to the union and especially to Margaret Haley, who had long supported immediate municipal ownership, and who not only vigorously supported Dunne's election but became one of his most important unofficial lieutenants. When he became mayor, no group was more pleased or had greater expectations than the CFT.[19]

Thus inclined and indebted, Mayor Dunne took what action he could when shortly after his election he selected seven new members of the Board of Education, five of whom were appointed "with special reference to the controversy between the union and the superintendent."[20] Among those appointed were Jane Addams, the acclaimed settlement worker of Hull House, and Dr. Cornelia De Bey, who was known to be close to Haley and Catherine Goggin. In 1905, however, there was little change in school board policy; under the law the mayor could select only a third of the twenty-one-member board in any given year. Cooley remained dominant, but to their credit, the mayor's appointees were able to cancel the board's ongoing effort to overturn the 1902 decision of Judge Dunne![21]

The Chicago Federation of Teachers were sustained by the reasonable hope that the mayor's second set of appointees would enable them to gain control. They were not disappointed. Among the six chosen were John P. Sonsteby, secretary of the garment workers local; Wiley Mills, an important single-tax advocate; and Philip Angsten, who was a prominent municipal ownership man. Also picked were Raymond Robins, a well-known social activist, and Louis Post. Robins in 1905 had supported Harlan because he believed that Dunne was being supported by the "underworld," but after the election he had written a conciliatory letter to the new mayor and had since become part of the administration's inner circle. Post was editor of *The Public*, a social reformist mouthpiece with a national circulation, and he was close to Mayor Tom L. Johnson. By the hostile *Chicago Tribune*'s count, there were now on the Board of Education ten friends of the CFT, three who were generally inclined to oppose Cooley, three independents, and only six friends of the superintendent.[22] Dunne's appointments met with little opposition in the city council; however, at least one alderman felt that the mayor's choices included too many "agitators" and "radicals."[23]

Although generally correct, the *Tribune*'s assessment greatly overrated the unity of purpose among Dunne's appointees. The mayor's choices fell into two groups: (1) community leaders like Jane Addams, Robins, and Post, each of whom had their own, albeit similar, political philosophy and constituency, and (2) relatively unknown and educationally unknowledgable people like Angsten and Sonsteby who represented groups loyal to the administration. The combination of highly individual community leaders and political friends of the mayor never truly came together into a united consensus. Emil Ritter, who was elected as the new board president at its first meeting on 10

July 1906, was a colorless, often-ignored figurehead, whose election offended no one. Dunne himself, as a politician, could exercise little direct authority over the board, and any attempt on his part would have left him open to charges of "pull" and interference. Adding to the potential for chaos on the Dunne board was that no one with the exception of Cornelia De Bey, who advocated the CFT line, seemed to have a clear plan of action. Even Louis Post, whose appointment was the most controversial, and who had long promoted the goals of the CFT in *The Public*, was vague in his thinking; when asked about his ideas for board policy, he replied that he did not know if he had any. Philip Angsten, when asked the same question, confessed his bemused confusion, adding that he had "never dreamed [I] was going to be a school trustee."[24] The consequences of this lack of purpose and leadership first became clear in the mismanagement of the minor, but delicate, issue of the choice of textbooks.

The question first appeared when Dunne appointee Shelly O'Ryan reported to the old board in early July that the Macmillan texts recommended by Superintendent Cooley's examiners were being sold elsewhere at considerably lower prices than those quoted to the city of Chicago. Moreover, O'Ryan had discovered technical violations of the board's code in the process of approval. His impressive comparison of the company's Chicago prices with those found in Indiana moved the board to suspend approval and defer the issue until the new trustees were appointed.[25]

The new board subsequently appointed a special textbook committee dominated by Addams and De Bey. Macmillan responded by explaining that the books offered to Chicago were of a higher quality than those sold in Indiana, and by submitting a new, much lower bid. The bid was then withdrawn in the face of a division in the special textbook committee between those, like Jane Addams, who purported to be seeking the best texts at the best price, and others led by Cornelia De Bey, who saw the issue in an ideological light, and who believed any acceptance of the Macmillian bid would only strengthen "the system" and the "School Book Trust." After Macmillan withdrew the offer, the committee, now compelled to consider a dozen different texts, soon degenerated into argument and anarchy. Finally, just two weeks before classes were to begin for the fall term, they voted not to make a recommendation, and after limited study, the full board selected an offer from the Wheeler company.[26]

The affair did little to reflect credit upon the Dunne board. President Ritter publicly claimed that the failure to accept Macmillan's second bid was to cost the city an additional $100,000 over the school year. Philip Angsten angrily denounced the choice of the Wheeler text, and such important board members as Addams, O'Ryan, and Robins were pointedly absent for the final vote. The *Forum*, reflecting the attitude of many in Chicago, labeled the school board as "lilliputian."[27]

Nor was the Dunne board's image enhanced when charges appeared in *Weber's Weekly*, in September 1906, that Louis Post was being improperly compensated for his work on the Board of Eduction. The story, immediately reprinted in most of Chicago's newspapers, claimed that Post was being subsidized (and by implication owned) by Cleveland's Mayor Tom L. Johnson. Many Chicagoans had been alarmed already by Dunne's initial reliance upon Johnson in the formulating of traction policy, and the intimation that Cleveland's "radical" mayor was also involved in the conduct of the city's school board was disturbing. Post offered the explanation that he had originally felt unable to serve as a school trustee because of his duties as editor of *The Public*; Tom Johnson, with whom he had enjoyed a long friendship, came to the rescue at the bequest of Margaret Haley by offering to pay Post's wife, Alice Thacter Post, to take over most of the responsibilities of the publication under the title of managing editor. The explanation quieted things, but the issue had served to reenforce a growing concern about the Dunne board's competence—and that of the mayor.[28]

This concern only deepened when the board began dismantling Cooley's promotional system through the particularly ill advised action of denying advancement to two hundred teachers who had in good faith passed their examinations.[29] That provoked angry criticism. Setting the tone was the *Chicago Tribune*, which in its editorial of 10 October 1906, attacked the mayor for appointing advocates of "cranky fads." "When Mayor Dunne," the newspaper wrote, "packs the Board of Education with freaks, cranks, monomaniacs, and boodlers and turns over to them the care of one of the greatest school systems in the country, he is doing much to bring Chicago into disrepute." The editorial went on to call his building inspector "another freak" and his appointees to the board of improvements "obviously unfit."[30] Although the school board rescinded their action concerning the promotions, the outrage of their opposition only increased as positive plans for replacing Cooley's system emerged.

It was Louis Post who provided the Dunne board with a basis for action through what became know as the "Post report." Introduced into Jane Addams's School Management Committee on 12 October, the report closely reflected the aspirations of the Chicago Federation of Teachers. It provided for (1) the elimination of Cooley's promotional examinations, (2) an automatic increase of salaries every five years for teachers rated in the upper two or three levels of performance classifications, (3) the replacement of secret markings with open "estimates," (4) a transfer of the burden of proof from the instructor to the superintendent in cases of involuntary termination, (5) the use of examinations only for those first entering the school system, or for those who wished to change their subject, and (6) an invitation to the board's finance committee to explore ways to increase salaries.[31]

The report intensified public debate, but Cooley himself, who privately thought the Dunne board "fools," even if he was willing to concede that Post was a "well-intentioned fool," remained sanguine.[32] He could afford to be relatively quiet; there was no serious suggestion that he should be replaced, and within the two weeks following the so-called Post report, his friends, or at least the enemies of the CFT, were organizing noisy public meetings of protest. Prominent in organizing these meetings were such groups as the Merchants Club, the Commercial Club, and elements of the religious community that were still smarting from Dunne's refusal to enforce the Sunday Closing Law, as well as an impressive array of former school board members. Two new organizations, the Teachers Club of Chicago and the Principals Club, were also formed to try to rival the CFT among school employees.[33]

Edward F. Dunne for the most part refrained from participating in the public debate. He did feel moved to defend his board from an attack from the president of Columbia University, Nicholas Murray Butler (a noted educational conservative), by suggesting at a speech before the City Club that the esteemed educator mind his own business and by offering that "presidents of colleges and scions of the wealthy" were less competent to judge the workings of public schools than "the hard-working and poorly paid teachers who come in daily contact with the children of the poor."[34]

Dunne's noble words aside, there were many even among those associated with the administration who harbored some doubts about aspects of the Post report. For instance, there was general surprise when Jane Addams sponsored in her committee a resolution that called for some means to compel "each teacher in the public school system to keep in step with the times by taking periodic courses." The resolution was accepted by the full board over the protest of Margaret Haley, who was present as a guest, and it was subsequently endorsed by Cooley. It was with this amendment that the Post report was passed on 5 December 1906 by a vote of twelve to five.[35]

The actions of his appointees to the Board of Education were clearly a mixed blessing for Mayor Dunne. On one hand, he had the eternal gratitude of the politically active teachers union; on the other, he found himself again accused of running an eccentric administration. He had tried in good faith to appoint a board reflecting the nearest thing to a group of experts in his political circle, and certainly a school board that included Jane Addams, Raymond

Robins, and Louis Post was one of easily recognized distinction. He would have been better served, perhaps, if he had worked to use his influence to have achieved more harmony between the board and the superintendent that could have brought about a compromise plan that might have stifled the storm of criticism. The real lesson of the school board fight, however, was that much of the mayor's opposition continued to be among the editorial staff of the *Chicago Tribune* and other structural reformers who emphasized "efficiency" over "democracy" in government.

Not all of the publicity associated with the mayor and his administration during the summer and early fall of 1906 was negative. His image as a family man, for instance, was greatly enhanced by a very public celebration on 16 August of his twenty-fifth wedding anniversary. In itself somewhat rare in those days of relatively early death, the anniversary provided Chicagoans with the endearing spectacle of their mayor bubbling with love for his wife and the institution of marriage. Calling himself the "happiest man in Chicago," he doubtlessly pleased women throughout the city by not only urging young men everywhere to follow his example but proclaiming his wife "the ruler of the family."[36]

At about the same time, Mayor Dunne began promoting the use of the public baths, which he saw as both an alternative to the saloons and dance halls for working people, and as a source of improved public health. Taking the idea from Cleveland's Mayor Tom L. Johnson, he briefly ordered the baths to remain open until ten o'clock in the evening, and he conducted grand tours to promote their usage. It was to be a short campaign.[37]

Less lighthearted were the successful efforts of the mayor and his corporate counsel, J. Hamilton Lewis, to negotiate in July a $400,000 repayment plan with the Chicago Telephone Company for overcharges covering the last five years. In September, following an Illinois Supreme Court decision granting the city additional powers to force lower telephone rates, Dunne went further and asked the city council to initiate an investigation into ways to force the telephone company to reduce their charges. He also hinted that a primary goal of his second term would be to introduce municipal ownership in phone service.[38]

For some Democrats, the mayor's plans for a second term were by now problematic. From being the darling of his party and the master of its city convention in February 1906, Dunne had become an object of disdain for many "regulars." The Harrison crowd naturally harbored resentments toward the man who had overseen the fall of their hero, but the members of the Sullivan organization that had supported him were by this point unrestrained in their scorn. It was not that the mayor was a bad man, of course, or even that he kept pushing harebrained schemes, but rather that he was "a child—politically" and eschewed such time-honored practices as levying a campaign assessment upon city employees.[39] Nor did he show much sense in his appointments. Instead of rewarding his hardworking backers and loyal servants of the party, he chose to fill the city rolls with idealists and political amateurs. Moreover, how could anyone understand a man who showed such a disinclination toward building his own political machine? That at least one could respect, but this mayor chose to rely upon a nonpartisan reformist clique. Clearly, there was something wrong with this fellow. Thus driven by mutual self-interest, the Sullivan and Harrison people had arranged a very fragile alliance and had largely taken charge of the party organization. In the city convention of May 1906, for instance, Mayor Dunne had been completely kept out of things.[40]

Mayor Dunne gave no sign that he was overly worried by the antipathy of the sachems of the Harrison and Sullivan factions. He had never depended upon the support of either group, and indeed, the backing of the Sullivanites during his election campaign had been a problem. Moreover, he knew he retained considerable strength among the party's rank and file. More worrisome in the fall of 1906, was the threat posed to his leadership among the city's social reformers by a new political organization called the Independent League.

William Randolph Hearst had always been an enigma among the social reformers. His power was certainly respected and his support of social reformist issues and candidates, including Dunne, appreciated. At the same time, many were suspicious of his motives and reliability. As early as 1901, Mayor Tom L. Johnson wrote George A. Schilling, an active Illinois social reformer, that he did not "believe you can depend on him." Dunne, too, while openly friendly and respectful of the New York City-based publisher—a respect expressed by occasional pilgrimages to consult with the Great Man—maintained his distance.[41]

In September 1906, Hearst seemed to justify this wariness by ordering the creation of Independent Leagues in those major cities in which he had newspapers. The leagues' stated purpose was to combat "Political bossism and Private monopoly," and among their goals were the municipal ownership of public utilities, stronger antitrust regulation, direct primaries, the direct election of United States senators, and the initiative and referendum.[42]

Given the fact that Mayor Dunne's personal platform was virtually identical and that the league threatened the delicate unity of Chicago's social reformers behind the administration, the organization's appearance in the nation's second city made little sense except in terms of Hearst's presidential ambitions. The previous spring the publisher had lost a close race for the mayoralty of New York City, and he was even now making a bid for the governorship of his state. It was especially distressing to Mayor Dunne when the Chicago League began putting together a slate of candidates for the November Cook County elections. It was even more disquieting when his father, P. W. Dunne, a hearty seventy-three, agreed to become a league candidate for county commissioner.[43]

Edward F. Dunne was *always* a loyal Democrat. It was one of the secrets of his success in a political environment dominated by bosses and machines. He could hardly, as the titular head of the city party, support the maverick political organization. At the same time, he depended upon Hearst's newspaper support and some of his friends had joined the league. Moreover, he had very little voice in the selection of the Democratic County slate. Thus, trapped by events, the mayor made public statements in support of his own party's slate, while offering a few occasional words of praise for Hearst. In the end, however, it did neither the mayor nor the social reformist cause much good among regular Democrats when, in part due to the league, the Republicans swept the county elections.[44]

In truth, as Dunne well knew, neither his troubles with the Independent League nor his troubles with the chiefs of his party would count for much if his administration was able to bring about a successful traction settlement. As the year drew to a close, that seemed more than possible; Walter Fisher was at last concluding his arduous negotiations with the companies, and in December, he presented his proposal to the city.

In many respects, the agreement that emerged was a victory for the city. Its provisions included (1) twenty-year franchises for the Chicago City Railway, Union Traction, and Chicago Railway systems, with the city having the right to purchase during the last five years of the charters at six months notice for about $50 million; (2) a complete rehabilitation of the lines at the estimated cost of $40 million; (3) compensation to be paid to the city for the use of the streets at a rate of 55 percent of annual net profits; and (4) the establishment of a permanent board of engineers with the power to oversee and veto the companies' actions.[45]

Dunne was at first profuse in his praise of the proposal, calling it "a good one." He went further and gushed that "had I predicted one year ago that we could secure a settlement with the traction companies on a $50,000,000 basis, I would have been laughed at and called a fit subject for a lunatic asylum." In his judgment, the mayor asserted, "nothing short of an earthquake could prevent a settlement."[46]

While no earthquake occurred like the one that had recently destroyed San Francisco, his euphoric mood soon passed as he and his advisers developed serious reservations. Within a few weeks, he was demanding that the city council place the proposed settlement on the ballot in the upcoming April elections. This notion was handily defeated by a vote of forty to twenty-eight, and subsequently a movement emerged led by the Referendum League and Margaret Haley to gather signatures for a petition to bring the question to the voters. Three nonbinding propositions were sought; one that asked whether the city should immediately begin condemnation proceedings against the traction companies to form the basis for a municipally owned system; another that asked whether the city council should submit any traction settlement to the people; and a third that inquired whether the state legislature should repeal the Sunday Closing Law. This latter proposition was a rather clever political ploy, reportedly suggested by Dunne, as a means of facilitating the gathering of the necessary 58,000 signatures—equal to one-fourth of the electorate at the last election.[47]

The mayor next openly turned against the Fisher settlement itself. Further study had revealed serious flaws. In the first place, the $50 million valuation was deceptive. With the costs of rehabilitation added on, the city would have to pay as much as $90 million for the traction lines. This effectively made municipal ownership impossible, since the city was only authorized to issue $75 million in Mueller bonds. Moreover, there was no protection for the city against costs incurred by any subcontractor hired by the companies for the rehabilitation. Dunne also objected to the use of percentages in calculating the city's compensation, preferring a set figure. Overall, he proclaimed, "these ordinances are not municipal ownership measures, but ordinances masking under the guise of municipal ownership, while really and in fact giving the present companies a franchise for twenty years."[48]

The city council did not agree. First, the Committee on Local Transportation, despite the passionate oratorical elegance of Margaret Haley, voted by nine to three to recommend the settlement, and then the full council, in a noisy session that was vibrated by galleries filled with traction workers chanting their support of the mayor, passed the ordinance by a margin of fifty-six to thirteen. The mayor used his veto, and Walter L. Fisher resigned. Subsequently, the council not only hired Fisher as *their* special traction counsel but, on 11 February, overrode the mayor. The vote was even more overwhelming with only the "twelve apostles" of municipal ownership, led by Alderman William Dever, voting to sustain Dunne.[49]

Superficially, it seemed that the rejection of the Fisher settlement was, at best, ill advised and, at worst, unbalanced. It appeared to some that had he embraced it, he could have assured his reelection as the man who successfully concluded the traction controversy. The settlement was in many circles unquestionably popular; it won immediate praise from all of the newspapers except those owned by Hearst, and the council's enthusiasm was now a matter of public record. Why then would he sabotage what could have been the crowning achievement of his administration?

One part of the answer to the question resided in Dunne's continuing commitment to social reformist goals and ideals. Certainly it is difficult to understand why he expected more from Walter Fisher, a man on record as doubting the feasibility of public ownership, and he clearly made a mistake in praising Fisher's work too quickly, but the fact remained that the agreement did not provide for anything like immediate municipal ownership. His understanding of his political reality also doubtlessly intruded into his thinking. Most of the newspapers, the city council, as well as the structural reformers did, it was true, applaud the settlement. However, that was no guarantee that group, many of whom were Republican, would back, under the circumstances, Dunne's ambitions for a second term. On the other hand, the social reformers, his real base of support, were decidedly not pleased. Raymond Robins and Louis Post, for instance, were scathing in their critique of the settlement, and the evidence even suggests that the mayor was stampeded into calling for a referendum by the independent activities of Haley and the Referendum League. Another worry was Hearst's Independent League, which was unfriendly toward Fisher and the results of his efforts, and which was making noises about running their own mayoral candidate. Altogether then, it was not unreasonable for Mayor Dunne to believe that his best chances to assure his reelection and, therefore, municipal ownership lay in reassembling the social reformist coalition that had first elected him, and to do that he had to reject the Fisher plan.[50]

That, in fact, he was in the race had already been long established. Since the previous December, his campaign manager, William L. O'Connell, and his campaign committee had been busily organizing for the race. Their first obstacle was the Democratic nomination, and here their chief opponent was the ubiquitous Carter Harrison. Fortunately, the delicate détente between the former mayor and Roger Sullivan had dissolved, and Harrison's hopes were largely dashed when the boss declared his neutrality. With surprising ease, Mayor Dunne swept the precinct primaries, gathering 624 delegates to 249 for Harrison.[51] At the city convention held on 23 February, he was renominated by acclamation on a self-penned platform, which proclaimed the party to be "unalterably pledged to municipal ownership of all public utilities" and opposed to "granting franchises to Wall Street stock jobbers."[52] Three days later, the Independent League declared for him unanimously but declined to do the same for the Democratic candidates for city clerk and treasurer, or for any of the many Democratic aldermen who had voted for Fisher's settlement.[53]

The mayor's strategy was clearly based upon reigniting the popular passion for municipal ownership. One sign that the issue might lack its previous potency was the Republican's decision to ignore it in their nomination of a man who, unlike John Harlan in 1905, had no record at all on the traction issue. Fred Busse was in fact a machine politician, having at various times been allied with both the Lorimer and Deneen factions. He had risen from the ranks serving first as town clerk of north Chicago followed by stints as state assemblyman, state senator, and state treasurer. In 1902, he was appointed by President Theodore Roosevelt as postmaster of Chicago, and he used the patronage-rich position to build his own "federal faction" based in the northern wards. Such was the momentum for Busse that he easily won the nomination despite serious injuries from a railroad accident in February that kept him from actively campaigning.[54]

Although the Republicans did not directly address the traction question in their choice of a candidate, they were quite willing to take advantage of the issue in a platform that put the party squarely behind the Fisher settlement. Other campaign themes also quickly emerged. One of the most effective was their linkage of the mayor with Hearst. Many Chicagoans who had been dismayed by the extent of the influence of Tom L. Johnson upon the administration were frankly appalled at the specter, however unrealistic, of William Randolph Hearst ruling the city through a puppet mayor. Nor was the Dunne school board neglected by Republican speakers and editors, who used its activities to illustrate Dunne's "radicalism." Another basis for attack, though considerably more minor, was Mayor Dunne's alleged disregard of law and order, as illustrated by his supposed abuse of his pardoning powers.[55] Overall, the Republicans sought to portray Edward F. Dunne as a likable person who was frankly incompetent, or as one speaker put it: "He may be good at shedding tears, may have a sweet smile, and be good to his family, but that does not prevent him from being the 'rottenest' mayor Chicago ever had. . . . We want a man who will use his own brains!"[56]

Thus armed, the Republicans set forth to do battle with unusual unity throughout the ranks. Busse's factional rivals, Congressman William Lorimer and Governor Charles Deneen, endorsed him and campaigned enthusiastically on his behalf. Even this paled, however, before the intervention on the eve of the election of the party's greatest vote-getter of them all, President Theodore Roosevelt, who praised the candidate not only as the best postmaster in the country but also as potentially "one of the best and most efficient executives any city could possibly have."[57]

By contrast the Dunne campaign was a fragmented collection of elements. At the heart of things was his own personal committee that after the convention became officially associated with the Democratic Party. Headed by O'Connell, it was made up of from fifteen to twenty-five members from each ward. The city's social reformers rallied to the cause through the Municipal Ownership Central Committee. Representing the Chicago Federation of Labor, the Municipal Ownership Delegate Convention, and the Referendum League, the Central Committee included among its most prominent leaders Haley, Robins, John J. Fitzpatrick, head of the CFL, and Louis Post. Although it held its own meeting and distributed its own literature, this group cooperated closely with the mayor's campaign committee and contributed much of the necessary legwork.[58]

Then there was the Independent League, which true to its name conducted its affairs outside of the mayor's control. Their insistence upon addressing their own agenda and their opposition to Democratic aldermen who had voted for the Fisher settlement (they even supported the Republicans who had voted to sustain Dunne's veto) were constant sources of embarrassment. At one point, for instance, the mayor found himself in the uncomfortable position of speaking at a major rally for the First Ward's notorious alderman Michael "Hinky Dink" Kenna, whom the league had especially targeted for defeat.[59]

Hearst and his vehicle added to the already considerable anger felt by many "regular" Democrats toward the administration. Reflecting that, the Sullivan-dominated county committee, despite the presence of O'Connell in his capacity as chairman, met on 23 March and reportedly laid down an official policy of nonsupport. Within days, Dunne appeared before the body but failed to win a ringing endorsement. Similarly, the Harrisonites were given the fulsome advice by their leader to support the mayor but to also vote for the settlement.[60]

As fractured as the Dunne campaign was, it put on a good show. Its star attraction was the mayor himself. Campaigning was something at which he excelled, and he was now an experienced and charismatic speaker. Once again, he lost his voice from his appearances at numerous public meetings (sometimes as many as six a day), where he decried the Fisher settlement as a mere ploy that served the interests of the traction companies and their Wall Street backers. His crowds were generally large and friendly, and his faithful friends, notably Haley and the Chicago Federation of Teachers, labored mightily for his cause. Yet from the beginning, the mayor was on the defensive. As a controversial incumbent, he was, of course, naturally vulnerable. More important, however, was the fact that with the exception of the two Hearst papers, all of the city's newspapers, and especially the "school-children, real-estate cheating *Chicago Tribune*," were either neutral or supporting Busse.[61] In 1905, Dunne had ridden the crest of a popular crusade, and that more than canceled out the Republican control of the media. Now in 1907, the mayor's political strength was much more limited with the consequence that his opposition was successful in defining the campaign's issues.

It was his antipathy toward the Fisher settlement that did his reelection bid the most apparent harm. It was difficult for many independents and Republicans who had voted for him in 1905, as the best man to solve the traction tangle, to understand his objections or his devotion to the ideology of immediate municipal ownership. For those citizens, the issue was efficient, comfortable streetcar service, which seemed guaranteed by Fisher's agreement. Under those circumstances, it was not difficult for the enemy press to portray Dunne as an opportunist controlled by Hearst and Tom L. Johnson to the detriment of the true interest of the people of Chicago. Even some of those firmly in the mayor's camp could not agree with him on this point. For instance, J. Hamilton Lewis, corporate counsel and among his most trusted political friends, sought to downgrade the issue of the ordinances, which he tacitly supported, while recommending the mayor for reelection on the basis of his own intrinsic worth.[62]

Dunne's efforts, then, to conjure up the spirit of popular outrage upon which he had ridden to the mayor's chair in 1905, were unsuccessful. The forces that had first elected him were no longer united. The irony of the situation was that the main source of this disunity was the proposed traction ordinances that had originated within his own administration.

For their part, the Republicans made little effort to match the number or magnitude of his public rallies; their control of the media was assurance enough that their message would be heard. On the other hand, their vituperation more than matched even that of the Hearst press as Republican speakers and newspapers alike pressed home the theme that "the trouble with Dunne is that he belongs in public life no more than a square plug does in a round hole."[63] Busse himself was still recovering from his injuries and did little campaigning. That was a double advantage: first, he was a poor speaker even when fit, and second, it made any personal attack upon him seem ungracious. An attempt early in the campaign by the mayor to question the sincerity of the Republican candidate's vote as a legislator on the Allen law made him look like a bully, and only the *American* and the *Examiner* continued to try to impeach Busse's character. Even that, however, seemed to emphasize once again the dangers of Hearst's influence.[64]

By the week before the election on 2 April, the signs were unmistakable; it was not only possible but likely that the mayor would be defeated. In public he was optimistic, but in private it was a different story. Dunne himself later related a conversation he had shortly before the election with William Loeffer, a former city clerk and party "regular," in which both men conceded the probability of defeat. Loeffer's solution was to spread a few hundred thousand dollars among the boys of the river wards. To his credit, Dunne declined.[65]

As expected, when the votes were counted, Edward F. Dunne had been rejected. In all, Busse received 164,839 votes, or 49 percent, while the mayor was given 151,823 votes, or 45 percent of the total. Even worse, the ordinances to implement the Fisher settlement passed by the even larger margin of 165,846, or 56 percent, to 137,720 votes, or 44 percent. Asked to explain the results, Mayor Dunne attributed them to "unlimited money."[66]

The demographics of the defeat were almost identical to those of the 1905 victory. Once again, Dunne ran very well in the city's Irish and working-class wards. He did suffer some losses, however, among middle- and upper-class areas, and this can be explained in terms of the popularity of the Fisher settlement among those groups. In all, he carried fourteen of thirty-five wards, a loss of just three from the earlier year. Far more significant to his failure were the dramatic declines—as much as 30 percent—in voter turnout in wards he carried in both elections. In light of the Democratic success in retaining control of the city council and in electing John Traeger as city treasurer, it would seem that much of the reason for the defeat may be directly attributed to the inaction on his behalf of his party's leadership.[67] About three weeks after the election, the aforesaid Loeffer affirmed this at a stormy meeting of the county committee when he stated that in Dunne they had

> a man who could see only William Randolph Hearst of New York, the Hearst newspapers, and the streetcar question. . . . Can you blame democrats [sic] for not being enthusiastic when he ran again? . . . I will acknowledge that if I had spent more money and done harder work the Ninth ward probably would have made a better showing, but there was no special reason why I should . . . I voted for Dunne. As far as I know, my personal friends did. But we felt when we had done that we had done our entire duty.[68]

After an abortive Republican attempt to take power early, Mayor Dunne formally surrendered his office to Busse in the city council chambers on 15 April 1907. He also submitted in writing a final message that covered virtually every aspect of the city government. Its emotional core, however, lay in a last appeal for municipal ownership of the traction systems. "The history of the street problem in Chicago," he wrote:

reeks with bribery, corruption, and rottenness. It is to be hoped that by the rigid enforcement of ordinances and police powers of the city, the companies will be brought to realize that their best interests lie in faithfully performing their public duties until such time as the municipal ownership and operation of the streetcars of Chicago will become, as it inevitably will an accomplished.[69]

The council unanimously voted to order the printing of five thousand copies of the message for public distribution.[70] Edward F. Dunne now became a private citizen for the first time in fourteen years.

4

D TOWARD THE GOVERNORSHIP

Social reformism that had achieved such success in Detroit, Cleveland, Toledo, and other cities, clearly failed in Chicago. In part, this was due to Mayor Dunne's self-confessed lack of "political finesse." More importantly, however, the complexity and tribalism of the city's political culture made it virtually impossible for any reform movement to sustain power without betraying the ideals upon which it was founded. Even the broad popular support that Dunne enjoyed in his first year meant little against the intransigence and indifference of the established political order, and his refusal and inability to play the game only made his failure something like inevitable. The influence and ideas of social reformism remained, but it was never to be the significant force that it had been between 1905 and 1907.[1]

Ironically, for Dunne himself the defeat inaugurated a period of broadening political horizons. Freed from the daily scrutiny and responsibilities of the mayor's office, he could now, at the age of fifty-four, assume the role of elder statesman and address the wider issues of the day. With a spark of political genius, he used this role to rise above his image as a social reformist ideologue and political amateur to become a leading spokesman for a broader demand for progressive change in Illinois. This process led to a spectacular, if unsuccessful, campaign for his party's nomination for mayor in 1911, followed by a triumphant march to the governorship in the following year.

In the summer of 1907, the promising nature of the future was not so apparent. For the moment, however, Dunne seems to have experienced relief upon his return to private life. He was by nature a sensitive and good-natured man, and he was doubtlessly pleased to be spared the attacks and controversies that plagued his term as mayor. Nearly thirty years later, his sense of frustration was still evident in his reference to "the arduous and vexatious annoyances which I encountered while I occupied the office of mayor of Chicago."[2]

His refusal to become disheartened was greatly abetted by his loyal circle of friends. On the first of June 1907, a grand banquet was organized in his honor that underscored both the affection felt for him and his continuing importance as a political figure. It was an elaborate affair, fit for a conquering hero. Held at the Chicago Athletic Club, of which he was a member, this "dinner of commiseration" included more than two hundred of his personal and political friends. Numerous short talks with such titles as "Dunne as a Friend," "Dunne as a Lawyer," and "Dunne as a Public Official," were delivered by such personages as J. Hamilton Lewis, William Dever, and Judge Samuel Alschuler. Prince Henry of Prussia and Sir Thomas Lipton, both of whom Dunne as mayor had welcomed to the city, sent congratulations, as did William Jennings Bryan. To climax things, the former mayor was presented with a silver loving cup, after which he responded with a few appropriately jovial remarks.[3]

As similar to a retirement dinner as the gathering was, it was clear that Dunne was not a dead political commodity. None present was as yet prepared to speak of a return to power in the city, an event that in any case under the newly revised municipal charter could not take place for four years, but neither did anyone make any reference to a glorious private life. Regardless of the uncertainty of his political prospects, he, it was well understood, still enjoyed considerable political strengths. His hard core of followers among the city's Irish, laborers, and social reformers, while failing in 1907 to turn out in such numbers as 1905, remained loyal. Moreover, the defection of the party "regulars," while fatal to his chances for reelection, afterward did not have much importance; they had never been particularly fond of him in the first place, and in the years ahead, their opposition was to constitute an asset. Nor did the simple truth that he had lost the election disqualify him from future political power. As a member of a party whose greatest living figure, William Jennings Bryan, had already lost two presidential bids and, in 1907, was headed for another, Dunne was not disgraced by defeat.[4]

Greatly aiding the restoration of his stature were the policies of the new mayor. With a passion not unlike that of the restored émigrés after the fall of Napoleon, Busse seemed bent upon eradicating all traces of social reformism from the government. Most controversial was his almost immediate discharge of the larger part of Dunne's appointees to the school board. Although this was illegal and was eventually overturned by the Illinois Supreme Court, it demoralized the Board of Education and effectively ended any plans for further change. It was greatly resented in the social reformist circles and it alarmed others. Dunne's image improved in comparison, and it became a not too difficult task to see him as a martyr for good government.[5]

He, himself, did not participate in the public altercations that followed Busse's rape of the school board, nor was he to become extensively involved in the city's politics for the next two years. Not only did he, of course, lack a ward-level machine that dictated daily attention to local affairs, but municipal ownership, the issue that had largely shaped his interest in city politics, was no longer viable. In the first place, the election had been lost, but more importantly, the Illinois Supreme Court declared significant sections of the Mueller law unconstitutional.[6]

It was for those reasons, perhaps, that his first pronouncements on municipal ownership, besides the occasional statement condemning the Fisher ordinance, were lukewarm. Speaking before the annual meeting of the American League of Municipalities (of which he had been elected president while mayor) on 18 September 1907, he dutifully affirmed his belief that the public ownership of utilities was the wave of the future, but the passion and commitment of his previous declarations on the subject were missing. While denying that his defeat was any kind of real referendum on municipal ownership, he made no reference to reigniting the crusade himself in Chicago. Of much greater interest, to the reporters present at least, were his thoughts about the upcoming 1908 presidential race. On this he expressed a rather vague support of Bryan.[7]

Two months later, he had become openly fanatical for the Bryan candidacy, and it was this campaign that was to be the arena of his reentry into active politics. His decision to avoid, for the moment, the miasma of Chicago politics and to concentrate upon the national campaign was astute. In supporting Bryan, he earned the gratitude of important figures within the Democratic Party, while further establishing himself as a respected regional and national figure. If Bryan won, he would have the president of the United States in his debt; if Bryan lost, he could still present himself as a champion of party and reform.

The advantages of this strategy became clear when Dunne rose to speak, on 5 December 1907, at a massive meeting at Freeport, Illinois. With Bryan and as many as three thousand Democrats present, he found himself introduced as a future governor of Illinois.[8] This was the first public indication of a growing movement among his friends, both within and without the Democratic Party, to elect him the state's chief executive in 1912. His attractiveness as a candidate was founded upon the wide esteem with which he was now beginning to be held. The Republican newspaper, the *Inter-Ocean* (Chicago) explained: "With all his rainbow chasing as mayor, the Hon. Edward F. Dunne left his office with public respect undiminished and even increased. However misguided in municipal administration, his personal sincerity was so transparent, and in his hands government power was so visibly impartial, that it could not be otherwise"[9]

Throughout 1908, he continued to campaign for Bryan, striking his theme that Taft and the Republicans were to blame for the economic panic of the previous year. His schedule, while not overwhelming, was fairly full. His itinerary included Philadelphia, St. Louis, Milwaukee, and Joliet, Illinois. At the national convention itself, held between 6 and 8 July 1908, his enthusiasm as a delegate earned him a place on the notification committee; it was an enthusiasm he maintained through election day.[10]

Bryan's defeat did little to slow his efforts to maintain a high public profile. In late 1908, and early 1909, he became involved in two issues of some local interest. The first concerned the extradition to Imperial Russia of Christian Rudowitz, a socialist opponent of the czarist regime. Dunne, together with Jane Addams and Raymond Robins, spoke and petitioned to keep Rudowitz in the United States. Although the socialist was deported, the former mayor had underscored in the public mind, especially among the city's laborers, his willingness to defend personal liberty and opinion.[11]

He was less generous to Jacob M. Dickinson. A Democrat, he had accepted the nomination of President-elect William Howard Taft to serve as secretary of war. The Iroquois Club held a banquet in his honor. Dunne refused to attend, stating that he found it "highly ridiculous for a Democratic organization to tender its congratulations to a gentleman because of his recent abandonment of his party." This caused some comment, but having made his point, he returned to active involvement in the club within a couple of months.[12]

For the rest of 1909, when not working in the law firm he had established with his son Edward F. Dunne Jr., he maintained an active speaking schedule. On 8 January 1909, he was in Rockford, Illinois, speaking before the Knights of Columbus on the virility of the Catholic Church in America. In February, he appeared before the Knox County Bar Association to discuss Abraham Lincoln's virtues as a lawyer. In April, he engaged in a debate, in Council Bluff, Iowa, with Ben L. Winchell, president of the Chicago, Rock Island and Pacific Railroad, over the benefits of public ownership, and in May, he spoke before the City Club of Kansas City, Missouri, on the details of his City Plan. Over the course of those and other speeches, he began showing a greater inclination to attack the Busse administration. The first issue to draw him out was the financing of the subway construction in Chicago with the traction fund created by the 1907 settlement. He called the action illegal, but more importantly, his willingness to speak openly against the sitting administration indicated his renewed interest in municipal politics. Earlier in the year, he had, with some difficulty, halted attempts within his party to nominate him for state's attorney; it was beginning now to become clear that his sights might be set higher.[13]

It was now 1910. Besides being the year of Halley's Comet and the death of Mark Twain, it was also one of importance in the development of a growing national consensus for reform. It was the year in which former President Theodore Roosevelt and President Taft first showed certain indications of political antagonism, symbolized by the open feud between Taft's secretary of the interior, Richard Ballinger, and chief forester and Roosevelt loyalist, Gifford Pinchot. In the United States House of Representatives, 1910 was the year that young progressives led by George W. Norris stripped Speaker Joseph Cannon of his dictatorial powers. More positively, it was in November 1910, that an intellectual liberal named Thomas Woodrow Wilson was elected governor of New Jersey. In Illinois, as well, 1910 was an important time of awakening reformist sentiments. The single most important immediate cause for that was the Lorimer scandal.

William Lorimer was a powerful boss of Chicago's West Side. His power within his party rivaled that of Governor Charles Deneen, and in 1908, he had secured his election as United States senator from the Illinois legislature. After two years of undistinguished service, he was accused of having purchased his election. At first exonerated by his colleagues, Lorimer was finally expelled from the Senate in July 1912. The case dominated public attention in Illinois throughout 1910 and most of the following two years, creating in the process both growing doubts about the state's political structure and a reinvigorated demand for honesty in government.[14]

Scandal also plagued Chicago in 1910. An investigation made into the city's financial affairs by a committee headed by Charles Merriam, a University of Chicago professor-turned-alderman, found much wanting. Among other things, the committee discovered a $45,000 overcharge for sewer construction by a company owned by an old friend of Mayor Busse. Similarly, a conflict of interest was found between the mayor and his crony Thomas A. Cummings who managed to corner the market on Chicago's new manhole covers. Hitting even closer were charges that Busse's personal secretary, Harry A. Smith, had organized the Chicago Fire Appliance Company to be the city's exclusive supplier of office equipment, equipment that was not only inferior but also overpriced. In all, it was estimated that these kinds of practices had cost the city as much as $30 million. Busse himself was not directly implicated, and there was a tendency to give him the benefit of the doubt. Nonetheless, his chances for reelection in the spring of 1911, it was generally agreed, were greatly diminished.[15]

Busse's vulnerability intensified the maneuvering among the Democrats.

In July, there were attempts to unify the party in face of the fall judicial and county elections. Conclaves were held, and it briefly seemed that an agreement among the factions about patronage and candidates would be reached. It proved impossible, however, to bring together Harrison, Sullivan, and Dunne, and negotiations broke down ostensibly over the question of the party's choice for county sheriff. In truth, the pressure of "too many mayoralty booms" made such a working agreement impossible.[16]

The most widely anticipated and publicized mayoralty boom was for Carter Harrison. He had been maneuvering for the nomination virtually since his humiliating defeat in the primary of 1907. He brought to the contest not only his well-respected name and organization but also a new alliance with the previously hostile Hearst press. With guaranteed newspaper support and a fat campaign chest, he was felt to be the front-runner. Harrison's strength was most worrisome to Roger Sullivan. Sullivan, himself, had no ambitions for the mayor's office (as it proved, he had greater hopes), so after some searching, he chose as his standard-bearer Andrew J. Graham, a businessman whose public service had been limited to several terms on the West Side Park Commission.[17]

It had been speculated that Edward F. Dunne might also seek the nomination, but as he lacked a machine and therefore the financial support and a base in the wards, the notion of his candidacy was not taken too seriously; against the impressive resources of the "H-H" faction, as the Harrison-Hearst group was known, and those of the Sullivan organization, his chances seemed meager indeed. For that reason many were "startled" when on the afternoon of 19 November 1910 he released a public statement announcing that "in response to the urgent and repeated requests of my fellow citizens," he was entering the primary.[18]

Little premeditation appears to have been involved. He genuinely did not have an organization, and for two months not even a platform. When one was finally released in late January, it was very general and showed signs of hasty composition. Among its planks were demands for "honesty in government," the end of graft and "fake reform," as well as a call for measures to curb "bomb throwing"! More substantial were pleas for more streetcars and municipally controlled subways and park governments. For all of that, the thrust of his campaign was to be the "scandalous administration of the present," paraphrased in his speeches as "Busseism."[19]

His friends quickly responded, and a skeleton organization emerged under Alderman John J. Bradley, an old ally. Among those who rallied to the cause were Judge William Dever, Raymond Robins, Margaret Haley, Philip Angsten, and William O'Connell, presently the treasurer of Cook County.

Clarence Darrow, while not participating in the campaign, offered a written endorsement. As impressive as that list was, Dunne was still not expected to have much chance. At Jim O'Leary's stockyard saloon, the smart money at the onset of the race was on either Harrison or Graham, who were given about even odds.[20]

The Republicans had also been affected by the scandals of the Busse administration. Charles Merriam made a smooth transition from crusading alderman to becoming the leading candidate for his party's nomination for mayor. Under slogans of efficiency and honesty, the city's structural reformers, including Walter Fisher, flocked to his cause. In contrast, the "regular" Republicans seemed to have been stunned into inaction. Busse himself did not help matters with his refusal to withdraw from consideration until just before the primary. Eventually, two candidates came forth to represent segments of the traditional leadership. One, John F. Smulski, a banker and leader of the sizable Polish population, was supported by Governor Deneen, and the other, John R. Thompson, a prominent businessman, was endorsed by Mayor Busse. Neither candidacy engendered much enthusiasm, and it appeared that Merriam was virtually unstoppable.[21]

With the Republican primary largely decided, the public's attention was given over to the heated Democratic contest. Harrison, who was basing his campaign upon the promise of seventy-cent gas, set the tone with early attacks upon Graham as the tool of the corrupt Roger Sullivan. Graham, who did not appear to stand for much at all, retaliated in kind with strong barbs about the former mayor's record, delighting in the process of quoting from the Hearst press hostile editorials about Harrison from 1904 to 1907.[22]

Against the organizational and financial strength of Harrison and Graham, Dunne could muster neither newspaper support nor an army of workers. His total spending was just under ten thousand dollars, one-tenth of which came from his own pocket. For those reasons, he conducted a hard-hitting "populist" campaign using his now polished gifts as an orator to appeal to his fellow Democrats over the heads of their erstwhile leaders. With an energy not quite matched in any of his other election bids, he threw himself into the fray. Throughout as many as five speeches a day, his theme was consistent: "Busseism." As he explained at one early meeting, "I would not be here tonight seeking your suffrages but for the eruption of scandal, plunder, corruption, graft, and lawlessness that have shrouded the city of Chicago for four years." Nor did he exempt his opponents from tar of the same brush. "The Democratic Bussites need not flatter themselves that they can hide their guilt behind the pretense of opposing the man," he proclaimed, "there is no distinction between them; each contributed his share." More specifically, he directly labeled Roger Sullivan as a Democratic "Bussite."   Against Harrison, he charged party disloyalty because of the former mayor's refusal to actively support him in 1905 and 1907. Harrison rather weakly rejoined that he had been personally offended by Dunne's verbal assault of 4 September 1904 for advocating the "tentative ordinance."[23]

These attacks engendered little response from either the Harrison or Graham camps, both of which tried to ignore him. Hearst's *Chicago American*, which found itself in the awkward position of backing a candidate against a man it had four years earlier lionized as the savior of Chicago, did not acknowledge Dunne's candidacy until three days before the election. In a lengthy editorial largely given over to castigating Graham and Sullivan, the newspaper proclaimed Dunne "a disappointment as mayor" and assured its readers that "Chicago is not likely to repeat the experiment."[24] Two days later, Harrison struck a similar theme when he proclaimed that Dunne "can see nothing but sunshine and roses, and his campaign managers have evidently been inoculated with the virus of optimism."[25]

Dunne's campaign manager, John J. Bradley, had indeed been "inoculated with the virus of optimism," predicting that his man would take more than 60 percent of the vote. This was not just political hyperbole; Dunne was attracting overflowing crowds, and he had clearly defined the race's issue as "Busseism."   Although this new strength prompted charges that Graham's backers were secretly helping Dunne to split the Harrison vote, it was becoming apparent that the former mayor might just make a respectable showing on the basis of his own appeal.[26]

Nonetheless, many were surprised by the results of the primary that was held on 28 February 1911. Harrison won with 55,069 votes and Graham received 35,541, but Dunne was a close second with 53,513 ballots cast in his favor. The margin of victory was so small that at first neither Dunne nor his supporters accepted the results, and a recount was demanded.[27]

In the spirit of restoring party unity in the face of Merriam's victory in the Republican primary, Harrison agreed. The recount changed the totals but a little, and there was some discussion in the Dunne camp of an independent candidacy. Dunne, always a party loyalist, dampened any such idea, but he did, however, decline to actively support Harrison in the election. Moreover, a number of his friends jumped to the Merriam camp. For all of this, Harrison managed to win yet another term as mayor against the Republican.[28]

It seems clear that the late entry into the mayoral race was not part of a master plan to eventually achieve the governorship. Such a plan, because it would have failed to take into account the automatic resistance of downstate Illinois to a sitting mayor of Chicago seeking the state's first office, would

have been unsound. It appears probable that Dunne did harbor publicly un-
spoken ambitions for the governorship, but it seems equally certain that he set
these aside when he decided to take advantage of the opportunity offered by
the scandals of the Busse administration.[29]

Ironically, in losing the primary he secured advantages that greatly enhanced the prospects for a move to Springfield. First, his uncompromising
advocacy of clean government during the campaign helped reestablish him in
the public mind as a dynamic and progressive leader. At the same time, he
had captured the attention of the professional politicians of his party. Although they might not agree with him on many issues, they could not help but
be impressed with his vote-getting potential. One consequence of this was
that unless directly challenged, they were not likely to oppose him too strenu-
ously.

Even more importantly, he was now backed by a standing organization.
There was in fact almost no pause in the boosting activities of his supporters.
Just two months after the election, a banquet was held in his honor that was in
effect a private nominating convention. More than eight hundred attended
the gathering, held on 10 June 1911, at the La Salle Hotel, and speaker after
speaker praised his honesty, integrity, and commitment to the people, while
emphasizing his qualities as an administrator—qualities, they were careful to
point out, that might ably suit him for the governorship. Pleased as he was,
Dunne refused to commit himself, but he did feel constrained to point out the
need for change in Springfield.[30]

In normal times, if any period of Chicago and Illinois political history
can be characterized as normal, the gubernatorial nomination would have been
the province of the organized factions of both parties. In 1911 and 1912,
however, the cumulative effect of the Lorimer scandal, the recent introduction of the direct primary as the means of selecting candidates, and the general mood for reform seriously affected the operation of the machine system.
The Republicans, while still under the nominal leadership of Governor Charles
Deneen, had in the wake of the Lorimer affair become a battleground of discord and recrimination. That was ultimately to lead to a breakup of the party
in the summer of 1912.[31]

Among the Democratic factions, the most directly affected by the fallout
of the Lorimer scandal was the Sullivan organization. As the most visible and
successful of the Democratic machines, this group was a natural target for
reformist sentiment. Moreover, Roger Sullivan, himself, was accused without telling evidence of having played a part in the election of the discredited
senator. For those reasons, he declined to participate in the choice of candidates for state and city offices. Instead, the Sullivanites were directed to con-

tinue their war with the H-H faction for control of the party apparatus.

Mayor Harrison and Andrew Lawrence, Hearst's local representative and editor of Chicago's *American* and *Examiner*, on the other hand, tried to take advantage of the growing demand for change by an abortive effort to rally the party's reformers under their banner. To this end, a convention was held on 4 October 1911 in Springfield. Its expressed purposes were to rescue "the party from the management which had controlled it to its defeat for the past eight years" and to organize something called the "Progressive Democracy." More than two thousand Democrats attended and listened to passionate addresses against "Lorimerism" and "Sullivanism." The affair, however, served little purpose; few not already in the H-H camp attended, and because slate making smacked too much of machine activity, no candidates were endorsed. In any case, it was unlikely that any kind of unity behind any particular list of candidates could have been achieved. It was well known that Dunne, at this point almost Harrison's personal enemy, enjoyed wide support among the rank and file of the faction. He was not above taking advantage of this by conveniently being in Springfield on the day of the convention, ostensibly to give a speech elsewhere in the city but also to greet informally his many friends at the gathering.[32]

His by now obvious gubernatorial candidacy was not left unchallenged. Contemporary wisdom held that in 1912 the Democrats, because of the growing divisions among the Republicans, stood a real chance of taking the governorship for the first time in twenty years. There was, as a result, no lack of candidates. By the late fall of 1911, however, two men, Samuel Alschuler and Ben F. Caldwell, were generally recognized along with Dunne as major aspirants for the nomination. Alschuler was an attorney from Aurora, and he had headed the state ticket in 1900. He and Dunne had long been close, and the former mayor was careful to assure him privately "that the long-time personal friendship existing between us will in no way be disturbed by the concurrence of our political ambitions." Alschuler was eventually endorsed by Carter Harrison for reasons apparently less rooted in political judgment than in a desire to spite Dunne. Caldwell was a banker and farmer from Sangamon County. He had served as a congressman and he was perceived and presented as the downstate candidate. Dunne was later to call him a man "of high standing and excellent character."[33]

By the end of January 1912, all three candidates had officially entered the primary. Dunne's announcement came on 17 January, and it was reflective of both the themes of the upcoming campaign and the spirit of his governorship as well. The main thrust of his attack was to be upon "Jackpot government," a phrase that emerged during the Lorimer affair and one that he was to use consistently. In his eyes, of course, "Jackpot government" was the result of sixteen years of Republican governors. He mourned the vast increase in the cost of state government since the "last Democratic governor and true friend of the people, Altgeld." The reference to Altgeld was calculated, and he would continue to present himself as the heir to the great Democratic chief executive. More positively, he promised to return the government to the people by working for

> the enactment of laws governing corrupt practices at elections, election of Senators by direct vote of the people, the abolition of that instrument of venality and favoritism in taxation, the Board of Equalization, the enactment into law of the initiative and referendum and other progressive measures which will restore representative government.[34]

He began to actively campaign on 22 February with a swing through "Egypt," or southern Illinois. That was logical, since as a Chicago-based politician he needed to try to establish himself as a statewide figure. In the course of a week, he toured twelve counties, and he was to maintain a similarly arduous schedule through the day of the primary election.[35]

His message was almost exclusively that of the dangers of "Jackpotism" and "Lorimerism." If he mentioned his rivals at all, it was in a vaguely complementary fashion. There was in actuality almost no ideological differences among them; they were all progressives. Things got so gentlemanly that the three candidates agreed to coordinate their first speaking tours so as not to visit the same place at the same time.[36]

Despite the spirit of cooperation and equality among them, it was Dunne who gained and held the initiative. As the best known with the strongest reformist record, he could and did set the tone of the campaign. By the middle of March, he had introduced a new angle on the larger theme of "Lorimerism"— bipartisanship. He claimed, with some merit, that had there not been collusion between politicians of both parties Lorimer could not have been elected. This breakdown in the two-party system, he argued, thus cheated the people of Illinois of a fundamental safeguard. A return to healthy competition could only work to protect democracy. It was not an especially original argument (Deneen had himself used it in 1910), but it did gain some public attention. It was also, of course, self-serving, since he had always been an advocate of party and party loyalty.[37]

The dynamics of the contest were soon apparent. With little ideological difference among the candidates, the race became dependent upon personal popularity and the regional loyalties each could command. Caldwell was unquestionably the downstate candidate. Alschuler enjoyed some support in Chicago, chiefly from the fractured and embattled H-H faction, and he was also strong in northern Illinois. Dunne from the beginning was dominant in the Windy City. Not only was he genuinely admired by many of the city's Democrats, but the organization that had originated in the 1911 mayoral race was vigorously promoting his cause. At the same time, although he had pockets of support throughout the state, he was the weakest candidate outside of Cook County.[38]

All three men entered the final stretch of the race with some hope of victory. Things naturally became more passionate, especially between Dunne and Alschuler. By late March, the two had entered into an ongoing polemic that centered on the question of which one was the more progressive. Alschuler argued that he "had been up to his neck fighting corruption, graft, boodle, and 'Jackpotism'" in the state legislature while Dunne was "droning away on the bench." Dunne responded by pointing out that Thomas J. Dawson, an "attorney and mouthpiece of the 'Jackpotter'" William Lorimer was running Alschuler's campaign in several downstate counties. However, when the two met at a gathering of Chicago freight handlers shortly before the primary election, it was clear that the rhetoric had not affected a fundamental mutual respect.[39]

When the ballots were at last counted on 9 April 1912, the results were curiously lopsided. On one hand, Dunne, the victor, only carried pluralities in 14 counties, while Caldwell took 45 and Alschuler, with 43, was a close second. On the other hand, Dunne's popular vote of 131,212 overwhelmed Caldwell's 71,972 and the 87,127 given to Alschuler. In all, 106,253 of Dunne's total (enough in their own right to assure victory) came from Chicago. He took all of the city's wards with the exception of the Twentieth, which was controlled by Harrisonite alderman Dennis J. Egan, which went for Alschuler by a thin margin. Obviously, his friends in Chicago had done their work well.[40]

The candidates quickly reconciled. Alschuler became part of Dunne's campaign team, and Caldwell soon announced his support. Downstate there was disappointment, but no bitterness. The *Mason County Democrat*, an Alschuler backer, reflected the general attitude when it wrote that Dunne "was a good man for standard bearer, and his nomination means a united Chicago Democracy for governor which in the estimate of everyone versed in Illinois politics spells success."[41]

The downstate paper was correct in its assertion that Chicago Democrats were united behind their former mayor; neither the H-H faction nor the Sullivan machine was inclined to break ranks. That did not mean that they were in the least inclined, however, to set aside their differences in their own private war with each other. Indeed, their conflict intensified after the primary into a comic-opera concatenation of events related to the Cook County and state conventions that were to ultimately affect the selection of the Democratic presidential nominee.

When neither faction secured in the primary a majority of ward committeemen, who served as delegates to the county convention, they began intense maneuvering to try to dominate the upcoming gathering. On 15 April, the appointed day, the Harrison forces arrived early at the Seventh Street Armory to seize control. They found the doors locked and guarded by an officer of the Illinois National Guard; the Sullivan forces had obtained an injunction to forestall just such an effort. Having arranged for their own injunction that directed the admission to the hall of all persons certified by the Harrison-run Board of Election commissioners, the Harrison people called upon the chief of police and the Cook County sheriff to force an entry. This was done without violence, and the Harrisonites held a convention that endorsed the initiative and referendum, Dunne for governor, and Champ Clark for president. They then elected delegates for the state convention. Meanwhile, the Sullivanites, finding the armory being held by hostile forces, held their own convention across town, which also endorsed Dunne and elected state delegates.[42]

At the state convention on 19 April, in Peoria, the Sullivan organization was victorious. In all, the Central Committee, where Sullivan's influence was especially strong, seated 334 of the boss's delegates and only 70 from the H-H group. Once again a rump convention was held, this time by the Harrison people. The issue was finally resolved by the Democratic National Convention in Baltimore, where with the help of the supporters of New Jersey Governor Woodrow Wilson, the Sullivan slate, which like that of Harrison's included Dunne, was recognized as valid representatives of the Illinois Democracy. Sullivan returned the favor by swinging the Illinois delegation into Wilson's camp, thus greatly aiding his nomination for president.[43]

Throughout, Dunne refused to become involved, realizing that to take sides would imperil his chances for election. Instead he made spirited attempts to bring the factions together. In September and October, he was finally able to arrange a temporary truce that, however, only applied to Cook County.[44]

For all of the emotional fury of the discord among the Democrats, it paled in comparison with those found in the state Republican Party. Incumbent Charles Deneen, who was seeking a third term, had won the preferential primary easily enough over seven opponents, but he came under serious attack from his party's progressive wing. He had been in public life as a legislator, state's attorney, and governor and on the whole had a good record.[45] However, he had been compromised in the eyes of many progressive Republicans by the Lorimer scandal. To be sure, he had not been implicated, but he had become a symbol of a disreputable system. Although an opponent of Lorimer of long standing, he was still a machine politician, and when he first acted in a way many saw as disloyal to Theodore Roosevelt at the ill-fated Republican National Convention held in Chicago in late June, and then when he refused to break with President Taft and follow T. R. into the Progressive Party, he was openly rejected by the very strong reformist element of his party. Even before the quickly organized National Progressive Convention (called to affirm Roosevelt's independent candidacy for president), the progressives of the state Republican Party met in Chicago on 3 August to nominate their own complete state ticket. Among those mentioned for the governorship were Harold Ickes and Walter C. Jones, the progressive standard-bearer for governor in the recent Republican primary. In the end, in part because Jones had done so poorly, Frank Funk, a state senator and farmer from Bloomington with a record as a moderate, was given the nod.[46]

As the breakup of the state Republican Party and the nomination of Funk would suggest, the gubernatorial race was from its inception overshadowed by the contest for presidency of the United States. This was reenforced by the frequent appearances during the campaign by members of the national tickets and politicians of all parties of similar stature. Woodrow Wilson, the Democratic nominee for president, first came to Illinois to get acquainted with the state ticket, as well as to lend his voice to the call for unity among the state's "regular" Democrats who were still badly divided between the Sullivan and Harrison Democrats. Dunne also spoke and apparently impressed all present including his party's nominee for president. Wilson returned in September and then in October for a massive rally at the state fairgrounds in Springfield that climaxed the Democratic campaign in Illinois. More than ten thousand attended, and such was the magic of the occasion that Carter Harrison and Roger Sullivan agreed to share the platform. Dunne, of course, was a featured speaker, and it was he who introduced Wilson. Of more direct help to Dunne was William Jennings Bryan who stumped the state on his behalf for more than two weeks. He, in addition, benefited by a visit by the man who had been his and Bryan's first choice for the presidential nomination, Champ Clark.[47]

The Progressives also brought in their political stars. Theodore Roosevelt came to the state, first in September and then on 13 October, or immediately before an assassination attempt in Milwaukee, and his running mate,·Hiram Johnson, had earlier come to Illinois to tour and speak for Funk. In contrast to both of his rivals, Governor Deneen could muster only a letter of endorsement from President Taft.[48]

Notwithstanding the national aspect of the campaign, Dunne's own strategy included little that was new or unexpected. He had been campaigning virtually since December 1910, when he had unexpectedly declared himself for the mayor's race, and his approach had been successful. Once again, he committed himself to an exhaustive schedule in which he visited more than four hundred communities and traveled more than fifteen thousand miles.[49]

His theme remained "Jackpotism," and most of his fire was directed against Governor Deneen. It was not that the governor was himself corrupt, he repeatedly argued, but that he had done nothing to root out corruption in the state government, and in this he had failed in his responsibilities. Moreover, was not Deneen a leading member of the political system that had elected Lorimer in the first place? This tactic, which was essentially the old political saw of "drive the rascals out," proved effective but left him vulnerable to the recurring charges of vagueness as to what he would do as governor.[50]

He had less to say about Funk. The Progressive candidate had a clean record, and Dunne gave every indication of wishing to draw as little attention to him as possible. The favor was not returned. As the representative of a party, the existence of which testified to a widely held belief that the bipartisan system was a failure, Funk felt compelled to try to discredit Dunne's record as a reformer. The former mayor of Chicago was, according to Progressive rhetoric, a hypocrite in his tirades against Governor Deneen. Had not he, for all of his good intentions, sheltered corruption in Chicago's government by his inefficiency and indifference? It had just been his good fortune that the revelations of widespread "boodle" in city hall had emerged after he had left office. Even his battle for municipal ownership, Funk reminded the voters, had been ultimately a failure, and what guarantee was there that he could do any better as governor?[51]

As cynical as the Progressive candidate was about Dunne, it was Deneen who bore the brunt of his fury. Indeed, Deneen, as the standard-bearer immediately at hand of a party many saw as discredited by the Lorimer scandal and the Taft administration, was the whipping boy for almost everyone. Besides the barrages of Dunne and Funk, he was forced to endure Olympian thunderbolts from Theodore Roosevelt who labeled him as "unfit." Even some of his supporters were less than enthusiastic about his candidacy. The *Chicago Tribune*, for instance, which had adopted the schizophrenic position of endorsing Roosevelt and Deneen, admitted on 18 October that the governor was not its ideal choice.[52]

In face of these obstacles, the governor waged what can only be characterized as a valiant effort. Always on the defensive, his schedule was matched only by that of Dunne as he tried to overcome his political handicaps by a personal appeal to the voters. Like Funk, he questioned his Democratic opponent's record as mayor, while pointing out that the Progressive candidate's tenure as a state legislator, while clean, was not a paragon of reformism.[53]

While intense, the campaign was for the most part gentlemanly. The moderate caliber of the personal attacks was illustrated by one downstate Republican newspaper's description of Dunne speaking locally. The "repudiated mayor of Chicago," this newspaper insisted, was "short and stocky with a poor voice for public speaking and an unattractive delivery," this about a man whose political career was founded upon his charisma and oratorical skills![54]

Near the end, things were marred by a rumor that the Democratic candidate as a member of the Knights of Columbus had taken an "oath of obligation" that could impair his performance as governor. Asked about the matter by a Lutheran minister in Mendota, Dunne dismissed the allegation as "insane." He was to be Illinois's only second Roman Catholic chief executive, and his religion had been of concern to some even back when he won the primary, when Samuel Alschuler felt it necessary to reassure a downstate supporter that he did not believe "that the average American Catholic is in any way less loyal to our institutions than the average person of any other faith."[55] Dunne's well-deserved reputation for honesty and devotion to family doubtlessly relieved the apprehension of many, and as neither Deneen or Funk (both mindful of the considerable body of Catholic voters in Chicago) sought to raise the issue, it never became important.

With the Republican Party first bruised and weakened by the Lorimer scandal and then torn apart in the summer of 1912, a Democratic triumph in the fall elections was a virtual certainty. For all of their vituperation toward each other, both Deneen and Funk conceded that Dunne was their chief opponent, and as early as September, the Democrats were claiming victory barring "overconfidence."[56] The voting, as a result, brought no surprises. In the presidential race, Wilson carried Illinois by a narrow 1.63 percent, and Dunne, running ahead of his party's national ticket by 3 percent, easily secured the governor's chair, while bringing with him all of his fellow Democratic candidates for the state cabinet. In the Illinois House of Representatives, the party increased its number from 67 to 73 and thus secured a plurality it had not held since the beginning of the Civil War. In the Senate, there were now 24 Democrats, an increase of 7, in the 51-member body. Similarly, the party swept local elections throughout the state, including those in Cook County.[57]

Within the statistics of victory was the somber reality that the Democrats in Illinois, as in the nation, had won only because of the split in the Republican Party. Dunne may have carried 66 counties, but he secured majorities in only 23, all of which were downstate and all of which were traditional centers of Democratic strength. In the same way, the plurality in the Illinois House of Representatives disappeared if the 25 Progressives were added to the 52 Republicans. For the moment, however, these portents were forgotten as Democrats throughout the state celebrated the man who was only their second governor-elect since the Civil War.

5

CONSENSUS FOR REFORM
THE FORTY-EIGHTH GENERAL ASSEMBLY

As in 1905, Edward F. Dunne in 1913 found himself riding to power on the wave of a "revolution" that transcended the usual political rules; it was his unique place in history to have been the immediate beneficiary of the two most important reformist upsurges in Illinois during the progressive period. Unlike 1905, however, he was now to have the advantage of a legislative body that was at least generally sympathetic to his aims. The remarkable Forty-eighth General Assembly, while disappointing the governor in some ways, would nonetheless compile a record of reform that would represent the high point of his years in public service.

In the months following the election, it was politics rather than reform that dominated his attention. He first took upon the monumental task of attempting to heal the breach within his party. The rivalry between the Sullivan and H-H factions, complicated further by the new prospects of federal and state patronage, defied all of his attempts at arbitration. For the moment, he maintained his neutral stance, but eventually he would be compelled to choose sides. As fundamental as this factional strife was, its importance soon dwindled in the face of what became a major political crisis that centered in the selection of a Speaker of the Illinois House of Representatives.[1]

The speakership in 1913 was a very powerful and coveted position. The Speaker appointed the members of all committees, and this gave him considerable control over the fate of the session. This year, the usual scrambling for the job was complicated by the fact that with 73 Democratic members, 52 Republicans, and 25 Progressives, as well as 4 Socialists, there was in the House no clear majority party. In addition, there were antagonisms and mutually exclusive agendas in every direction. The Republicans and Progressives were naturally at odds, and among the Democrats there were the usual factional wars. Moreover, there were regional conflicts between those from Cook County and those from downstate. Ideology also played its divisive role, as did the question of whether one was a "wet" or a "dry" on the liquor question. For all of that, however, it was the personal ambitions of the body's prominent members that were to be often decisive.

Not unreasonably the governor-elect resolved to steer clear of the matter; his participation could only, so he reasoned, win unnecessary enemies. However, he soon came under pressure from his progressive friends, most notably William Jennings Bryan, when it became clear that the leading candidates were men who in 1908 had voted for Lorimer. On 6 January 1913, he therefore issued a cautious statement urging House Democrats to rally behind a man who would support J. Hamilton Lewis for the United States Senate, and who had not helped to elect the fallen Republican boss.[2]

While that action assured that no one who had voted for Lorimer, including Sullivan's candidate, John J. McLaughlin (Cook County-D) could win, it also failed to cause the election of a suitable Speaker. John Rapp (Wayne County-D), a leading progressive member, came the closest in the seemingly endless balloting that followed when on 17 January he came within "an eyelash" of victory. Unfortunately, his "dry" stance hurt his cause, and the prospect of an indefinite deadlock became very real.[3] This was a source of growing concern for Dunne. Originally scheduled to be inaugurated on 13 January, he had already lost four days of his term because the Illinois Constitution required that the House canvass the election returns before the new state administration could take office; and that they could not do until they had elected a speaker. There was an attempt to circumvent this by an agreement with Governor Deneen to let Dunne take his oath. Deneen was agreeable, but lame-duck Attorney General Charles Stead vetoed the idea as unconstitutional.[4]

Next the governor-elect sent William O'Connell to Springfield to negotiate an agreement among the three acknowledged progressive Democratic candidates: Rapp, William Hubbard (Green County-D), and Charles Karch (St. Clair County-D). It was decided that the three men would support each other in turn until one was elected. After some heated discussion, Rapp was chosen to go first. It did him little good; he again went down to defeat eight votes short of a majority. Subsequently, Karch and Hubbard's efforts also failed.[5]

Throughout, Dunne was urged by his supporters to openly endorse a candidate. That, so it was felt, would force most Democrats into the fold, if not for reasons of party spirit, then certainly for the prospect of having the governor with all his state patronage in their debt. It did not work. John Rapp, who gained the public endorsement, again failed to gain a majority. Not only did the hard-core McLaughlin forces unexpectedly withhold their nineteen votes, but the Socialists, contrary to all expectations, voted for their own candidate.[6]

Things were becoming truly desperate; there was even an attempt to drag in President-elect Wilson, but he wisely declined to intervene. The fight had now gone on so long that the bitterness it engendered seemed to threaten any prospect of a fruitful session. Something like panic began to creep into the public statements of all concerned. At that point, Roger Sullivan stepped in and arranged a compromise in the person of William B. McKinley (Cook County-D).

McKinley had been a minor candidate whose name had regularly appeared during the balloting. While a Sullivanite, he was also a close friend of Dunne's. While a "wet," he won the grudging approval of the Illinois Anti-Saloon League. On the evening of 28 January, with the governor-elect's tacit support, the Republicans, who had been standing behind Homer J. Tice (Menard County-R), agreed to back the Chicago Democrat. The majority of Democrats were also brought into line. The next day he was elected. In all, he received votes from 46 Republicans, 36 Democrats, and 1 Progressive. Seventeen Democratic "drys" as well as 4 McLaughlin supporters failed to jump on the bandwagon.[7]

The mechanics of this minor political miracle are not completely certain. There was some suggestion that a deal was struck with the Republicans concerning the upcoming senatorial elections (that before the Seventeenth Amendment being a function of the legislature). Subsequent events make that unlikely. Promises were probably made about committee appointments, but it is even more certain that Republicans crossed over because they, too, had a stake in getting down to business.

Dunne's initial instincts to stay out of the speakership fight had proven to be correct. He had, it was true, kept any who had voted for Lorimer from the office, but that had to be measured against the revelations of Roger Sullivan's mastery and of his own inability to control the House Democrats. For the moment that was not especially important—the political boss was not concerned about reformist issues, and the governor-elect showed little inclination to wrestle away control of the party machinery. Still, it was not a propitious beginning.

McKinley's selection set the long-delayed plans for the inauguration into motion. Having arrived in Springfield the previous evening in a blinding snowstorm, Dunne rose to take his oath at an outdoor celebration at noon on 2 February 1913. As if to compensate for the vagueness of his campaign and his role during the speakership fight, he offered a vigorous address that spelled out an ambitious and specific progressive program.

He assigned the highest priority to an amendment that would introduce the initiative and referendum into the state constitution. Of almost equal importance was his call for a Public Utility Commission to be granted wide regulatory powers, and that would guarantee considerable autonomy for Chicago and permit municipal ownership. He also asked for the replacement of the elected Board of Equalization as the agency of property tax assessment with a smaller, appointed tax commission. In addition, he endorsed a long list of political reforms, including the simplification of the process of amending the state charter, the ratification of the Seventeenth Amendment that authorized the direct election of United States senators, the introduction of shorter ballots upon which the names of candidates would be rotated, the extension of civil service, and the enactment of a stringent corrupt practices act. His reformism reached an unusual height when he called for a law to punish with imprisonment any elected official who broke a written campaign pledge. More practically perhaps, he made strong pleas for better roads and for more humane treatment of criminals, juvenile delinquents, and the insane.[8]

The inauguration was followed by a furious round of festivities. The Democrats had not controlled the state administration since 1897, and they were fully willing to celebrate. From the Sullivan-dominated Cook County Democracy came 250 "silk-hatted patriots." Not to be outdone, the H-H faction sent 272 of their number to march. Also present were numerous delegations from other county committees and seemingly endless streams of bands and fire companies. In sharp contrast to the last transfer of power between the parties when Republican Governor-elect John Tanner snubbed outgoing Governor John Altgeld, the mood was friendly, and Deneen and Dunne were full of mutual praise. Later that night a "brilliant reception" was held at the governor's mansion; the next day both the new governor and his wife had to seek medical attention for two very sore right hands.[9]

Before Dunne and the legislature could get to work on his program, it was politically necessary to elect two United States senators—one for the usual six-year term and the other to complete the last two years of Lorimer's. That did not promise to be an easy task. Not since 1818 had the state elected two senators at the same time, and the lack of precedent only added to the situation's complexity. Joint balloting of the two houses of the legislature began on 11 February, and an immediate deadlock ensued as political self-interest came to the front.

The Democrats, with the encouragement of President Wilson were united in their determination to secure not only the long term for their preferential primary victor, J. Hamilton Lewis, but the short term as well for the national committeeman Charles Boeschenstein of Edwardsville. For their part, the Republicans were intent upon electing their primary choice, Lawrence Y. Sherman, to one of the seats, while holding on to the hope of taking the other as well. The Progressives with far less unity were committed to the candidacy of their recent nominee for governor, Frank Funk.[10]

If another fracas like the speakership fight was to be avoided, compromise was in order. Governor Dunne therefore proposed a division of the seats. Lewis, as the representative of the victorious party in the November election, was to be given the long term, and Sherman was to be elected to the short.[11] The regulars of the Democratic Party were not pleased with a scheme that gave away so much potential federal patronage. Arthur W. Charles, chairman of the state organization and a Sullivanite, explained: "I do not believe that after the magnificent victory of last fall, the Democrats of Illinois will look with approval on the bartering of the short term senatorship in order to complete a bipartisan alliance."[12] The charge that the governor was trying to negotiate a "bipartisan alliance" was simply unfair; rather he just saw no other way to resolve the matter.

His proposal was further frustrated by the reluctance of the Republicans. They had hopes of coming to terms with the Progressives. That idea, however, was laid to rest on 26 February, when Theodore Roosevelt made his disapproval known. Roosevelt's pronouncement was in fact a source of relief for some Republicans as well as Democrats, since it was felt that to elect Funk was to guarantee his reelection in 1914.[13] So things stood when the General Assembly adjourned until 11 March to allow the governor and Speaker McKinley to attend the inauguration of President-elect Wilson.

From all appearances, the governor and his party, which also included Mayor Harrison and two hundred or so representatives of the Chicago and Cook County Democracies, had in Washington, D.C., a wonderful time; this despite the fact that the Illinois contingent, led by Dunne "upon a superb horse," somehow lost its place in the inaugural parade and only arrived in front of the reviewing stand as Woodrow Wilson was leaving. The timely intervention by the new secretary of state, William Jennings Bryan, saved the day.[14]

The next evening, Governor Dunne accompanied by William O'Connell and McKinley met with the new president at the White House. Wilson indicated his reluctance to intervene into the senatorial elections; he did not want to be placed in the position of standing between the state organization controlled by Sullivan, to whom he owed so much, and Dunne who led the state party's reform wing. He did agree that if absolutely necessary he would try to do something to end the impasse.[15]

Thus it was that after the General Assembly resumed its session and its deadlock for an additional week, William Jennings Bryan arrived in Springfield on 18 March to speak before the body. In what the governor called a "great speech," he, without openly endorsing Dunne's compromise, did indicate the administration's strong interest in getting J. Hamilton Lewis to the capital as soon as possible.[16]

The regular Democrats reluctantly took the hint. The fears of the Republicans that the Seventeenth Amendment might be soon ratified, resulting in the governor appointing two temporary senators, were played upon, and a deal was struck giving the long term to Lewis and the short to Sherman. To the end, seventeen House Democrats refused to go along.[17]

The resolution of the senatorial question unquestionably rebounded in the governor's favor. It helped to erase the image of indecisiveness and weakness created during the speakership fight, and it strongly reenforced the loyalty of J. Hamilton Lewis, who became Dunne's liaison in Washington.[18] More importantly, the legislature, almost three months after the session began, could at last address the administration's program and especially Dunne's pet project: the initiative and referendum.

The initiative (by which the citizenry could petition the legislature to place laws on the ballot for a direct vote) and the referendum were solutions that the reformers had found to the problem of "interest controlled" legislatures. Based upon the example of the Swiss, seventeen states by 1913 had enacted either the initiative or referendum or both.[19]

Illinois had experimented with the spirit of the initiative and referendum with the Public Opinion Law of 1901, which gave voters only an advisory vote. Under that measure, however, the people had twice indicated their desire for a binding initiative and referendum. In response, the General Assembly in 1911 had come within nine votes in the House of passing the measure. Governor Dunne, who supported the idea since at least 1902, was determined to see it enacted.[20]

The proposal's only openly organized opponent was the Civic Federation of Chicago. An upper-class group (its honorary president between 1883 and 1896 was socialite leader Mrs. Potter Palmer), the Civic Federation was dedicated to governmental efficiency, chiefly expressed in working to keep taxes as low as possible, as well as such minor philanthropic projects as a Penny Savings Society and a campaign "of educational publicity against harmful food for babies."[21]

Officially, the organization's opposition to the initiative and referendum in both 1911 and 1913 was that it stood in the way of a constitutional amendment to reform the state's tax structure (the law only allowing one revision of the state charter per legislative session). The Civic Federation, however, widely distributed bulletins that attacked the measures as dangerous to representative government and as surrendering Illinois to the volatile rule of the urban masses led by "quacks in politics and social reform."[22]

Far more threatening to the initiative and referendum was an ill-defined and informally allied cabal of conservatives and machine politicians, which included most of the leaders of the Republican regulars as well as several important downstate Democrats. Not daring to publicly flaunt popular demand, these people had and would again call upon the tactics of parliamentary maneuver and amendment to block passage. Generally Republican, their activities on this and other matters were to reformers like the governor justifications in themselves for the direct democracy promised by the measures.

However, the governor was optimistic. In the last elections, as he was to repeatedly point out, both the Democrats and the Progressives had called for the initiative and referendum in their platforms. Together the two parties had been given nearly two-thirds of the vote, which he interpreted as a resounding endorsement. His hopes seemed further justified by the support of such vociferous and widely separated groups as the Illinois Anti-Saloon League and the Chicago and Illinois Federations of Labor. Despite his experience as mayor, he continued to find it impossible to believe that the people's representatives could deny something their constituencies so strongly desired.

At first things went well. On 11 February, Senator D. Duff Piercy (Jefferson County-D) introduced an administration resolution (S.J.R. 17) that would permit 8 percent of the registered voters to bring proposed legislation to the ballot (contingent upon the approval of one-quarter of both houses of the General Assembly) and 5 percent to cause a referendum upon any law. It was quickly reported out of Piercy's Committee on Constitutional Amendments favorably. In the full Senate, it was amended, after some debate and opposition by Chicago's senators, to require that 50 percent of all signatures for petitions be acquired outside of Cook County. The measure passed in this form on 17 April by the impressive margin of forty to one.[23]

In the House, the resolution passed through Charles Karch's Judiciary Committee by a vote of twenty-four to three with little fanfare. On the floor, however, the verbal battle began. Representatives of the Civic Federation together with a dedicated core of opposition led by Representative Edward J. King (Knox County-R) decried it as the first crack of doom for the Republic, while such allies of the governor as Samuel Alschuler, John J. Fitzpatrick of the Chicago Federation of Labor, and Fred Kern, chairman of the State Board of Administration, praised the initiative and referendum as the salvation of the principles of democracy.[24]

Both sides were predicting victory. Governor Dunne issued another appeal to the House citing the clear record of the people's will on the issue, while asserting to reporters his belief in its imminent passage. George E. Lee, secretary of the Initiative and Referendum League, went further and claimed the resolution would pass with 115 votes, or 14 more than the two-thirds necessary. Donald Sutherland, secretary of the Civic Federation, on the other hand, proclaimed: "the proposition will be lost by from ten to fifteen votes."[25]

High noon, or rather high midnight, came on 13 May 1913. In a session lasting well into the night (the *House Journal* records adjournment at 11:59 P.M., while the newspapers insist events continued until about 1:00 A.M.), the House engaged in a political drama that in a real sense was the climax of the Forty-eighth General Assembly. The antagonists were the Republicans, who had caucused an hour before the chamber had convened that morning and agreed to support a series of amendments. All but one of those were relatively minor, but one, to be introduced by Representative Morton D. Hull (Cook County-R) was a genuine threat.[26]

In essence, this so-called Hull Substitute would predicate the passage of any proposal through either the initiative or referendum upon a majority of total registered voters rather than a majority of those actually voting on the proposition. The effect would be to transform a nonvote on any particular matter, a frequent enough occurrence under the Public Opinion Law, into a no vote. That formula had been discussed earlier in the Senate, but it had been overwhelmingly dismissed. Now the House Republicans pledged not to compromise in the full knowledge that it was completely unacceptable to Governor Dunne and his supporters.[27]

Having given over the morning to routine business (and backstage maneuver), the House did not address the Piercy resolution until 2:00 in the afternoon. At that time, it met as a committee as a whole to avoid the usual three readings, and this confined all remaining debate to the next hours. It was a challenge to which both sides energetically responded. Speaking for the measure were a team led by Progressive representative and future Republican United States senator, Medill McCormick (Cook County-P), Seymour Stedman (Cook County-S), leader of the state Socialist Party, and Charles Karch. The opposition was largely centered in the person of Representative King, who devoted four hours and eight glasses of water to a tirade that was characterized as "inhuman at times," and which at one point represented "Judas Iscariot's kiss and betrayal," "as the first referendum." Throughout, William O'Connell, whom the governor had called from his duties as Cook County treasurer, roamed the aisles marshaling support. At the same time, things were given a bizarre twist by the physical presence of former Senator William Lorimer, who moved about the chamber at will, and who was given a seat on the Speaker's platform.[28]

Shortly after ten that evening, the cascade of words trickled to a halt, and the Hull Substitute was introduced. Solidly supported by the Republicans, it was nonetheless tabled by a margin of 83 to 63. Speaker McKinley then tried to unilaterally force a vote upon the resolution. So much protest resulted that he was forced to allow the introduction of ten more amendments. Each of those were successively defeated. Finally, at some time around or after midnight, the roll call on the initiative and referendum commenced. As it ended, it appeared it had exactly the 103, or two-thirds vote, required to send it for final approval to the voters. A cheer went up, but the elation quickly died when Representative Hubert Kilens (Cook County-D) rose before McKinley could declare the measure passed and changed his vote to the negative column. Confusion prevailed, and the administration Democrats just managed to table the resolution for later consideration.[29]

Dunne never forgave Hubert Kilens. Other Democrats naturally blamed the Republicans, while the governor's social reformist allies were more specific and vehement. Within a week, the Chicago Federation of Labor issued a formal statement that directly attributed the defeat to the influence of William Lorimer upon key Republican legislators. Outraged, those representatives caused the summoning of the CFL's executive and legislative committees to the bar of the House to offer proof. A sizable delegation that included such close allies of the governor as Margaret Haley, who had composed the statement, John J. Fitzpatrick, and Daniel Cruice appeared and defiantly cited "common knowledge" of Lorimer's role. Finding this unsatisfactory, the House very late on the evening of 27 May, with many absent and despite the best efforts of the administration Democrats, voted by a margin of 45 to 44 to censure the CFL. Throughout, Governor Dunne made no public comment, but it was highly probably that he was in private agreement with his friends.[30]

Silence was good politics; not only was he dependent upon the good will of the Republicans for the success of the rest of his program, but he was even now engaged in lobbying for a second try at the initiative and referendum. Although serious in this, at least one associate was distressed by his refusal to ruthlessly pressure legislators for fear that they might "resent executive interference."[31]

On 5 June 1913, the Piercy resolution was brought again before the House for a vote. This time, the administration agreed to the inclusion of two minor Republican amendments, but it was to little avail. They still insisted upon the Hull Substitute, which was again voted down. This set the scene for the second defeat of the initiative and referendum. The margin was a discouraging 95 to 38, or eight votes short.[32]

The governor was "intensely disappointed," and the closeness of the first vote on the matter only made things more galling. There was some discussion of a future special session to reconsider the matter. Eventually, however, he was forced to the conclusion that the initiative and referendum was a dead issue in Illinois.[33]

Also disheartening was the General Assembly's failure to abolish the Board of Equalization. Responsible for property tax assessment, the elected twenty-five member board had long been the target of reformers. In 1909, a study group chosen by Governor Deneen had recommended its replacement with an appointed five-member tax commission, but the legislature had been apparently unwilling to dismantle such a fruitful source of power and patronage. Dunne resurrected this proposal and Michael Igoe (Cook County-D), one of his chief floor leaders, managed to steer it (H.B. 854) through the House, where it passed by a vote of 79 to 44. In the Senate, things went differently. Exiled to the Committee on Elections, it was never allowed to reappear.[34]

A similar fate befell the administration's hopes to define and regulate corrupt electoral practices. House Bill 914 made it to a second reading easily enough, but Representative Lee O'Neil Browne (La Salle County-D), one of the chambers most powerful conservative voices, managed to delay further consideration. Through the mysteries of cloakroom politicking, it thereupon disappeared forever from the House agenda.[35]

Despite those setbacks, the governor was nonetheless able to inspire the Forty-eighth General Assembly to enact an impressive set of progressive legislation. His greatest success came with the creation of a Public Utility Commission, which extended the authority of the old Railway and Warehouse Commission to most utilities. Attempting to capitalize on existing support (the legislature in 1911 had passed a joint resolution in favor of a new board), the governor announced his appointment of a study group that included Professors David Kinley, John Fairlie, and Walter F. Dodd, as well as the noted economist and former associate of Mayor Tom L. Johnson, Edward Bemis.[36] Working from the recommendations of the governor, who was not unfamiliar with the issues of utility regulation, the group eventually presented a carefully crafted proposal that created a state Public Utility Commission of five members to be appointed by the governor and confirmed by the Senate. The bill provided for extensive powers to oversee all public utilities, which were defined "to include transportation, telegraph, telephone, light, heat, cold, power, electric, water, pipe-line, grain warehouse, and wharf companies."[37]

The measure (H.B. 907) attracted wide support, but its provision to allow Chicago and all municipalities with populations that exceeded 100,000 to create their own independent utility commissions aroused instant downstate opposition. The legislature subsequently deleted this "home rule" article, and neither Dunne nor the Chicago lobby was able to restore it. The entire political spectrum of Chicago pressured for a veto. At one point the governor was forced to endure a heated visit from Mayor Harrison and almost the entire city council. After due consideration, however, he signed the measure on 30 June 1913. He explained that the positive features, which included a recognition of the possibility of municipal ownership (which was directly provided for in a separate bill), far outweighed the unfortunate lack of "home rule."[38]

In addition, Dunne was a vocal proponent of three road laws (H.B. 608, 679, 894) drafted by Representative Homer J. Tice (Menard County-R). The Tice bills were based upon a plan proposed by Governor Deneen and modified by the Illinois Highway Improvement Association at its convention in Peoria in September 1912. The final version of the bills provided for a state commission to finance half the cost of county road construction done in accordance with state standards as enforced and overseen by county highway commissioners. The governor, who had been a delegate at the Peoria convention (as had been Charles Deneen and Frank Funk) not only worked to pass the law but championed the cause of better roads throughout his term. In 1919, more than a year after he left office, the Illinois Highway Improvement Association recognized him as the "first good roads governor of Illinois."[39]

Governmental efficiency was another priority. He urged the creation of the Legislative Reference Bureau (S.B. 274) that like Wisconsin's Legislative Reference Library, created in 1901, was charged with researching relevant information for the legislature and with preparing a biennial budget. Similarly, he approved the Efficiency and Economy Commission (S.J.R. 22), which was to find means for streamlining the state's governmental apparatus. In 1917, under Governor Lowden, the commission's report was the basis for a complete overhaul of Illinois's administrative structure.[40]

Dunne was also a strong champion of prolabor legislation. He endorsed, for instance, the Illinois Federation of Labor's successful efforts to upgrade the Workman's Compensation Law. Easily passing, the IFL's bill (H.B. 841) included among other things "the creation of a non-political Industrial Board of three members appointed by the governor for terms of six years to administer the law and the enactment of definite insurance provisions." For his old friends of the Chicago Federation of Teachers, he promoted the Teachers Pension Act (H.B. 881), which required cities of 100,000 people or more to match dollar for dollar each teacher's contribution toward a pension. To administer the law, local pension boards were created.[41]

Ironically, the governor had relatively little to do with the passage of statutory woman suffrage, which was unquestionably the most widely heralded progressive accomplishment of the Forty-eighth General Assembly. By his own account, he had been a private convert to the cause of votes for women since his association as mayor with Margaret Haley of the Chicago Federation of Teachers. He had, however, never become a public advocate. For one thing, he was a politician from "wet" Chicago, where the powerful liquor interests and liquor consumers alike feared the impact of women voting. For another, he remained at heart a traditionalist about the social role of women. As the son of a still-living patriarch and the head of a family of nine children and a wife who was "boss" of his home, he was genuinely uneasy about any change in the relationship of men and women that might disrupt the existing patterns of family life. That was a point he later underscored when he vigorously vetoed the introduction of sex education into the curriculum of the University of Illinois.[42]

For those reasons, he allowed the omission of a woman suffrage plank in the 1912 Democratic platform upon learning that the Republicans had ignored the issue in their convention, and he failed to raise the issue in his inaugural address. Nonetheless, he was not uncooperative with Illinois Equal Suffrage Association. In early March 1913, he met with the organization's president, Grace W. Trout, and agreed to give his unofficial blessings to an attempt to secure "statutory suffrage." Statutory suffrage was a device the women had evolved to bypass the Illinois Constitution's reference to "male citizens." The theory, later upheld in court, was that the legislature could extend suffrage to women for offices not specifically mentioned in the state charter. Unlike a constitutional amendment, statutory suffrage requires only a majority vote in the General Assembly. Moreover, in light of the fact that the law allowed only one amending proposal per legislative session, it did not threaten the governor's plans for the initiative and referendum. After that point, as far as Dunne was concerned, the women were on their own. Their successful fight has become a classic in legislative tactics.[43]

The governor became directly involved only after the women's bill (S.B. 63) passed the legislature in mid-June 1913. After nearly two weeks of being "importuned in many directions" to veto the act, he courageously signed the bill into law at a public ceremony attended by his wife, Elizabeth Kelly Dunne (a strong supporter of votes for women), Mrs. Trout, Speaker McKinley (whose fiancée had reportedly threatened to break things off if the bill did not pass), and others. With a stroke of a pen he added as many as 1,600,000 new voters.[44]

Throughout the country the Illinois victory was seen as a "turning point." With recent defeats in Ohio, Wisconsin, and Michigan, the movement had been in the "doldrums," and some had begun questioning the strategy of pursuing suffrage on the state level. This triumph, the first in a major state east of the Mississippi River, changed everything. As one contemporary explained: "The effect of the victory upon the nation was astounding. Suffrage sentiment doubled overnight."[45] Thus it was that Edward F. Dunne, somewhat despite himself, made an important contribution toward a more equal balance of rights between the sexes.

The General Assembly began winding down its work in the last week. Immediately before it adjourned, the governor delivered a record of twenty-three vetoes. Some of those applied to measures like a Chicago park consolidation (S.B. 304), which he had supported but found constitutionally flawed. The vast majority, however, reflected his concern for economy. As early as April, he had warned of the need for tightening the budget as a result of conditions, so he stated, left over from the previous administration. Finding himself largely unheeded, he now trimmed state appropriations by more than a million dollars—a considerable sum in those days of three-figure yearly incomes for some wage workers. If there was any inclination to override him, it escaped public notice. Without much comment, the exhausted legislature formally ended its session on 30 June 1913.[46]

Contemporary judgments of the accomplishments of the Forty-eighth General Assembly were mixed. John Fairlie, who had helped to write the Public Utility Law, and who like so many of Dunne's associates had earlier worked for Tom L. Johnson, maintained that it had taken only "halting steps in the direction of both political and economic reform." The Illinois Manufacturing Association was pleased to note: "Business interest came through the Forty-eighth General Assembly remarkably well." Governor Dunne, himself, expressed some disappointment.[47]

In truth, the Illinois legislature in 1913 was the beneficiary of two more or less distinct reformist influences. The first and more liberal was based on the political "revolution" of 1912 that followed at least in part from the Lorimer scandal and saw the creation of the Progressive Party and the election of Dunne. The second influence was founded in a moderate but steady propensity toward reform in the state government that had been evident since at least 1909. For all of the governor's high hopes, it was this second and more conservative approach that prevailed.

Not one of the major reform bills offered in 1913 lacked a precedent in previous sessions. Moreover, virtually all of the successful progressive measures were oriented toward making government more efficient within the preexisting parameters of governmental power. In contrast, bills like, above all, the initiative and referendum, but also such things as an old-age pension bill, failed. It is ironic that Edward F. Dunne, social reformist that he remained, was to base his claims to success upon legislation that he endorsed but that more properly belonged within the ideological body of ideas of his old opponents, the structural reformers.

Nor was there anything like an absolute division between progressives and conservatives in the Forty-eighth General Assembly. There were legislators who supported every important reform bill, but there was no organized progressive coalition as such. By the same token, while there were some who opposed every reform, there was nothing like a structured body of reactionaries. Lee O'Neil Browne, a man who openly praised William Lorimer, could also find himself voting for the initiative and referendum. Similarly, Edward King, the leader of the fight against such "direct democracy," could also be the sponsor of the old-age pension bill. Reform measures were enacted, as a rule, by shifting coalitions representing different political and geographical interests, augmented as in the cases of woman suffrage and the cause of better roads by single-issue lobbying. In 1913, consensus was clearly the central theme of reform in Illinois.

For Edward F. Dunne, one positive feature of being governor, and one which stood in contrast to his troubled experience as mayor, was the fact that when the legislature was not in session, his official schedule was reduced to a relatively sedate round of ceremonial and administrative duties. He was to enjoy nearly six months of respite until yet another campaign, one involving a U.S. senatorial race in 1914, forced him back into the controversies of the political arena. For the moment, he was more than ready to relax. Indeed, during the summer of 1913, his official obligations were largely limited to two reviews of the Illinois National Guard at Camp Lincoln outside of Chicago.

His role as commander in chief was of special interest to at least one member of his family. P. W. Dunne, his father, was still alive and passionately committed to the cause of Irish independence. It is said that shortly after the inauguration, P. W. made the suggestion that it would be a fine idea to mobilize the Guard and send them to Ireland to fight the British.[48] Whether that actually occurred is problematic: Governor Dunne, however, was forced to take his command of the militia seriously in September 1913, when an ethnic riot threatened to break out in Benton, a town in Franklin County deeply placed in southern Illinois. Preexisting tensions between Polish and "American" miners were the source of this affair, and violence reared its ugly head when two "American" musicians were murdered after a dance. Poles became fair game, and as many as twenty-five were "severely beaten." On the appeal of the mayor, the governor sent troops in, who quickly quieted things.[49]

In the fall of 1913, his repose was disturbed again by reports of abuse at the Pontiac Boys Reformatory. An investigation was ordered, and more than forty boys testified to ritual beatings administered by Dr. James Marshall, the reformatory physician, the practice of a painful "initiation" for new boys, random and frequent "blackjacking" by the guards, and the punishment of forcing some boys to drink water taken from toilets. According to the report, one major source of difficulties at the institution was poor food, which resulted in "chronic constipation [among the prisoners and the guards] producing conditions so abnormal that this comparatively would account for the existence of the other conditions."[50]

At Governor Dunne's direction, a number of guards and employees, including Dr. Marshall, were discharged. More importantly, the use of corporal punishments was formally prohibited. The governor subsequently visited the facility himself to check on the implementation of the new policy. While there he addressed the boys in stern paternalistic tones but promised that in the future they were to be treated "as human beings, with a good measure of intelligence and as boys with souls that need help."[51]

Dunne's response to the situation at Pontiac was entirely consistent with his beliefs about penology. Like many progressives, he believed in improving the human environment to reduce crime and in the state's duty to rehabilitate criminals. As he phrased it: "Regeneration rather than vengeance is the watchword of the State in dealing with its convicts." As mayor he had ordered a cleanup of the city jail, and now he was prepared to reform the functioning of Illinois's prisons.[52]

In April 1914, he appointed Edmund M. Allen as warden of the main state prison at Joliet. With the appointment came instructions from the governor to make the institution a model for the entire state prison system. By the end of the year, much had been accomplished. The state had abolished for all of its prisons the rule of silence, the task system, and striped clothing. Inmates were allowed extended letter-writing privileges and recreations hours with more frequent visitors without the encumbrance of a twenty-five-cent admission charge. At the Chester penitentiary, night schools for the illiterate were replaced with day schools taught by convicts. At the Pontiac reformatory, professional teachers were hired for elementary classes and vocational training. Sanitary conditions were also improved throughout the state. Whitewashed walls were painted, pure water was made available at all times, barbershops were established, and clean underwear was issued once a week. Many of the reforms were directly "recommended by Governor Dunne."[53]

The governor's plan to create camps for honor convicts to do open-air work on the state roads had been authorized by the Forty-eighth General Assembly, and Camps Allen, Hope, and Dunne were built in the spring of 1914. A policy was initiated by which inmates received a day off from their sentences for every three days of road work. The governor, however, had his limits. At one point he had to step in and put a halt to the practice of allowing inmates to leave the work gangs to see a movie at the local theater![54] Even as his reform program for the prisons was being implemented, however, his attention was increasingly given over to weightier political matters, for on 18 January 1914, Roger C. Sullivan had announced his intention to seek the Democratic nomination for United States senator.[55]

6

GOVERNOR OF ILLINOIS

The years 1914 and 1915 were to be a period of declining political fortune for Edward F. Dunne. While he retained his personal popularity, events conspired to severely undercut his position. First, he found himself embroiled in a futile effort to deny Roger Sullivan the Democratic nomination for United States senator, a fight that served only to reveal publicly his relative weakness within his own party. This was followed by heavy Republican majorities in the fall of 1914, elections that exacerbated any hopes for further reform. Even more portentous were the subsequent defeat of his ally Mayor Carter Harrison for mayor and the resignation as secretary of state of William Jennings Bryan. These events left him dangerously isolated as he faced with increased uncertainty his dawning campaign for reelection.

Roger Sullivan was, of course, the leader of the most powerful faction of the state Democratic Party and a man who was anathema to Illinois's reformers. Born on 3 February 1861, on a farm near Belvidere, Illinois, he had never, because of the needs of his family, been able to undertake higher education. Nonetheless, displaying a rare political talent, he had begun his rise to real power in the reelection campaign in 1884 of Grover Cleveland.[1]

By 1914, he was considered a wealthy man. His fortune was centered in the Ogden Gas Company of Chicago, which was the only definite source of the charges of corruption that followed him throughout his career. In 1895, the city council of Chicago voted an advantageous franchise for the company, and it soon came out that Sullivan and the current mayor and Sullivan ally, John Hopkins, as well as several important aldermen were major stockholders. Protests by the reformers were vehement, but in vain.[2]

In part because of this scandal, but also because he so successfully cornered power in the Democratic Party, his enemies were legion. Chief among these was his rival for leadership, Carter Harrison. More important, however, was the enduring hostility of William Jennings Bryan. The Great Commoner considered his native state of Illinois a special concern, and he was naturally opposed to a political boss like Sullivan. More directly, Sullivan worked hard to successfully subvert Bryan's hopes for the 1904 presidential nomination.[3]

Despite the enmity of Bryan, Harrison, and most of those who called themselves progressive in the state Democracy, Sullivan brought some impressive assets to the race. First, there was the machine, which was not only powerful throughout the state but also controlled the party organization. Second, there was the fact that he had a reasonable claim upon the support and loyalty of President Woodrow Wilson, whose nomination he helped secure. Third, he felt able to present himself with some small merit as a progressive. He had, of course, assisted Wilson, but in helping the governor resolve the speakership crisis and in not openly opposing any reform measure, he had been useful to Dunne. It did not seem inappropriate, therefore, for him to seek the highest post the state could offer. Thus it was that Sullivan, for only the third time in his career (he had been elected probate clerk for a single term in 1890 and had run unsuccessfully for county clerk in 1897), prepared to present himself to the voters.[4]

Dunne's initial inclination was to remain neutral regarding Sullivan's candidacy. He was, it was true, uncomfortable with the kinds of machine politics the boss represented. However, he had never made a practice of opposing entrenched leaders within his own party, and there was no certainty that he could defeat Sullivan should he become involved. Moreover, alienating the leader could only complicate his own hopes for reelection.

Others were not so complacent. On 9 February 1914, the Wilson-Bryan League was formed at a meeting in Springfield for the specific purpose of opposing Sullivan. Attending were such progressive figures as Carl Vrooman, George Sikes, Congressman Henry T. Rainey, and Fred Kern, as well as Oklahoma Senator Frank B. Owen and Joseph Folk, a former governor of Missouri who was close to Dunne. Much noise was made, Sullivan was denounced, but little else was achieved.[5]

Bryan himself declined to endorse the league (as did Woodrow Wilson), and it quickly faded. Nonetheless, he was gravely concerned, and he was soon in touch with Mayor Harrison and Governor Dunne. There was some speculation that the three might back a bid by the governor, but this was an honor he vigorously declined. He did agree at last to work with the other two in finding a suitable candidate to endorse in opposition to Sullivan.[6]

There was certainly no lack of aspirants. Three members of the state administration, Lieutenant Governor Barret O'Hara, Secretary of State Harry Woods, and Attorney General Patrick Lucey had all declared as had numerous others, but none was deemed initially acceptable to carry the progressive

Democratic banner in the primary election. Throughout the late spring and early summer of 1914, Dunne with Harrison and Bryan searched for an appropriate candidate. Bryan's personal choice was Carl Vrooman, who was even now vigorously campaigning against Sullivan. However, the fact that he was relatively new to the state and that he had "been so thoroughly stamped with the 'dry' idea that his candidacy would be a difficult one to make effectively in Cook County" eliminated him from consideration.[7] More acceptable to the three was Congressman Henry T. Rainey of Illinois's Twentieth District. A dynamic man with a progressive, but noncontroversial, record, Rainey, however, refused even Bryan's direct blandishments to enter the contest.[8] Next, the secretary of state urged the governor and the mayor to consider Judge Owen P. Thompson. Although not a declared candidate, Thompson was widely admired without any factional enemies. Dunne had appointed him to the Public Utility Commission but questioned the viability of his candidacy because of his "dry" propensities. Nonetheless, he dutifully called him in and offered his endorsement. Thompson, however, refused to run, not only because he was happy in his current vocation, but also because he felt entering the contest would be "a political mistake."[9]

Finally, they settled upon Congressman-at-large Lawrence B. Stringer. He had been considered earlier, but because of his past association with Sullivan he had been placed at the end of the list. With Rainey's and Thompson's refusals, he became the best choice. Having been the party's unsuccessful candidate for governor in 1904, he was well known. Although a former ally of Sullivan, he had a generally good record, and he enjoyed cordial relations with Bryan. Moreover, he met a new criterion set by Harrison that Sullivan be opposed by a downstate man to offset the boss's wide power outside of Cook County. Perhaps just as important, he was already an active candidate and clearly wanted the job. On 16 July, Dunne together with Harrison and Senator J. Hamilton Lewis formally endorsed Stringer. Five days later, Bryan's announcement of support followed. Those actions clarified the campaign. All other candidates running against Sullivan, with exceptions of James Traynor, O'Hara, and Woods, dropped out.[10]

Unlike Harrison, the governor did not immediately take the stump on Stringer's behalf. When he did at last begin campaigning nearly a month later, he seemed more concerned with exacting revenge for the defeat of the initiative and referendum by going to Chicago to "nail Hubert C. Kilens if it [is] the last act of his life." Among other things, he called Kilens "the worst traitor we had in the last General Assembly."[11] Much to his disgust, Kilens was to be renominated and reelected.

It was not until 28 August that Dunne turned his attention to Sullivan, and from that point until a massive closing rally on 7 September, he attacked Sullivan as a traitor to the party, citing various occasions when the boss had failed to support Democratic nominees. This theme expanded into larger attacks upon bossism.[12]

While the loose anti-Sullivan forces were unsteadily maneuvering their way toward the primary, the Chicago leader was conducting a disciplined, highly effective campaign. On 11 May 1914, he began a seven-week swing through southern Illinois. As the only major candidate without a college education who had worked his way up from poverty, he presented himself as a true man of the people. Without a set speech, he instead spoke on curbsides to small groups. By the end of the primary campaign, he had visited every county in the state and each ward of Chicago.[13]

For the most part, his themes were positive. Of course he was a progressive; after all he helped Woodrow Wilson get the nomination. Was he not, therefore, the best man to support the president in the Senate? When attacked by Vrooman, who followed him around the state in the early phases, or by Stringer or even by Dunne, he could as the clear front-runner blithely ignore his opposition. Only late in the campaign was there any serious attack upon Stringer, and it came not from Sullivan but from his ally Attorney General Lucey, who accused him of somehow (he was not very specific) helping William Lorimer become senator.[14]

Not surprisingly, all things considered, Sullivan won with 47 percent of the vote. Stringer was second with 37 percent, followed by Woods with 8 percent, O'Hara with 5 percent, and James Traynor with a bare 3 percent. The "downstate strategy" had worked; Stringer carried pluralities in most counties south of Chicago, but this was more than offset by Sullivan's majority of 35,000 votes in Chicago over the combined totals of his opponents. On 19 September, Sullivan's nomination was formally endorsed by the state party convention in Springfield on a progressive platform that echoed and enhanced that of 1913.[15]

Sullivan's major opponent in the campaign was Lawrence Y. Sherman, a Taft Republican backed by a party united in their determination to rectify the 1912 debacle. It was the candidate of the Progressive Party, Raymond Robins, however, who added a national dimension to the contest. Robins was, of course, an old friend of Dunne's, and he attracted the support of many in the Democratic Party who could not stomach Sullivan. With elements of the Wilson-Bryan League and of the labor movement, a Robins-for-Senator Democratic League was formed creating some publicity.[16]

It was the sense the 1914 elections were a test of the viability of the

Progressive Party, however, that especially excited interest. This interpreta-
tion was reenforced by the presence on Robins's behalf of some of his party's
most famous figures. First into the state was former Senator Albert Beveridge,
who toured in late July. The following month, Theodore Roosevelt invaded
and spoke throughout Illinois to increasingly enthusiastic crowds. At the end
of October, he returned to address in Chicago a crowd of perhaps 150,000
people.[17]

For his part, Edward F. Dunne participated as little as possible in the
campaign. While always a guardian angel of party loyalty, he could not find
it in his heart to condemn those Democrats who were supporting Robins. Indeed, in his private thoughts, he probably wished his old friend the victory.
His speaking schedule was very limited, and his talks seemed to avoid men-
tioning Sullivan. For instance, in Carlinville his theme was primarily the sins
of the previous Deneen administration, while his speech in Chicago centered
on the need for better roads. If the governor was merely dutiful toward the
Sullivan campaign, Carter Harrison did his best to ignore it completely. Refusing to speak for his party rival, or even to appear willingly on the same
platform as the boss, he did work extensively for other candidates.[18]

In the end, the rivalry of politicians counted for little against the return of
many of the voters to the Republican Party. Sherman won with nearly 39
percent, representing an increase of the Republican vote of about 10 percent
over that of two years earlier. Robins's total of just about 20 percent signaled
a Progressive loss of slightly over 6 percent. Sullivan's 37 percent indicated
only a slight loss from Dunne's 1912 total.[19]

The same pattern appeared in the congressional elections. In 1912, Illinois elected twenty Democrats, five Republicans, and two Progressives to
Congress. After the elections of 1914, there were sixteen Republicans and ten
Democrats. Symbolic, perhaps of this shift to traditional patterns was the
return to Congress of former Speaker Joseph Cannon, a man whose very name
spelled reaction.[20]

Even more troubling for Edward F. Dunne was the Republican recapture
of the Illinois House. In all, they now controlled seventy-seven seats, while
the Democrats held seventy-two, and Progressives and the Socialists had only
two each. In the Senate, there appeared to be a tie between the two main
parties.[21]

The governor's annual New Year's reception was usually a joyous affair.
The main rooms of the mansion were filled with conversation and light. Punch
and hors d'oeuvres were served, while in the library "something more inspi-
rational" was made available for those so inclined. At the reception of 1915,

however, the reality of imminent Republican dominance of the legislature cast a shadow over the festivities, and it was to that that the talk among the prominent Democrats present inevitably turned. The year 1915 did not seem promising.[22]

For their part, the Republicans were well pleased. The elections had shown that the split of 1912, at least as far as the voters were concerned, was well on its way toward mending, and that the GOP had regained its status as the state's majority party. The return to power in the legislature, however, brought new problems; like the Democrats in 1913, the Republicans would quickly find themselves embroiled in a lengthy fight over the choice of a Speaker of the House. Unlike the Democratic altercation, it was primarily ideology rather than faction that was to play the central role as the antiliquor forces for the first time in the state's history sought real control of the General Assembly.

The effort to ban the manufacture, transportation, sale, and ultimately the consumption of alcoholic beverages was founded in the same reformist impulse as that which spawned the progressive movement. Armed with political, economic, and social evidence, the proponents of Prohibition, who were usually, but not always, structural reformists, made a convincing case that the removal of alcohol as an intoxicant not only would promote moral uplift but would also go far toward eliminating political corruption and social misery. In Illinois, such organizations as the Woman's Christian Temperance Union and the Prohibition Party worked hard for the cause, but in state politics the major "dry" voice came from the Illinois chapter of the Anti-Saloon League.[23]

Organized in 1898, the league had achieved its first major victory in 1907 with the passage of a township option law, which allowed townships and precincts in counties not organized in townships, to vote themselves "dry." In the two years following passage, more than half of the state geographically had prohibited the sale of alcoholic spirits; however, this represented only about 30 percent of the population. After the elections of 1909, the group's efforts were centered upon an ongoing seesaw battle against powerful and now alerted "wet" organizations like Chicago's United Societies for Local Self-Government, and while conquering rural Illinois, the movement made little headway in the population centers. On the other hand, the Anti-Saloon League had been successful over the years in convincing the legislature to prohibit such things as drinking on trains and the sale of liquor near state institutions of higher learning. Despite those gains, they continued to be frustrated in achieving their next major goal—the county option—and having lost once again in the Forty-eighth General Assembly, they were determined not to fail in the Forty-ninth.[24]

For the governor, as for most other mainstream politicians, the liquor question was a perilous trap to be avoided if at all possible. He had been fortunate in the past that the issue had never emerged in strength during any of his campaigns. If pressed, however, he was by inclination and political self-interest a "wet." As a social reformer he had never shown much interest in official attempts to eliminate private vice. Moreover, he was naturally antipathetic toward any movement that concentrated its attention upon what was largely interpreted as a working-class problem, at the expense of addressing the issue of the corruption of the rich. He had used just this argument to justify his refusal as mayor to enforce the Sunday Closing Law. Nonetheless, as a rule, he did his best to stay above the issue.[25]

The Republicans of the Forty-ninth General Assembly were not allowed this luxury, and their battle over the liquor issue was to set the tone of the session. The Republican "drys" had been frustrated by their failure to pass the county option in 1913, and they were now determined to secure a friendly Speaker in the House. On the other hand, the well-organized Republican "wets" were equally intent that this was not to be. The collision of the irresistible force and the immovable object came at the first caucus of the House Republicans (which also included the two Progressive representatives). Seventeen "wets," led by Thomas Curran (Cook County-R), refused their support for any of the candidates for the speakership promoted at the meeting. Most important of those were Edward Shurtleff (McHenry County-R) and Walter Provine (Christian County-R). The Curran group instead backed David Shanahan (Cook County-R), who not only declined to enter the fray but strongly supported Shurtleff.[26]

In the House chambers, a deadlock quickly ensued. After two days, with the Curran "wets," voting for James H. Vickers (McHenry County-R), Shurtleff withdrew, leaving only Provine as a major candidate. However, without the Curran "wets" he was unable to obtain the necessary two-thirds majority. His near miss brought about an attempt to arrange a compromise behind William P. Holaday (Vermillion County-R), but many "drys" refused to go along. Equally unsuccessful was Provine's subsequent attempt to win with Democratic "dry" votes; in 1915, there was a far stronger consciousness of party than in the previous legislature, and he lost as many Republican votes as he gained from the Democrats. By the end of January, his base of support had become so small that he too withdrew.[27]

The fact that Provine's tactic of seeking support across party lines had helped to destroy his candidacy did not discourage some Democrats from seeking to achieve a measure of power through contributing to the selection of a Republican Speaker. In 1915, as in 1913, they were divided on the liquor question into three general groupings, hardcore "wets" and party regulars led by Lee O'Neil Browne (LaSalle County-D), an equally hardcore body of "drys" headed by William Hubbard (Green County-D), and the "administration Democrats" who were generally "wet" and led by Michael Igoe (Cook County-D). In late January and early February, Browne made repeated efforts to unify bipartisan "wets" behind David Shanahan. To their disappointment, Shanahan still maintained he was not a candidate. There were similar attempts to create a bipartisan coalition of "drys," but it was unsuccessful as well.[28]

As things became heated, long-held personal animosities began to erupt in the chamber. On 3 February, for example, Representative Curran entered in an apparently good mood only to be outraged at the sight of Representative Edwin Perkins (Logan County-R). Curran immediately began a tirade that questioned not only Perkins's politics but also his manhood for allegedly signing an Anti-Saloon League pledge to work for a "dry" Speaker. For a moment, the specter of physical violence loomed, but the two were restrained, and the House returned to its fruitless balloting.[29]

By mid-February, all concerned had enough; there was no desire to repeat the three-month battle of the last session. On 15 February, the Anti-Saloon League officially announced its withdrawal of interest. Meanwhile, David Shanahan had agreed, at last, to become a candidate and to accept Democratic support. On 16 February, he was elected with one hundred of one hundred twenty votes cast. Ironically, considering his earlier refusal to become involved in any kind of bipartisan deal, the abstention of twenty "dry" Republicans resulted in his receiving seventeen more votes from the Democrats than from his own party.[30]

It was a major victory for the "wets." The Anti-Saloon League claimed a triumph of sorts in "perfecting" the liquor issue for the elections of 1916, but it was unquestionable that the Curran group had been successful, first, in blocking the candidacy of anyone unacceptable to them, and then, in electing their first choice as Speaker. At the same time, the speakership altercation underscored the return to more traditional patterns of power in the state government. By virtue of that contest and the strengths and weaknesses it revealed, David Shanahan, for the Republicans, and Lee O'Neil Browne, on the Democratic side, became the two most powerful men in the Illinois House of Representatives. This stood in sharp contrast to the progressive leadership exercised in 1913 by such men as Charles Karch, Michael Igoe, John McLaughlin, and Medill McCormick.[31]

Also contrasting sharply with 1913 was the governor's biennial message that arrived following the election of Shanahan. Gone were the clarion calls for reform and change; indeed, there was no significant mention of either the initiative and referendum or the abolition of the Board of Equalization—his two priority issues during the Forty-eighth General Assembly. Instead, he concentrated upon reviewing the accomplishments of his administration, with special mentions of the improvement of conditions in the prisons and on the state's roads. He did, it was true, recommend the modification of the constitution to allow more than one amendment per legislative session, and the enactment of the report of the Efficiency and Economy Commission to reorganize the state's administrative structure, but neither of those inspired much passion in his message. Rather than expending energy on what he must have perceived as ultimately vain efforts at new progressive reform, he reserved his warmest recommendations for proposals that had bipartisan, and even conservative, support. By far, the most important of those was his call for the construction of a waterway to connect Lake Michigan with the Mississippi River.[32]

The vision of a direct water route between the lake and the river can be traced back to the seventeenth century and the French explorers Louis Joliet and Father Marquette. Two centuries later this vision was sufficiently compelling to induce the legislature of the young state of Illinois to begin construction, in 1836, of the Illinois and Michigan canal. Completed in 1848, it was soon made obsolete by the new railroads and became a continuing expense—it was also completely inadequate for the needs of an industrializing Illinois. For a long period, there was added to the symbolic bad odor that surrounded the canal a literal stink brought about by Chicago's practice, after 1865, of pumping in raw sewage. The completion of the Chicago Sanitary and Ship Canal, which ran between Lake Michigan and the Des Plaines River, solved that in 1871, but the goal of a truly efficient water route remained unfulfilled.[33]

By the first decade of the new century, strong political forces were developing in support of a new and modern canal. In November 1906, the first convention of the Lakes-to-Gulf Deepwaterway Association met under the leadership of Congressmen William Lorimer and Henry T. Rainer. Proposing a coordinated regional system "connecting the Great Lakes and the St. Lawrence River with the Mississippi River and the Panama Canal," the organization enjoyed a major success in November 1908, when the state's voters amended the constitution to include a provision for a deepwaterway. Subsequently, the issue became lost in the Republican factional fight between Lorimer and Governor Charles S. Deneen, and the legislature, in part, also over the question of whether the canal should be twenty-four or fourteen feet deep, was unable to take action. Although the concept of the canal became a dormant political issue (the Lakes-to-Gulf Deepwaterway Association failed to meet after 1911), it retained a latent power.[34]

Until almost his second year as governor, Dunne had ignored the canal issue. In his 1913 inaugural address, he made no mention of it, and he seems to have become publicly involved only after December 1913, when he attended the National Rivers and Harbors Congress in Washington, D.C. By the fall of 1914, he had become a fervent advocate, and in his biennial message, he gave it his highest priority. The canal, as he envisioned it, was to be eight feet deep and would cost a little more than $3 million.[35]

He made numerous speeches for his version of the deepwaterway throughout the state, while trying at the same time to resolve local objections along the proposed route. In the process he even managed to convert some of those who were initially opposed. The General Assembly responded in late May 1915 by passing the canal measure (H.B. 914) by substantial margins.[36]

While the bulk of the legislature and probably most of the people in the state were receptive, there was a small but very vocal group who were not. Surprisingly, most of the public opposition came not so much from downstaters, who might be expected to be less than enthralled with a project using tax money that would primarily benefit Chicago, but from among some of the longest-standing advocates of the canal. Chief among those was Congressman Henry T. Rainey, who soon assumed the role of spokesman. While the canal measures were under consideration, Rainey had appeared before the Senate to state his objections. In the first place, he argued, the eight-foot depth of Dunne's proposed canal was completely inadequate. This "tadpole ditch," as some would come to label it, could never effectively serve the purpose for which it was intended. Rather, Rainey argued, a depth of at least fourteen feet was required. In the second place, he strongly objected to the bill's provisions for power development, which he felt played into the hands of such "waterway parasites" as Samuel Insull and the North American Water Power group at Marseilles.[37]

The governor had tried to anticipate Rainey's objections by having earlier pointed out that the eight-foot depth had been recommended by the Army Corps of Engineers in 1908 and by holding out the hope that the canal, once built, could always be deepened. Rainey and his group remained unconvinced. For the moment, however, Dunne was triumphant, and he promised that construction could begin as early as August 1915.[38]

The deepwaterway law was the governor's major accomplishment of the Forty-ninth General Assembly. He was less successful in other areas. For instance, he had called for greater regulation of lobbyists. Although he was able to persuade the House to change its rules and keep lobbyists off the floor, no comprehensive lobbying law was forthcoming. On the whole, Governor Dunne was not very involved in the legislative process of 1915. As a result, he enjoyed excellent relations with Speaker Shanahan and most legislators of all three parties. He even had something like cordial interaction with Representative Hubert Kilens, the Judas of the initiative and referendum passion play of the previous session. All of that was founded, of course, in the domination of the legislature by conservative and Republican forces. It made no sense for the governor to court defeat with innovative proposals. The political winds were clearly not blowing in his favor, and during the spring of 1915, there were two events that only underscored his insecurity. The first was the replacement of Carter Harrison by Republican William Hale Thompson as mayor of Chicago.[39]

Harrison's defeat had its foundation in his antagonism with Roger Sullivan; the boss was clearly determined to exact revenge for the mayor's opposition and foot-dragging during the senatorial primary and election campaigns. To oppose the five-term mayor, the Sullivan organization lined up Robert M. Sweitzer, clerk of the Cook County court. They then vigorously pushed his candidacy with blatant appeals to Chicago's German-American community. Not only was Harrison accused of being anti-German, but considerable effort was expended upon presenting him as a threat to the city's extensive liquor interests. Harrison tried but failed to counter those charges with an endorsement from the municipality's leading "wet" organization, the United Societies for Local Self-Government.[40]

Governor Dunne was in much the same awkward position as in the beginning of the 1914 senatorial primary fight. With an eye to his own upcoming campaign for reelection, he had no wish to alienate the Sullivanites. On the other hand, Harrison had become an ally (at least most of the time), and so Dunne dutifully offered his endorsement in a letter made public in mid-February. He did not, however, travel to Chicago to speak.[41]

In the primary, Sweitzer and the Sullivan machine buried Harrison by a margin of nearly eighty thousand votes. That defeat effectively ended Harrison's career and the already shaky H-H alliance. Vestiges of the faction with the participation of Harrison, who went into semiretirement, and later of Dunne, would continue to play a much reduced role, but the primary signaled the absolute triumph of Roger Sullivan in his conquest of the Chicago Democratic party.[42]

Meanwhile, the Republicans had nominated the man who was to be the most controversial mayor in the city's history. William Hale Thompson came from a wealthy family, and he had first attracted public notice as an athlete and as president of the Chicago Athletic Club. In 1899, he decided to capitalize on his popularity, and allegedly on a bet, he successfully ran for a seat on the city council. His term was largely undistinguished, but he did work hard for the city's first municipal playground. As an alderman, he became an associate of William Lorimer, who backed him in a vain attempt, in 1902, to become a Cook County commissioner. Ten years later, Thompson lost again when he attempted to secure a seat on the Cook County Board of Review. However, the campaign brought into being a new organization under the leadership of Frederick "Poor Swede" Lundin grandly called "The Republican Club of Illinois." Its sole purpose was to elect Thompson as mayor in 1915.[43]

His opponent in the Republican primary was Judge Harry Olson, the choice of the Deneen faction. In a hard-fought contest, Thompson, with the unexpected help of the *Chicago Tribune*, won by less than four thousand votes. The election campaign itself was undistinguished by any substantive debate. Both candidates pledged to work for home rule in the regulation of public utilities, something that Thompson was subsequently unable to wrench from the Forty-ninth General Assembly, but most of the "debate" was centered in such emotional questions as Sweitzer's Catholicism and whether or not the Democratic candidate was too pro-German; an issue that had helped in the primary, but which was to hurt him in this, the second year of the European war. Those tactics apparently struck a responsive chord among the voters as Thompson was elected mayor by the highest plurality yet achieved by a candidate for the office.[44]

For Governor Dunne, who had briefly campaigned for Sweitzer, the election was an ominous sign indeed. In the course of the last five months, his party had lost two important campaigns by substantial margins. Moreover, without Harrison, he faced Sullivan almost alone, and without a Democratic mayor of Chicago, the power of his party was greatly reduced.

The second portentous event of the spring of 1915 occurred far from the heated, often petty, arena of Illinois politics—on the cold North Atlantic and on the killing floors of Europe. Beyond the depressing daily routine of reading about it in the newspapers, Dunne and political Illinois had been largely unaffected by the ongoing horrors of World War I. This sense of distance was shattered on 7 May 1915, when a German submarine sank a British liner, *Lusitania*, killing 1,198, including 102 Americans. On 8 May, Dunne issued a short statement that labeled the sinking a "grave calamity," and which expressed confidence in President Wilson's ability to avoid the "awful calamity of war." Even before the sinking, the governor had begun to show an awareness of the magnitude of events in Europe. In March, for example, before the Irish Fellowship Club of Cincinnati, he had called for a suspension of Irish-American agitation against British rule in Ireland. As he phrased it: "Let us in this crisis suppress our racial sympathies, place American patriotism above all other consideration, and confine our energies to working for the restoration of peace in war smitten Europe."[45]

Beyond shaking the complacency of Dunne and all Americans, the *Lusitania* incident had little direct impact upon the governor's political situation. However, the crisis created by the event eventually led to the resignation on 9 June of William Jennings Bryan as secretary of state, and that had profound implications. He had always been a loyal Bryan man, and he counted on the Great Commoner's help in the capital and in the state. One result had been Dunne and Harrison's domination of federal patronage in Illinois. Now with Bryan out of the Wilson administration and Harrison out of office, the governor was becoming isolated, with only Senator J. Hamilton Lewis as a last remaining major ally. The isolation severely compromised any hopes he may have entertained to maintain his influence over the state party.[46]

For the moment, however, neither Harrison's defeat nor Bryan's resignation greatly affected Illinois politics, where the focus remained upon the state legislature. Despite the governor's relative inactivity, it did manage to achieve by adjournment on 20 June a fairly substantial record. After the deepwaterway law, the most important accomplishment was a constitutional resolution (S.J.R. 24) that called for legislative power to be extended to include the right to establish different classifications for the assessment of property taxes. Also important was the consolidation of Chicago's park systems and township governments under the authority of the city council (H.B. 162). In the area of reform, the House adopted new rules that required the registration of lobbyists with the clerk and that restricted the powers of the Speaker and the chairmen of the various committees to table legislation (H.R. 57). If the record of the Forty-ninth General Assembly paled in comparison to that of the previous session, nonetheless it had worked hard. In all, more than fifteen hundred bills were introduced, and as Speaker Shanahan pointed out, "absolutely no bad or vicious legislation crept through."[47]

Governor Dunne approved most of the major legislation enacted by the session. This time, he pleased Chicago by signing the parks consolidation bill. However, as in 1913, he returned a record number of vetoes. Among those were the Calumet Harbor bill that he saw, in 1913, as a source or private profit, and a bill introducing the censorship of moving pictures. He also once again trimmed appropriations, cutting more that two million dollars (including three thousand for his own office) from the state budget.[48]

With adjournment, the governor could turn his attention to finalizing plans for a trip to San Francisco to attend the Panama-Pacific Exposition on 24 July, or "Illinois Day." Leaving Chicago on a train, he took with him a party of twenty-five that included most of his family, Speaker Shanahan, and William O'Connell, in his new capacity as chairman of the Public Utility Commission. Following an indirect itinerary that involved stops at Vancouver and Seattle, the party arrived in California on 23 July. A grand ceremony to dedicate the Illinois Pavilion was scheduled for the next day. Before the festivities could begin, as fate would have it, word arrived of the capsizing of the steamship *Eastland* on the Chicago River. Eight hundred twelve men, women, and children had been killed, and the stunned delegation immediately prepared to return home. Dunne, in his words, was "grieved beyond expression by this terrible calamity." Once back, he added moral force to the state and federal investigations of the tragedy.[49]

The *Eastland* disaster set the tone for the remainder of his year. Since 1913, in manner paralleling the course of President Wilson and the New Freedom, Dunne had been moving steadily toward the middle of the political spectrum and away from the more fervent reformism that characterized his election campaign and his first six months in office. In cynical terms, he was being an opportunist and following the political tides as manifested in recent elections, or to put it another way, he was being a good public servant and obeying the expressed will of the people. In either case, he had begun embracing issues and positions that either had a broad base of support or were, at the least, generally inoffensive. His proposed deepwaterway, for instance, enjoyed the strong approval of the business community, a group not noted for their support of Edward F. Dunne. Similarly, he continued to try to make the good roads movement his own. Although proposing nothing substantially new to the legislature, he did make numerous speeches as well as publicized inspection tours of work already completed. Sadly for Dunne, events conspired to prevent him from achieving the more moderate, statesmanlike image that he actively pursued. In the latter half of 1915, he found himself compelled to divert most of his time to a series of increasingly serious controversies that were neither flattering in their impact nor conducive to political success.[50]

His season of diminishing fortunes began with the angry resignation of E. N. Allen, the warden of the state penitentiary at Joliet and the architect of the administration's plan of prison reform. In June, Allen had lost his wife in a fire set in their quarters by a prison trustee named "Chicken" Joe Campbell. Now on 6 August, Allen unexpectedly resigned claiming, first, that the governor had refused to approve an appropriation to build a new residence for the warden—thus insensitively forcing Allen back into the home where his wife had died—and second, that Dunne had interfered with the interrogation of Campbell by sending Representative Joe Devine (Lee County-D) to protect the then alleged murderer from physical abuse. Moreover, Allen claimed, the governor had always been jealous of the publicity the warden had gained for the changes made at the prison. Allen's charges quickly faded as a public issue, but the subsequent trial and conviction of "Chicken" Joe in late 1915 (he was not executed until after Dunne left office) was a frequent headline item. That virtually ended a small campaign that the governor had begun with his biennial message against capital punishment.[51]

As unfortunate as the Allen affair was, it was insignificant compared with the conflict stirred up by Congressman Rainey in his efforts to undermine Dunne's canal program. Shortly after the adjournment of the legislature, Rainey and his circle implemented a two-pronged attack. First, they challenged the deepwaterway law in court with the argument that the proposed eight-foot depth did not meet the definition of "deepwaterway" as called for in the 1908 constitutional amendment. Second, they worked hard to get the War Department, which had the final say in such projects, to veto the plan. Throughout the summer and fall of 1915, this fight raged, sometimes quietly and sometimes very openly, and it became increasingly certain that Rainey and his circle were winning. By October, there were reports that Secretary of War Lindley M. Garrison was looking "coldly" upon the scheme.[52]

For the governor, the fact of the battle was in itself a frustrating disappointment. Not only was he compelled to give over considerable time to the conflict, but the waterway was supposed to have been a crowning achievement, one upon which he could base his reelection campaign. Instead, it became yet another source of public controversy. Making things worse was Rainey's expansion of his criticism in the fall to include the state administration's response to a serious foot-and-mouth epidemic.

Foot-and-mouth disease is a not necessarily fatal disorder that primarily affects livestock. In this period, it was a recurring problem; the last outbreak having occurred in the Midwest as recently as 1908. In late 1914, it appeared again near Niles, Michigan, and by October of that year, it was discovered in the Chicago stockyards. Initially unalarmed, state officials, including the governor, were rudely surprised in January 1915 to find that the malady had spread throughout the state. Illinois, with 59,042 animals infected, was to prove to be the state most affected.[53]

Recognizing at last the seriousness of the situation, Dunne called a joint meeting of the General Assembly on 19 January to ponder the matter and to listen to a panel of experts. As the panel explained, the only effective method of eradicating the disease at the time was to slaughter and burn or bury the infected animals while inoculating those uninfected. This process had already begun, and the legislature voted more than a million dollars to cover half of the incurred expenses; the other half to be paid for by the federal government. It was a difficult task. In August, just after it was thought to have been checked, the disease broke out again due, according to the United States Department of Agriculture, to faulty serums. It was not completely eradicated until the end of the year.[54]

In October, the epidemic was politicized by Rainey when he charged the state veterinarian, Dr. Oscar E. Ryson, with having helped spread the illness through apathy and through ignoring the advice of the Agriculture Department. The governor leaped to his appointee's defense, but he was somewhat undercut when Ryson was subsequently indicted by a Springfield grand jury for improper disposal of the carcasses of test animals used to make serum.[55]

Even as he was leveling barrages against the administration over its handling of the matter, Rainey's real target remained the waterway issue. Once while charging Ryson with incompetence, for instance, he also claimed the existence of seven hundred thousand dollars of graft in the planning of the canal. It was an allegation Governor Dunne labeled as "extraordinary."[56]

While he was defending of his canal and his administration, the governor was also facing the specter of a major constitutional crisis. A series of lawsuits had been filed in June and July, by John Fergus, a Chicago taxpayer, ably assisted by Fayette S. Munro, an attorney and former member of the legislature, that alleged unconstitutional practices by Dunne and the Forty-ninth General Assembly. Both men asserted that they were merely acting as public-spirited citizens, but unnamed state officials were reported as claiming that Munro's involvement, at least, was founded in his disappointment that the legislature had not established a state park in his home county of Ogle. Regardless, things became serious when the cause was taken up by the Citizens Association of Chicago.[57]

The association had been founded in 1874 by structural reformers dedicated to governmental efficiency. In recent years, they had been beating the drum for a convention to rectify some of the constitutional inadequacies that were at the root of the Fergus suits. Disappointed in their hopes for a convention during the sessions of 1913 and 1915, they now saw in the suits a means to force change.[58]

On 28 August 1915, they were first tested in court. Circuit Judge James Creighton in Springfield ruled (1) that the governor, contrary to customary practice, had no right to veto portions of an item in an appropriation bill; (2) that the state legislature could not vote themselves travel pay above and separate from their salaries; (3) that salaries for state officials not mentioned in the constitution could not be included in the same appropriations with those who were named; (4) that the legislature could not create commissions by mere resolution. The decision had the potential of completely disrupting the function of the state government. The governor's budget cuts thrown out, and 106 state offices were declared, in effect, nonexistent. Dunne ordered Attorney General Lucey to appeal.[59]

The issue was resolved when, on 5 November and 15 December, the Illinois Supreme Court affirmed completely the Creighton decision and added some points of its own. Among those was the ruling that the legislature had erred in the past by creating special legal counsel for the various state commissions. All of the state's legal business belonged instead to the office of attorney general. That eliminated even more state officials. The governor and the entire political establishment were, understandably, greatly disturbed by the judgment that now left the government in confused array and without a clear budget. The only solution was to reconvene the General Assembly to pass constitutionally correct appropriations and to reinstate the affected state officials and commissions.[60]

The first meeting of the First Special Session of the Forty-ninth General Assembly was brief; the House met continuously from 22 November to December 1, but the Senate only sat for three days. Dunne's budget was restored, and the vast majority of state offices were re-created. Despite those accomplishments, the session, in the forceful opinion of many legislators, was a failure because it had left so much undone. Downstate legislators were very concerned by the neglect of further funding to cover outstanding expenses incurred during the foot-and-mouth epidemic, and a sizable body of "highbrows" were dismayed that the Efficiency and Economy Commission had not been reinstated. Concerning the latter, Dunne took the view, which was not inconsistent with his fundamental social reformism, that since the original session of the Forty-ninth General Assembly had been unwilling to act upon the commission's report, preferring merely to perpetuate the body, he was not going to be further involved. Another question left unresolved was an important Chicago bond issue that had recently been declared illegal. More distressing to the governor, who in years ahead would establish himself as a lay historian, was the necessity to veto as potentially unconstitutional a bill to provide for a centennial commission to plan for Illinois's birthday in three years time. The First Special Session resolved to meet further on 23 February 1916, but the signs were clear that a Second Special Session might have to be called before then.[61]

His third year in the governor's chair had not been good for Edward F.

Dunne. His political strengths had been enervated by a succession of events, including Bryan's resignation, Harrison's defeat, and the rise to almost complete power within the state Democratic Party of Roger Sullivan. Moreover, all of his attempts to create a broader power base beyond his reformist backers had been frustrated. As the new year began, it was becoming increasingly problematic whether he could recover the political strength necessary for any reasonable hope to retain his office in the fall election.

7

ILLINOIS RETURNS TO "NORMALCY"
THE ELECTIONS OF 1916

Edward F. Dunne was not one to go quietly into the good night. In the face of what was to be an irresistible Republican resurgence and the stranglehold on his party by machine politicians, he returned to the strident social reformism of his early career and waged an energetic battle for survival. Motivated as much by pride and principle as by any expectations of victory, he first overcame an effort to replace him as head of the state ticket and then undertook a courageous, if lonely, campaign for reelection, which, while in vain, underscored the respect with which he was held by the people of Illinois.

Under the circumstances, it was not surprising that as the new year of 1916 dawned, the governor was uncertain about his future. While he felt he still had much to give in the public's service, neither could he ignore the changing political realities. In January, the death of United States Supreme Court Associate Justice Joseph Lamar seemed to offer an ideal opportunity for escape. Within a week of Lamar's death, the *Illinois State Register* began promoting the governor for the seat on the High Court, arguing not only that the state deserved a place but also that Dunne because of his "admirable personal character, his large judicial experience, and his familiarity with all the important questions of the day and the recent past" was an ideal choice. Senator Lewis soon promised his help, although because of an ongoing disagreement with the Wilson administration over the postmastership of Chicago, his voice did not carry its usual weight. Even more impressive was a unanimous resolution of the Illinois Senate (now meeting in a second special session) endorsing the governor.[1]

In the nation's capital, this small flurry of activity had almost no impact. Lamar's seat was generally considered to belong to the South, and speculations centered upon men from that region. Any hope Dunne may have had was dashed when President Wilson announced on 28 January the controversial appointment of Louis Brandeis of Boston. Clearly, if the governor were to continue in public life, he would have to work within the boundaries of Illinois.[2]

The focus of state politics on the opening of the new year swiftly shifted from the legislature in Springfield to the parties in preparation for the coming primaries and elections. Consequently, when the General Assembly was called into a second special session by the governor on 7 January, it met without the conflict that seemed inevitable after adjournment the previous December. Technically in session between 11 January and 14 February, the legislature was actually convened for just five days. Nonetheless, it was reasonably productive in restoring funding for the remaining state agencies affected by the Fergus suit, including the Centennial Commission, and in voting additional compensation for destroyed livestock during the foot and mouth epidemic. Unfortunately, in the view of many, including the governor, the legislators failed to consolidate the two state primaries that were now scheduled for April and September. That was to make this year's political season difficult for all concerned.[3]

Oddly, after the Second Special Session adjourned on 14 February, the General Assembly met again as a resumed First Special Session on 26 February in response to its own call in December. All that was accomplished was the appointment of a committee to study Chicago's bond difficulties. Meeting again on 9 May and 10 May, as the First Special Session, the legislature declined any action on the bond issue and at last disbanded permanently.[4]

Governor Dunne echoed the general complacency that characterized the reconvened legislature. He offered nothing new to be acted upon, and he was not even moved to extensive comment when two events fatally wounded the previously all-important deepwaterway law in late January. First, Representative William A. Hubbard (Green County-D) filed suit in the Sangamon Circuit Court of Sangamon County on behest of Congressman Rainey that claimed the deepwaterway law did not meet the criterion of a deep waterway as voted into the state charter in 1908. A final ruling was not forthcoming until December 1916, but the litigation had the effect of ceasing all preparatory work on the canal. Even more devastating was the decision of General Daniel C. Kingman, chief of the Army Corps of Engineers, made public on 28 February not to recommend the construction of the project without direct congressional approval on the basis that the toll provisions of the law were contrary to national policy on international waterways. The governor ordered an appeal, but for all effective purposes the canal was dead.[5]

As disappointing as the death of the deepwaterway law was, the real center of the governor's concern in the early months of 1916 was his party's factional fight. The Sullivan Democrats opened things up on 14 January at a meeting of the State Committee, during which they selected an "official" slate of eight delegates-at-large for the national convention scheduled to meet on 14 June in St. Louis. On the slate were Sullivan and four loyalists as well as Congressman Henry T. Rainey, Senator J. Hamilton Lewis, and Governor Edward F. Dunne. Missing was even token representation for the Harrison faction. The governor had sent a letter to the gathering pleading for party unity, and he now issued a disclaimer separating himself from the results. "Neither myself nor any of my friends entered into such an agreement," he insisted, nor would he be party to any effort to exclude the former mayor from the state delegation.[6]

The Harrisonites, now for the most part led by Chicago Congressman Adolph J. Sabath, who had been recently chosen as chairman of the Cook County Democracy, had signaled their intention to fight Sullivan at a banquet held in December, and they took this slate making as a declaration of war. Within two days of the announcement by the State Committee, they held their own conclave, during which they vowed "to battle Mr. Sullivan in every war and congressional district in Illinois." They drew up their own list of delegates-at-large that included, besides Carter Harrison, such notables as Secretary of State Lewis G. Stevenson, Congressman Lawrence Y. Stringer, Senator J. Hamilton Lewis, and Governor Edward F. Dunne.[7]

Both Lewis and the governor tentatively approved the Harrisonite list, but neither man wished to fuel factional fires. Observers found it significant that Harrison was not invited to share the railway platform with the senator and the governor to greet Woodrow Wilson on 31 January as he passed through Chicago. Lewis now asked for his own name to be struck from both slates, and with the approval and support of Dunne, he attempted to arrange a compromise at a meeting of downstate Democrats in Peoria. However, the Harrisonites rejected Lewis's plan because it recognized the relative strengths of the two factions and left Sullivan essentially in control of the national delegation.[8]

In truth, Harrison and his followers were not much interested in maintaining the status quo but instead were determined to reverse the current balance of power. They strove mightily in seeking support throughout the state, and they repeatedly sought to draw the governor to their side. As bait, they, like the Sullivan organization, offered their backing for his renomination and reelection. Dunne, who had yet to declare his intentions, resisted all such blandishments and maintained a stance of neutrality.[9]

The primary to select delegates in March continued his judgment as the Sullivanites swept all before them. Harrison did win enough votes, it was true, as did Rainey and the governor to serve as delegates-at-large, but seventeen of the twenty district delegates were solidly behind Sullivan. Even more impressive, the Sullivan organization carried twenty-eight of thirty-five wards in Chicago and effectively displaced the Harrison faction from its last bastion of strength. Not only was Sullivan left in control of Chicago, but his margin of power in the state committee had been increased to where nine of its ten members were his liege men.[10]

In the weeks that followed, the temporarily humbled Harrisonites announced that they would no longer oppose the boss in Cook County. Sabath's resignation as chairman of the county organization soon followed. As a kind of ultimate recognition of his supremacy, Sullivan was called to Washington, D.C., on 12 April to discuss the fall campaigns with the Wilson administration.[11]

Not surprisingly, the state convention, held in Springfield on 20 April to confirm the primary results, was dominated by the boss. The governor was, of course, invited to speak, which he did in very general terms of party loyalty, and he was cordially received. In deference to the fact that the primary election to select the state ticket was not to be held until September, no platform was written, and only a vague endorsement of the state administration was passed.[12]

Dunne may have been very aware of Sullivan's power, and he may have had no intention of challenging him, but neither was he prepared to become the pawn of the organization. That was illustrated at the national convention when he and Harrison led twelve other delegates in opposition to Sullivan's barely serious pretensions to the vice-presidential nomination. Supporting incumbent Thomas Marshall, the governor argued that if any son of Illinois should be considered, it should be Senator Lewis. Fortunately for all concerned, the boss's candidacy ceased to be an issue before balloting began.[13]

Shortly after returning to the state, the governor on 20 June, at last announced his intention to seek reelection. Basing his case for a second term upon his accomplishments, most of which dated back to the Forty-eighth General Assembly, he also proposed a platform that included calls for the redistricting of state senatorial and congressional boundaries, the consolidation of the two primaries, the extension of the state practice of rotating names on ballots to local elections, and (yet again) the abolition of the Board of Equalization. Even as he was laying the groundwork for his campaign for renomination, however, Governor Dunne found himself diverted by the demands of his duties as commander in chief of the state militia. The occasion was the Mexican crisis.[14]

In his final year and a half as governor, he came to take his military responsibilities with increasing seriousness. Unlike his mentor, William

Jennings Bryan, he had become a firm advocate of preparedness in general and the strengthening of the Illinois National Guard in particular. He had first endorsed both ideas in face of the growing threat of the war in Europe at a governors conference held in Boston in August 1915, and he had made an even stronger plea in a speech on Washington's Birthday before the National Security League in Chicago, where he called for a "Federal Standing Army" of fifty thousand men augmented by a system of powerful and modern state militias. In the same spirit, he participated in the preparations for massive preparedness parades held on 3 June 1916 in Chicago and Springfield.[15]

When President Wilson ordered troops to the Mexican border and beyond in response to Pancho Villa's raid on Columbus, New Mexico, in pursuit of his policy of teaching the Mexican people "to elect good men," Governor Dunne reacted with enthusiasm. The state's troops were ready, he proclaimed. "Illinois learned a lesson in 1898," he insisted, and it was ready this time to answer the president's call should it come. It came in late June, just as the governor announced his bid for reelection, and war fever swept the state. Two thousand men were gathered at Camp Lincoln near Chicago, and ten thousand at Camp Dunne, which was built outside Springfield as the primary reception center. Dunne was involved in all phases of the mobilization. On 26 June, the first Illinois troops were sent to Texas. Very soon, however, the governor's attention was diverted from the very real prospect of his troops engaging in combat by a serious challenge to his candidacy from within his own party.[16]

It was clear to all concerned that the Democrats were facing an immense test in Illinois in the approaching November elections. The Republicans had clearly regained their status as majority party, and in the summer of 1916, this resurgence was greatly helped by the breakup of the Progressive Party following Theodore Roosevelt's refusal to try again for the presidency and his subsequent endorsement of the Republican nominee, Charles Evans Hughes. The situation was alarming not just to Illinois Democrats but to the national party, which was very concerned about the state's twenty-eight electoral votes.[17]

In July, a plan emerged from within the Sullivan organization that, so it was felt, would enhance Democratic chances and allow the boss "to accumulate a certain amount of respectability in his remaining years." It called for the replacement of Edward F. Dunne as the head of the state ticket with the popular Progressive leader, Raymond Robins.[18] A bemused Robins soon found himself the object of petitions, telegrams, and letters like that from a Danville Democrat who swore that "the Democratic men here especially Sullivans [*sic*] main man of the local Daily newspaper" were going to do everything in their power "down this way" to see him nominated. Far more worrisome to Dunne were messages from "citizens of substance and merit" in the progressive wing of the party who saw in the possibility of Robins's candidacy a way to replace a governor who, however admirable in his intentions, "has not got the punch," and who "has not made a successful executive."[19]

The momentum for Robins reached Washington, D.C., from where the Democratic national chairman, Vance C. McCormick, intervened on behalf of the Wilson campaign. Replacing Dunne with Robins, a figure of national stature, fit neatly into McCormick's strategy of drawing one-third of the overall Progressive vote into the Democratic column. The problem with all those hopes and machinations was that Governor Dunne was simply too popular to confront in the primary. State Chairman Arthur Charles of Carmi, who was a Sullivanite and a candidate for state treasurer summarized things: "I am for Roger Sullivan when it comes to a matter of personal friendship, but it looks to the downstate men as if it would be very foolish to start a Sullivan candidate against Dunne in the primaries . . . I can't find any general sentiment out in the state for a fight on Dunne in the Democratic ranks."[20]

If it were not feasible, then, to run Robins against Dunne for the nomination, perhaps, so McCormick reasoned, the governor could be persuaded to step aside for the sake of the party. Meeting with him in Chicago, apparently on 11 July, he did his best to persuade, and he sweetened things with an offer of a place on the newly created federal farm board.[21]

For his part, Edward F. Dunne was perhaps willing to consider the idea if he were appointed to Charles Evans Hughes's vacant Supreme Court seat, but otherwise he was firm in his refusal. Not only did he believe himself the best possible candidate and the most likely Democrat to win, but also he held to his conviction that he, himself, would attract a substantial portion of the Progressive vote. Undaunted, McCormick soon induced Secretary of the Navy Josephus Daniels to write William Jennings Bryan on 17 July, as the person who had "more influence" with Dunne "than any man," to persuade the Great Commoner to bring the governor into line.[22]

It was naturally hurtful for the Wilson administration to be so willing to push him aside, especially as he had been a loyal supporter. On the day before Daniels wrote Bryan, the governor emotionally announced he was in the race to stay, that he had no "yellow streak" and that he would not be driven out by anyone. Subsequently backed up in his determination by Senator Lewis, it was clear Dunne meant just as he said.[23]

The issue became meaningless when Robins, who had "never considered the suggestion of my nomination as a candidate for governor on the Democratic ticket seriously," announced on 5 August his support of Hughes and his conversion to the Republican Party. He explained: "My home state of Illinois is an illuminating example of the general experience. We have had able Progressive Democratic leadership and within the past decade have won both the city and state governments. Yet the permanent gains for progressive principles have been practically nil."[24]

The reason for that was because the "heartsick minority" of progressive Democrats had been overwhelmed by a "corporate boss" in service of "selfish personal and corporate interest," aided by the "present administration in Washington".[25]

Although successful in thwarting the efforts to remove him from the campaign, the Robins affair soured relations between the governor and the national administration. Until the spring of 1916, federal patronage had been largely given over to a division among Dunne, Lewis, and Harrison. Sullivan's victory in the April primaries, and the subsequent indication by Dunne that he cared as much about his own political survival as that of Woodrow Wilson, changed things. In the months ahead, the Wilson campaign in Illinois, whether conducted through McCormick or through Democratic western chairman, Senator Thomas J. Walsh of Montana (who was based in Chicago), was to rely upon the boss and his organization. Dunne was rarely consulted, frequently ignored, and allowed only the barest ceremonial courtesies.

In the end, only two other Democrats filed in the gubernatorial primary, and neither was much of a threat. The first was James Traynor of Chicago, generally considered to be a very minor candidate, and the second was William B. Brinton of Dixon, who reportedly entered the contest "just to see how many votes he'd get," and who promised that at no time would he "have a thing to say against Governor Dunne and his administration."[26] With this quality of opposition there was little apparent cause for worry; far more important was a ruling on 29 July, by Judge Normal L. Jones of the Circuit Court of Sangamon County, that upheld the Hubbard suit against the deepwaterway law, which the administration immediately appealed.[27]

Things were so relaxed that the governor, together with Mrs. Dunne, Adjutant General Frank S. Dickson, Mrs. Dickson, a daughter-in-law, and three advisers from the National Guard, departed on 15 August for a ten-day visit to the troops in Texas. Disdaining all "frills," the party slept in tents, and from all accounts enjoyed meeting the troops and local politicians, all the while reaping favorable publicity. Following the trip, Dunne immediately took up the question of extending the franchise to the men in the field. Promising at first to call yet another special session, he let the matter drop after its constitutionality was widely questioned. Fortunately, when negotiations were begun with the Mexican government in late September, Illinois's troops began returning home without having had to fight.[28]

On 31 August, the governor at last opened his campaign with a speech in Chicago. It was one of but a small handful of addresses he would deliver before the 13 September primary election. His theme throughout was simply that he had been a "clean and progressive" chief executive, and that he deserved, therefore, to be reelected. It seemed that it was all to be perfunctory. On 8 September, however, the Sullivan organization's latent frustrations with Dunne burst forth.[29]

The immediate source of this emotional shift by the Sullivanites, who had given every sign of fatalistically accepting Dunne as the Democratic gubernatorial candidate after the Robins affair, was a pamphlet written by Philip J. McKenna, a Harrisonite and former president of the Chicago Sanitary District. Entitled "Save the Honor of Chicago," it was a scathing attack on Roger Sullivan. Ironically, the pamphlet was a last feeble effort of the Harrison faction, which had broken their pledge and fronted candidates for Cook County offices only to withdraw most of them by September. The governor immediately disclaimed any knowledge or endorsement of McKenna's work, but the Sullivan ward leadership at a very intense meeting of the Cook County Democratic managing committee voted by a margin of twenty-five to seven to back Brinton in the primary election, now just three days away. Brinton, who had the good fortune of being in Chicago at the time, gratefully accepted their support.[30]

The governor did little openly to propitiate the Sullivanites. The state's major labor leaders, John Walker, president of the Illinois Federation of Labor, and John J. Fitzpatrick, president of the Chicago Federation of Labor, did remind their membership of the administration's efforts on their behalf, while at the same time, they linked Brinton to the presence of federal troops in Chicago in 1894 during the Pullman strike. However, they, like Dunne, remained confident.[31]

When the votes were counted the governor easily won renomination with 151,763 votes to Brinton's 65,639 and Traynor's 21,105; even in Cook County, his margin of victory was of landslide proportions. On the other hand, with the exception of Louis G. Stevenson's successful bid for the nomination for secretary of state, Sullivan's candidates won every other seat on the state ticket.[32]

Mutual self-interest now dictated that the governor and the Sullivan organization relegate their differences to the past and achieve a semblance of unity at the party convention on 26 September in Springfield. Dunne, by the grace of Sullivan, was in complete control of the platform. It included, besides the expected review of his administration's accomplishments, calls for a constitutional convention; changing the amending process of the state constitution; full suffrage for women and members of the National Guard serving out of state; the implementation of the report of the Efficiency and Economy Commission; more and better roads; the eight-hour day for working men and women; and the extension of gubernatorial powers to include line-item vetoes regarding appropriation bills.[33]

Also written into the platform was what was to be the governor's central campaign theme. In a return to the crusading progressive spirit of 1912, this plank attacked the "Invisible Government" of Illinois that had achieved the Republican gubernatorial nomination of their candidate, Frank O. Lowden, through "enormous expenditures of money." Only "constant vigilance" (and the reelection of the administration) could "protect the people" from their "oppression." The real issue, as he was soon to define it in his speeches, was simply "whether money could buy the governorship."[34] Clearly, the governor hoped not.

Meanwhile, the Republicans, too, had stirred up their share of factional discord in their nominating process. Since his election as mayor of Chicago in 1915, William Hale Thompson had brought about something of a revolution within the state party. Reorganizing and rebuilding upon the faction of William Lorimer, he had created a powerful machine, and he had gone far toward overthrowing the entrenched power of former Governor Charles Deneen and Roy O. West. He had already taken West's office of national committeeman, and beginning in the spring of 1915, the mayor and his followers had dedicated themselves to capturing the governor's chair with their candidate, Frank O. Lowden.[35]

In the primary, the Deneen group, backed by the *Chicago Tribune* and many returning Progressives, supported Morton Hull, a prominent legislator in the Forty-eighth and Forty-ninth General Assemblies. Also running was Frank Smith, who counted upon the support of the remnants of the organization of the late United States Senator Shelby M. Cullom. Lowden, who did pick up the endorsements of such important downstate Progressives as Frank Funk, easily won the primary after a bitter and expensive campaign.[36]

In many ways, Frank O. Lowden was the perfect "straw man" for the progressive crusade Governor Dunne was trying to create. Of relatively humble origins—born to a farming family in Sunrise, Minnesota, and educated in rural schools and at the University of Iowa and the Union College of Law in Chicago—Lowden experienced an epiphany of lifestyle with his marriage in 1896 to Florence Pullman, daughter of George Pullman of Pullman Car and strike fame. He soon was a wealthy man, holding, besides his wife's extensive fortune, directorships that included the Pullman Company, the National Bank of the Republic, and the Kansas City, Pittsburgh, and Gulf Railroad.

Having achieved financial security so easily and so early in his life, he turned to politics.[37]

A conservative Republican by inclination and now by social class, Lowden soon associated himself with William Lorimer. In 1904, he was Lorimer's candidate for the Republican gubernatorial nomination. Although unsuccessful, he was shortly elected a Republican national committeeman. In 1906, he got himself sent to Congress from the rural Thirteenth District in which his country estate was located. He served in the House of Representatives until 1911, when he retired ostensibly because of his health, but also in response to the mood created by the ongoing Lorimer scandal. [38]

At the 1912 Republican convention, Lowden elected, like Charles Deneen, to remain with the party and Taft when Roosevelt bolted. Unlike Charles Deneen, however, Lowden was able to avoid any association with the Lorimer scandal and the progressive outrage that followed. When the tides began shifting back to the Republicans in 1914, he recovered his ambition, and at a meeting with Thompson at Eagle Rock, Wisconsin, in mid-May 1915, he agreed to become the mayor's candidate for governor. Now, following a hard primary battle, this wealthy businessman and Taft Republican, backed by the most notorious and ruthless machine in the state, was his party's choice to face Dunne in the election.[39]

The governor did his best to inflame reformist sentiments against Lowden. He began with a tour of southern Illinois in September. In contrast to his triumphant processions of 1913, this trip was very modest; he used public transportation and traveled with only a small staff. Often quoting Lowden's primary opponent, he insisted that his opponent had been nominated by "the public utility corporations, the great packing interests, the warehouse combination, the railroads, the Pullman company . . . the consolidated financial interest known as 'Big Business,'" as a tool to rob and cheat the people of the state. The means by which these nefarious forces conspired to loot Illinois was through gaining control of the Public Utility Commission. But as Dunne so accurately pointed out, under the law Lowden was not allowed to serve on the commission because he was a director of the Pullman Company.[40]

Dunne also tried to exploit the ambiguous attitude many former Progressives were believed to hold toward the Republican candidate. He enjoyed pointing out that Lowden had yet to have been endorsed by Theodore Roosevelt. At the end of October, he was forced to drop this theme when a reporter in Chicago bluntly asked the former president whether he backed his party's gubernatorial candidate. Showing some irritation, Roosevelt barked that "of course I am for Lowden. He is a Republican, and I am for the Republican ticket."[41]

In contrast to Roosevelt's faint praise were the efforts of William Jennings Bryan for Dunne. Originally scheduled by the Wilson campaign to speak in Illinois and other vital eastern states, the Great Commoner's itinerary had been shifted to less important areas, but remained full. Nonetheless, he interrupted his tour to come to the state to speak for his old friend. In just two days, the pair appeared in ten towns, primarily in southwestern Illinois—traditionally strong Bryan territory. Like the governor, "Colonel" Bryan attacked Lowden as the mouthpiece of the rich while insisting that Dunne was "one of the best governors you've ever had."[42]

Senator J. Hamilton Lewis also did his best to help with a ringing endorsement during a speech delivered on 3 November in Freeport. Unfortunately, he was unable to do more as the Wilson administration had drafted him to appear almost continuously throughout the Midwest. On the other hand, about the only direct advantage Dunne derived from the national campaign was being allowed on the platform when President Wilson made appearances on 4 and 19 October in Chicago.[43]

It was in the state's chief city that he concentrated his efforts in the last week before the election. There he appealed to his traditional constituency among the workers. John Walker, president of the Illinois Federation of Labor, who was not unmindful of the governor's "own private and official acts to justify Labor's cause," strongly restated his support. It was there that Dunne, on election eve, concluded with a speech that again defined the primary issue as whether the people would elect a man "whose sympathies are wholly with the corporations."[44]

In contrast to the governor's rather facile efforts, the Lowden campaign was a well-financed circus. The Republican candidate began with a three-week tour on a private train. Accompanying him were a baby elephant, a fife and drum corps, and a changing chorus of other Republican candidates that included Medill McCormick, a former Progressive leader and now a GOP candidate for congressman-at-large. Lowden, despite Dunne's attempts to paint him as such, was no reactionary, and he was in personal agreement with most of the accomplishments of his opponent. Consequently, he had some difficulty developing his attack. At first, he could do little more than criticize the handling of the foot-and-mouth epidemic. Soon, however, he hit upon the hackneyed theme of a wasteful extravagance and inefficiency in state government. It was Governor Dunne, he insisted, who was responsible for a fifteen-million-dollar increase in appropriations in 1915, for an advance of "four million dollars a year" in state spending since 1913, and for padding the state payroll with temporary appointments. When in Chicago, Lowden added the charge that the governor had proven himself an enemy of home rule by his refusal to veto the Public Utility Law.[45]

The charges of extravagance were, as Lowden doubtlessly knew, cynical. Not only had the upward surge of appropriations been caused by increases in services of which he approved, but they had been voted by legislatures largely controlled by Republicans. Moreover, he conveniently overlooked the fact that the incumbent held the record for the number of vetoes of appropriations. Dunne could hardly be held to account that in 1915 his efforts in that direction were wiped out by the Fergus suits. Perhaps for those reasons, as well as a result of a growing confidence, Lowden let this extravagance theme drop in the latter part of the campaign, preferring to concentrate upon such wider questions as the increasing costs of living and the foibles of the Wilson administration.[46]

Both sides entered election day with the usual prophecies of impending victory. Vance C. McCormick, the national Democratic chairman, went so far as to predict that the Republicans not only would lose in Illinois but would carry only six states in the entire country. Only slightly less grandiose was the statement by William O'Connell, once again Dunne's campaign manager, that the governor would win with a seventy-five-thousand-vote majority in Chicago.[47]

It was not to be; both Wilson and Dunne lost in Illinois. In all, Lowden received 696,535 votes, while Governor Dunne was given 556,654. Wilson did slightly better, running about 1 percent ahead of the governor. With Lowden was elected the entire Republican state ticket as well as heavy majorities for his party in both houses of the legislature. Governor Dunne accepted defeat gracefully and without apparent surprise, wiring his congratulations at 9:00 P.M. from the La Salle Hotel in Chicago.[48]

The defeat was not founded in any personal antipathy; indeed, the governor managed to increase his total by more than 100,000 votes from that which he received in 1913. Rather, it was clear that he was liked and respected by citizens of all political stripes, a fact emphasized by the *Chicago Tribune* in its editorial wrap-up when it wrote:

> Governor Dunne went under with the national ticket of the Democratic party, but he has the consolation of . . . an honorable record and the knowledge that the people of the state would have been willing to have another term of him if he had separated from the general camp of his party.[49]

The *St. Louis Globe-Democrat*, another strongly Republican paper, struck a similar theme:

Gov. Dunne, has throughout his administration of four years, been an official of integrity and high aims. Clean-handedness has marked the work of the executive office throughout his entire term. He has failed in getting done not a few things he has ardently desired to have done, and not one of these defeated efforts was inspired by any other motive than to serve the public interest.

His failure to be reelected was not due to any personal fault, the paper assured its readers, but to his inability "in spite of Gov. Dunne's efforts," to root out "extravagance, cutting cancers, warts, and pustules of all kinds from the body politic, and relieving that body of a swarm of parasites which have for so long preyed on it."[50]

Although the growth of the Sullivan machine may have influenced some voters, the results were instead centered in the rather obvious fact of the re-unification of the Republican Party. Most of those who had voted Progressive in 1913, and in lesser numbers in 1914, had followed their national and state leaders, including Theodore Roosevelt, Raymond Robins, Frank Funk, and Medill McCormick back into the GOP ranks. It was a process that Dunne and his party were simply unable to meaningfully influence.

Similarly, there were unmistakable and relevant diminutions between 1912 and 1916 in the progressive passions of the voters. In 1912, in part because of the Lorimer scandal and in part because of the circumstances surrounding the formation of the Progressive Party, the citizenry was emotionally committed to reform in a manner not seen before and not seen afterward for at least sixteen years and the election of Franklin D. Roosevelt as president of the United States. It was this consensus for reform that was most directly responsible for the nomination and election (albeit by a minority of votes) of Edward F. Dunne as a visible symbol of honesty and progressive policy. By 1916, reformist passions had faded, and try as he might, Dunne was unable to resurrect them. Instead, he found himself overwhelmed as the voters returned to the "normalcy" of pre-1912 politics that meant relatively conservative, Republican state government.[51]

The last weeks of his term were quiet and routine. On 7 December, he hosted a meeting to celebrate the state's ninety-eighth birthday, and on 16 December, he represented Illinois for the last time at a governors' conference in Washington. He used the occasion to make a final plea for the Illinois Waterway.[52]

Not surprisingly, the Fiftieth General Assembly, with its large Republican majorities, organized quickly, and the date for Lowden's inauguration was set for the eighth of January. As he entered into his final weeks, Dunne made 118 appointments, all of which were eventually approved by the legislature, and characteristically, his last official act was to commute the life sentence of a very ill wife-murderer.[53]

Inauguration day belonged to Frank O. Lowden, but Governor Dunne was graciously thanked in a joint legislative resolution read by Speaker David Shanahan for his services to the state. At noon, Lowden took his oath, and at 2:45 P.M., Edward F. Dunne, to the cheers of a small group of well-wishers, boarded the train for Chicago.[54]

8

FINAL YEARS

Edward F. Dunne never sought elected public office again. He made this decision consciously; as he explained in a letter to William Jennings Bryan just days after the election: "I am determined, however, to retire to private life and do not believe that this intention will be changed. The responsibilities and worries of official life and the strenuous work in the campaigns have all recently become somewhat irksome."[1] Even after the hurt, apparent in this quote, of having been abandoned by some of his progressive friends (including the president of the United States) faded, he remained determined. In the next years, he would repeatedly quash efforts to run him yet again for this position or that. While he always reserved the right to become involved with public questions that interested him, his role in politics was to become increasingly peripheral. Instead, for his remaining twenty-one years, his family and private law practice were the real focus of his life.[2]

Upon becoming governor, he had dissolved his partnership with his son and namesake, Edward F. Dunne Jr., who then brought in a new associate, Daniel F. Murphy. Despite occasional criticism that the pair represented clients before state boards appointed by the senior partner's father, the firm prospered. On the morning following the inauguration of Frank O. Lowden, Judge Dunne, as he was again known, appeared at the firm's office bright and early. In 1919, Edward Jr. went east into manufacturing to be replaced by the former governor's son-in-law William Corboy. "Dunne and Corboy" soon established new offices at the famous Rookery Building, where for the next decade and a half they practiced completely nonpolitical, but successful, family and business law.[3]

It was while Dunne was working to reestablish himself as an attorney that he felt moved to speak out publicly for the first time after his defeat. In April 1917, soon after the entrance of the nation into World War I, he delivered a strong appeal for conscription at St. Paul's Episcopal Church in Chicago. The next month while in Springfield doing work for a client, Dunne was surprised by a hastily called banquet on his behalf by his friends in the legislature. This was followed by an invitation from Governor Lowden to help greet Marshal Jacques-Joseph Joffre then on a tour of the United States. Dunne and his family remained consistent supporters of the war effort and of President Wilson's efforts to assure a just peace.[4]

In the late summer of 1918, he reluctantly joined the remaining fragments of the Harrison faction in yet another attempt to confront Roger Sullivan and his machine. Grandly calling themselves the "Allied Democracy" in an obvious attempt to identify their cause with that of the Allied fight against Germany, they drew up a list of candidates for the September primary and set out to defame and defeat the boss. Dunne began the attack with one of his few speeches in which he labeled the boss as "Gas Chieftain" out, as ever, to despoil the party and the state. He promised that the Allied ticket was not "gold plated, gas baited, or traction tainted." Carter Harrison took a similar tone in his addresses around the city. In response, Sullivan's supporters, in one of their massive rallies, dismissed Dunne and Harrison, in a remarkable oxymoron, as "Grand Dukes and Bolsheviki." The primary results were a "walkover" for Roger Sullivan, as he once again demonstrated his hegemony over the Democratic Party.[5]

Among the victors was J. Hamilton Lewis, who, with William O'Connell as his campaign manager, was seeking renomination to the United States Senate. There had briefly been rumors that he might not run because of ill health, and that Dunne would take his place. That did not happen, and such was the reality of Sullivan's domination that neither the senator nor O'Connell associated himself with the Allied Democracy. There had been no break between the former governor and his two closest political friends, but Dunne's relative retirement facilitated a pragmatic detente with the boss. Lewis was also openly backed by Woodrow Wilson, and that together with presidential endorsements of other Democrats around the country enraged and revitalized the Republicans, who had assumed politics was to be adjourned during the war. For once, Judge Dunne was not involved in the controversy, and Lewis went down to defeat to the Republican nominee, Medill McCormick.[6] Even as these campaigns were unwinding, Dunne was becoming involved with an issue of greater personal importance. It was an issue that was to bring him, briefly, international recognition for the only time of his career.

Agitation for Irish independence was a family tradition, but beyond involvement in fraternal organizations and the occasional speech, he had never allowed himself to become a leader. Shortly after the American entry into World War I, he had joined in with other prominent men in the Irish Fellowship League to publicly demand self-determination for Ireland. However, over the next two years he consciously sought to remain supportive without assuming a position in the forefront of the movement among the city's Irish. In this he was not unlike other well-known politicians, including Senator Medill McCormick and Mayor William Hale Thompson.[7]

In the spring of 1919, a third Irish Race Convention was scheduled by the nationally based Friends of Irish Freedom to meet on 22 February in Philadelphia to lobby for the old country's freedom. Unlike the first two gatherings held while the fighting was in progress, and which had been small, ineffective, radical, and tainted by charges of treason, this conclave was planned as a gathering of all mainstream Irish organizations from across the country. In Chicago, the Irish Fellowship League, the Ancient Order of Hibernians, and Clan-na-Gael met to choose delegates. Among those selected by the League was Edward F. Dunne.[8]

He did not want to go. In fact, he vehemently declined the honor, initially refusing even the blandishments of his father, P. W. Dunne. Eventually under great pressure from his family and friends, he surrendered, and against his better judgment, he departed for the City of Brotherly Love determined to limit his participation to his attendance.[9]

It was a noisy affair as 5,000 delegates cheered on such speakers as Senator David I. Walsh of Massachusetts and Senator William E. Borah of Idaho as well as a bevy of lesser luminaries and leading members of the Roman Catholic hierarchy. More constructively, it was decided that a committee of twenty-four should be appointed to meet with President Wilson, who was briefly back in the country from Paris. Dunne was included in their number.[10]

When the delegation arrived in Washington, D.C., the president refused to meet. He had just given assurances to the British ambassador that he would do nothing to embarrass his ally over the Irish question. Moreover, he was under an enormous strain from dealing with the territorial questions of the defeated Central Powers.[11]

Importuned by his personal secretary, Joe Tumulty, Wilson at last agreed to see the group on 4 March at New York City's Metropolitan Opera House following a scheduled speech. Things began poorly as Wilson insisted that one leading delegate, New York Supreme Court Justice Daniel Cohalan, who had during the course of the war attacked the administration's Irish policy, be excluded, and it was a visibly irritated president who at last met with them. Almost nothing was accomplished. While not ruling out the possibility of Irish independence being discussed at the conference, Wilson bluntly refused to bring the matter up. Nor would he commit himself to working to obtain passports to Paris from the English for representatives of the recently self-proclaimed but unrecognized Irish republican government.[12]

Dissatisfied with Wilson's replies and greatly strengthened in their resolve by a resolution passed in the House of Representatives calling for a
review of the Irish question at the peace conference, the delegation decided
to appoint three of their number to follow the president back to Paris. This
American Committee for Irish Independence was instructed to lobby for permission for representatives of the Irish provisional government to go to the
conference and, if failing in this, to present the case for a free Ireland at the
gathering of the Allies themselves.[13]

They showed some tactical sense in their choice of men—none of whom
was closely associated with radicalism, and all of whom had some connection
with the Wilson administration. As chairman, Frank P. Walsh of Missouri
was selected. He had headed the Commission on Industrial Relations, and he
had served on the National War Labor Board. Michael Ryan of Pennsylvania,
while having a record as an agitator for Irish independence, also had a respectable tenure on a public service commission in Philadelphia. The third
delegate was Edward F. Dunne, whose worse fears about participating in the
convention now seemed realized. They sailed from New York City on 1 April
and arrived in Paris ten days later.[14]

Their first act was to try to arrange a meeting between Walsh and Wilson.
He met instead with the president's chief adviser and "alter ego," Colonel
Edward House. Although sympathetic, House was unable to secure from the
British prime minister, Lloyd George, either passports to France for members
of the Irish provisional government or even a definite agreement for a conference with the Irish Americans. He was able, on the other hand, to secure
approval for the committee to visit Ireland. The British government granted
this in the mistaken notion that they would be impressed with the existing
conditions there; it was also a convenient way to get them out of Paris.[15]

They arrived in Dublin on 3 May 1919 and were scheduled to meet with
the Irish Parliament and the provisional Irish government ten days later. In
the interim, Dunne and Ryan made visits to Belfast and Limerick. Dunne,
accompanied by Irish republican President Eamon De Valera, also managed
to steal a visit to his alma mater, Trinity College in Dublin. Having pointedly
arrived with passports from both the British and the Irish republican governments, the three men were clear in their sympathies, and they were not reluc-
tant to cogently express their support of independence to the enthusiastic crowds
that met them everywhere. This was especially true when with great fanfare
they addressed the Irish Parliament.[16]

During the remaining three days of their visit, they attempted to visit
Sinn Fein prisoners being held by the British. On 11 May, they bluffed their

way into Mountjoy Gaol in Dublin, and the following day they tried to inspect the conditions of those allegedly being held in Westport, a town in a British "military area." In a tense moment, they found themselves turned back on the road by armed English troops. On 13 May, they left for Paris.[17]

The British were not amused by the quasi-revolutionary activity of the Irish American delegations. The press severely criticized Lloyd George for sanctioning the visit, and even His Majesty, King George V, questioned the wisdom of his prime minister's act. In response, Lloyd George refused any further dealing with the delegation. Similarly, Wilson and the American Peace Commission used the uproar following the visit as an excuse to withhold any further help as expressed in a very terse letter from Secretary of State Robert Lansing.[18]

Not to be discouraged, the delegates sent to Wilson preview copies of their *Report on Conditions in Ireland, With a Demand for Investigation by the Peace Conference*, which under seventeen headings sought to document the "atrocities" of English military rule. The report, called "grotesque" by the *Times* of London, was soon refuted in detail by the British government. Nonetheless, the report created some publicity in the United States when officially released in July.[19]

The Irish Americans' hand was greatly enhanced when on 6 June (the same day they sent their report), news arrived of a strong resolution by the United States Senate in support of representation for the Irish republicans. Fearing a loss of control, President Wilson now met with Walsh and Dunne for a frank discussion. When pressed on the point of self-determination, he confessed the limits of his power. Admitting the existence of a "great metaphysical tragedy," he told them that given the complexities of the situation, there was just little he could do. He did agree to have Secretary Lansing present the Senate resolution to the conference without comment or recommendations. The Irish American delegation next made a vain appeal to the French premier, George Clemenceau. Failing in that, they sent President Wilson another report and prepared to return to the United States.[20]

They arrived in New York City on 8 July 1919 to a greeting as befitted heroes as hundreds of Irish Americans crowded the docks. Looking tan and fit and met by his wife, Edward F. Dunne was particularly enthusiastic about the accomplishments of the trip. As he explained it, the American Commission for Irish Independence had been successful in drawing attention to the "story of English atrocities" and in forcing the English newspapers to admit the scandal of conditions in Ireland. Although it could have been argued that their main achievement was to give the British an excuse not to discuss Ireland at the Peace Conference, an unlikely event in any case, clearly the delegates had been successful in adding pressure on the London government for the inevitable freedom of Ireland.[21]

He returned by train to Chicago. Accompanying him were Walsh and President De Valera, who had begun a tour of the country to drum up support. They were scheduled to speak at a massive rally in the Windy City, and more than 25,000 attended and listened to the three, in addition to Mayor Thompson and Illinois Congressman William E. Mason, speak for the cause. Dunne fulfilled his final official duty as a commissioner when he appeared together with Walsh, Ryan, Cohalan, and John Murphy of Buffalo, New York, before the Senate Foreign Relations Committee in late August.[22]

His role as an advocate of Irish freedom, however, was not concluded. In 1920, at a state Democratic convention, most noted for the ascension of George Brennan into the late Roger Sullivan's position of power and for the nomination of former Senator J. Hamilton Lewis for governor, he was chosen as a national delegate. At the Democratic conclave in San Francisco, he, together with Frank P. Walsh and President De Valera, strove mightily for the inclusion of a platform plan favoring Irish independence. They had some trouble gaining a hearing. At one point, Dunne found himself physically barred from the room where the platform committee was meeting. Reinforced by Senator David Walsh of Massachusetts and others, he was at last allowed to make his presentation. However, both the Wilson administration and William G. McAdoo, secretary of the treasury and the president's son-in-law as well as a leading contender for the presidential nomination, opposed the plank, and it was defeated in the committee by a vote of thirty-one to seventeen.[23]

In the contest for the presidential nomination, Dunne initially supported Vice President Thomas Marshall with the explanation that neither of the two leading candidates, McAdoo and Governor James Cox of Ohio, could win the election. Following Marshall's withdrawal, he with most of the Illinois delegation first supported Attorney General A. Mitchell Palmer before switching to Cox, who became the nominee. He was relatively inactive during the fall campaigns; there is no evidence that he did anything for Cox, but he did speak at least once for Lewis in Chicago.[24]

If the election of 1916 killed progressivism as the dominant force in Illinois politics, then the election of 1920 was its wake. Nationally, Warren Harding, a Republican whose politics of "normalcy" more closely resembled those of William McKinley than Theodore Roosevelt, was elected president. In Illinois, Len Small, a close associate of Mayor Thompson, was elected by a landslide over J. Hamilton Lewis to succeed Frank O. Lowden as governor. Thompson, who had himself been only narrowly reelected as mayor in 1919, in large part because of his antiwar stance, was now the most powerful man in the state's most powerful party.[25]   Within two years, however, an issue appeared that seemed to belie the death of Illinois progressivism, and that drew Dunne back into the political arena.

It had long been accepted that the Illinois Constitution of 1870 was sadly inadequate and antiquated. Unsuccessful efforts to effect a call for a constitutional convention had been a regular feature of every legislative session for years. Finally in 1919, at Governor Lowden's urging, one was issued. Beginning on 6 January 1920, the delegates, who were for the most part conservative Republicans, wrestled with their complex task, and on 12 September 1922, they presented the state with their proposed state charter. The twelfth of December was chosen as the date for ratification by referendum.[26]

Upon perusing the convention's work, Dunne found many serious flaws. Not the least was that it "contained a gross betrayal of the rights of the citizens of Cook County to proportional representation in the legislature." He was also alarmed by what he interpreted as a dangerous increase in the powers of the state's supreme court, which were made even less desirable by a decrease in the court's accountability.[27]

Soon he, with Clarence Darrow, Harold Ickes, and others of like opinion, created the People's Protective League to combat ratification. Dunne served as chairman of the organization's executive committee, while Ickes was its president. The cause also brought together many who had been prominent during Dunne's tenure as governor, including Carl Vrooman, Charles Merriam, William O'Connell, and Fred Kern.[28]

An immediate and intensely public campaign was dictated by the fact that the proposed charter was being acclaimed by much of the sitting leadership of both parties. Even before the PPL was formed, Dunne, with surprising vigor for a sixty-nine-year-old man, accompanied Darrow in breaking into a meeting of the Cook County Democratic Central Committee to check a move by George Brennan to railroad through an endorsement. The two reunited allies not only stopped any endorsement but also were able to wrestle a vote of condemnation.[29]

It was decided that the best strategy was to take advantage of the generous supply of oratorical talent in the PPL and challenge the proponents of the constitution to a series of debates. Dunne debated, among others, former Senator Lawrence Y. Sherman and Congressman Morton D. Hull. He, like Merriam, Kern, Ickes, and Darrow in their debates, condemned the document both because it undercut representation for Cook County and for the powers of the Supreme Court, and also because it did not provide for the initiative and referendum, a fair income tax, or true home rule for Chicago.[30]

The anticonstitutional movement began attracting important support.

Numbered among those coming on board were Governor Len Small, Mayor William Hale Thompson, former Senator J. Hamilton Lewis, former Mayor Carter Harrison, Raymond Robins, Margaret Haley, the Chicago City Council, the American Federation of Labor, the Illinois Federation of Labor, the Chicago Federation of Labor, the "large majority or superior, circuit, and municipal judges," and the milkmen of Chicago. On the other side, the proponents, led by Illinois Supreme Court Justice Orin Carter, also had a top-heavy list of supporters. Those included Senator Medill McCormick, Senator William McKinley, former Governor Charles Deneen, former Governor Frank Lowden, George Brennan, Walter Fisher, the Citizens Association of Chicago, the Chicago Bureau of Public Efficiency and "most Republican and Democratic county organizations downstate."[31] The constitutional question, then, was roughly reflective of the ideological dichotomy between social and structual reformism found in Illinois progressivism before World War I.

From the beginning, the proponents were on the defensive. Even the most fervent advocates were forced to admit that the document had flaws. By mid-October, it was becoming plain that the tide was turning against the proposed state charter. Illustrative of this was the changing attitude of the *Chicago Tribune*. The "World's Greatest Newspaper" had initially greeted the work of the convention with enthusiasm, and it began featuring articles on the front page that outlined the benefits of the document. By the last week before the referendum, those articles had been replaced by an editorial advising the readership to vote against the constitution. Much to Dunne's satisfaction, it was defeated by a statewide vote of 921,398 to 185,298; Chicago's returns, with a vote of 541,206 to 27,878, showed an even more lopsided proportion.[32]

It would be a mistake to see in the constitution battle of 1922 a resurgence of Illinois progressivism. The presence of Mayor William Hale Thompson on the side of the opponents and the support of the charter by such old-time progressives as Walter Fisher would seem to render such a view as simplistic. At the same time, however, the constitutional fight did underscore that much of the state's reformist leadership from before World War I could still come together around the right issue and that the people in Illinois, even in those years of "normalcy," could still disregard most of their sitting leadership and protect their own interests. On a lesser scale, that point was demonstrated again in 1923 as Judge Dunne once again became involved in a political campaign.

As 1923 began, Mayor Thompson of Chicago was clearly vulnerable. His antiwar stance, his political "cronyism," not to mention the recent jailing of seven of his appointees to the school board, had earned him a wide array of determined enemies. Sensing victory, the Democrats nominated William E.

Dever, a man with a reputation for honesty and reform who had served as Dunne's council floorleader. His candidacy attracted the support of many who had fought the constitution and included such familiar faces as Raymond Robins, Margaret Haley, Michael Igoe, J. Hamilton Lewis, and Charles Merriam. With joy, Dunne joined the campaign, but because of his advancing age, he made fewer appearances and speeches than in the past. Dever easily defeated Republican Arthur C. Lueder, postmaster of Chicago, who had been nominated by his party following Thompson's withdrawal.[33]

The most remarkable aspect of Dever's victory, however, was not that he had won but that he had achieved his election with that rarest of things, a united Democratic Party. Not only was he backed by what had been the Dunne and Harrison wing, now mostly led by William O'Connell, but he was from the beginning boosted by Democratic boss George Brennan. Unfortunately, at least from Judge Dunne's point of view, Brennan was to be "prime minister of the Dever regime." The inevitable split between the new mayor and his old leader first came in the primaries of 1924 when Dunne was running for delegate-at-large for the national convention in support of the candidacy of William McAdoo and was defeated by a Dever-Brennan slate. The boss's influence became even more glaring when in the spring of 1925, Mayor Dever offered to the city a new traction ordinance.[34]

Dunne had remained personally close to the mayor, and he had received copies of the traction scheme well in advance of their public release. He was intensely disappointed. Dever had been elected on a platform that in part called for immediate municipal ownership, and in 1924, he had assured him that this remained an important priority. What he now got was in his judgment a blatant sellout to the traction companies. In the first place, the valuations placed upon traction properties were completely unrealistic and prohibitive in their own right to future municipal ownership, but even more disastrous, an envisioned municipal railway board was so designed as to place the streetcar systems beyond any direct control of the city government.[35]

Even before Dunne's "first formally written attack" on 31 March 1925, he in concert with others had helped to organize the People's Traction League to defeat the measure in referendum. Joining him were former Mayors Harrison and Thompson, while Dever could count on the support of Brennan, Samuel Insull (Chicago's popular utility baron) and Dunne's old nemesis, Walter Fisher. After a short but intense campaign, during which Judge Dunne issued written statements but did not speak, the traction scheme was defeated at the polls by a three-to-one margin.[36]

His opposition to the mayor did not end with this victory. In July 1925, he with Carter Harrison, J. Hamilton Lewis, and William O'Connell formed the Illinois Democracy to try to counter the power of the city's increasingly powerful Democratic machine. Not much was heard from the Illinois Democracy until February 1926 when they announced a slate for the Cook County primary. Most of their candidates were former governmental associates of the organization's leaders, but running for a nomination to the county Board of Review was Robert Jerome "Duke" Dunne, Edward's fourth surviving son, former captain of the University of Michigan football squad, current football coach at Northwestern University, and a future circuit court judge. Without directly attacking either Brennan or Dever, the group based their appeal for votes upon a fairly standard platform that called for home rule for Chicago, municipal ownership, the amendment of the Volstead Act to legalize beer, and "states rights in defining what the words 'intoxicating liquors' mean" in the Eighteenth Amendment to the United States Constitution that created Prohibition.[37]

The Illinois Democracy was not perceived as much of a threat by the Dever-Brennan machine. One Brennan lawyer summarized the attitude when, after the primary on 13 April 1926, he proclaimed: "They are not a faction, but only a flea bite." In actuality, considering that the group had done almost no public campaigning, their candidates' total of slightly more than 25 percent of the vote showed remarkable strength. After the primary, the Illinois Democracy faded, and until Dever's defeat for reelection by former Mayor William Hale Thompson in 1927, and Brennan's death in the following year, Edward F. Dunne remained in the void reserved for political "outs."[38]

In 1929, he became involved for a last time with Chicago's eternal traction question. A proposal had emerged to consolidate the city's systems into an early conception of the Chicago Transit Authority. While he certainly favored in the abstract such a goal, the details of the plan seemed in his opinion to perpetuate the control of the streets by private corporations. He disregarded ill health to appear before a committee of the state Senate to speak against the enactment of the laws to implement the proposal. His efforts were in vain, and he lent his name to a new People's Traction League, organized and led by Harold Ickes. In the referendum campaign, the former governor again took to his pen to make views known.[39]

By the time the referendum election was held, Chicago, like the rest of the nation, had entered into the long economic slide of the Great Depression. Capitalizing on this, the supporters of the scheme assured voters that the creation of the unified streetcar system would create jobs. Much to Judge Dunne's disappointment, the necessary ordinances passed overwhelmingly. However, as the two leading streetcar companies subsequently went bankrupt, the plan was allowed to lapse. Chicago was not to solve, finally, its public transportation question until a reconceptualized Chicago Transit Authority began operation in 1947, ten years after the death of Edward F. Dunne.[40]

The year 1930 saw the return to the United States Senate of Dunne's old ally J. Hamilton Lewis, who was elected over Ruth Hannah McCormick, widow of Senator Medill McCormick and daughter of the late Republican boss Mark Hanna of Ohio. In part because of Lewis's reelection, Dunne and Harrison were rehabilitated within the party, and both men were chosen as delegates-at-large to the 1932 Democratic National Convention. Initially they, like the rest of the delegation, supported Lewis as a favorite son candidate, but they found themselves taking a direct stand against the expressed will of George Brennan's successor as party boss, Anton J. Cermak. Cermak made it know that he wished to shift Illinois's vote to Alfred Smith for the presidential nomination. Edward F. Dunne, together with Harrison, Henry T. Rainey, and others, resisted, insisting instead on backing the governor of New York, Franklin Delano Roosevelt. Cermak's creature, Henry Horner (the Democratic nominee for governor who had beaten in the primary Dunne's legislative floorleader, Michael Igoe) used "Blandishments . . . warnings, and at time outright threats," but Dunne's willingness to "stand the pressure" excited the admiration of his colleagues. Illinois eventually went for Roosevelt.[41]

Two years later, President Roosevelt returned the favor by appointing Dunne as United States commissioner to the ongoing Century of Progress World's Fair being held in Chicago. The job was largely ceremonial, and he was ably assisted by his second daughter, Mrs. Mona Dunne Leonard. Nonetheless, the appointment gave him immense pleasure, and he liked to joke that having served as mayor, governor, and now as federal commissioner, he had fulfilled his ambition to serve on all levels of government. It was a fitting and graceful conclusion to his long years as a politician and a public servant.[42]

He was eighty years old when he was appointed. Already some of the sadder inevitabilities of his longevity had come to affect his life. In 1921, he had lost his father, P. W. Dunne, who had died with Mosaic irony on the eve of Irish independence, and every year seemed to bring the death of an old associate and friend, including William Jennings Bryan in 1925, whom Dunne had come to view as "erratic and extreme in some of his views" but still "a very great man," and William "Billy" O'Connell in 1936. Of far greater impact was the death on 25 May 1928 of his wife, Elizabeth Kelly Dunne. The couple had just returned from wintering in Florida, a frequent refuge for many Chicagoans (including Al Capone) in the 1920s, when she succumbed unexpectedly to a lingering "anemia" that may have been leukemia. They had been married forty-seven years.[43]

Perhaps prompted by her death, Dunne began to contemplate writing his memoirs. "Vaguely determined to entitle his book 'The Last Half Century in Chicago,'" he was convinced by the Lewis Publishing Company in Chicago to expand his original concept into a history of Illinois. Working with William L. Sullivan, who had been his private secretary during the governorship, he gave over most of the next five years to this work. It was published in 1933, under the title *Illinois, the Heart of the Nation* in five volumes. He was responsible for the actual survey of the history of Illinois that took up the first two volumes, while a "special staff of writers" composed the remaining three that consisted of seemingly unorganized biographical sketches of important citizens past and present.[44]

Dunne's part begins with a rather good survey of the events and circumstances leading to statehood, which includes discussions of geography and the American Indians of the region. He then switches to a strictly political account that advances through each gubernatorial administration down through that of Governor Louis Emerson in 1929. He includes a special discussion of his own term as governor, with a background that reviews his two years as mayor. He then offers some short essays on such quasi-political aspects of Illinois history as the rise of the state's utility companies as well as a few biographical abstracts of people like William O'Connell who had been important in his career. Those were clearly labors of love, and he writes fondly of virtually everyone, friend and foe alike, with whom he had ever had contact. The exception was Hubert Kilens, the state representative who, in 1913, changed his vote on the initiative and referendum.

It was published in an elaborately bound edition to limited and mixed reviews. Only John A. Zventina of Loyola University addressed it in depth. Writing in *Mid-America*, he found it to be "a rather pretentious history." Still, he was impressed with its "concise language," and while regretting the omission of any discussion of the economic, social, and cultural aspects of Illinois's development, he contended that it was "packed with solid information" about the state's political history. He found a greater source of disappointment in the biographies in the last three volumes.[45]

For the biographer, Dunne's *Illinois* is at once a treasure house and a source of frustration. He provides real insight into his associations and motivations, but he glosses over many of the controversies of his career while providing virtually no information of the periods before he became judge and that between his terms as mayor and governor. For all that, if the test of such works is related to its subsequent use by students of history, then, as one of the most cited sources in the study of progressive Illinois, it has proven to be a major contribution.

The year 1933 saw Dunne's new status as a published author and also his eightieth birthday party. By now, he had become genuinely regarded as one of the "grand old men" of the Democratic Party, and his birthdays had become occasions of press interest. This year the celebration was especially ebullient with ceremonies held at the University Club of Chicago. The crowd was large and the leading toastmaster was Carter Harrison. Speeches in praise of Dunne's honesty and service were given; telegrams of congratulations were read; and not a few toasts were drunk. The object of the occasion, "erect as a totem pole, waving his arms to the rhythm of the swing noises," joined in and sang a few choruses of "Auld Lang Syne," and "Hail, Hail, the Gang's All Here."

More seriously, his birthdays gave him the opportunity to express his opinion of the events of the day. He was especially supportive of the New Deal, which he saw as the logical extension of what he and other social reformers had tried to accomplish. On his eighty-second birthday in 1935, he made this clear when he applauded the "plainly developing tendency on the part of the American people . . . to bring about a socio-political situation under which there shall not be such tremendous contrast between the very rich and very poor."[46]

His joy on these occasions was not feigned. Always an optimistic person, in his remaining years he seemed to revel in life. He never formally retired as an attorney, but the Great Depression had hurt the practice to the point that his son-in-law and partner, William Corboy, was forced to go east in the mid-1930s to recoup his finances. Dunne, himself, never wealthy, was able to weather the economic crisis by securing an appointment as a counsel for the Cook County Board of Election Commissioners. It was more or less a sinecure that required only an occasional written opinion.[47]

One advantage of his son-in-law's relocation was the subsequent presence in his home of his daughter, Eileen Dunne Corboy, and her four children. Robert Jerome "Duke" Dunne, now a judge of the circuit court, already lived with his father at the house at 737 Gordon Terrace, and the addition of a daughter and a pack of grandchildren made for a lively and happy environment. The former governor found his days filled with the attentions of his loving and active family, especially those of his oldest and adoring grandson, Edward Dunne Corboy, as well as those of his many friends. He also found time to indulge his interest in poetry, producing verses with titles like, "I'm Eighty-Two, but Far From Blue."[48]

The spring of 1937 found him vacationing at the Hotel Alma in West Palm Beach, Florida. He had earlier been forced to move from the Hotel Nicholas because of poor service, but otherwise he was doing fine reading a biography of Peter the Great of Russia, whose brutality he found a "shock," and indulging himself as "a wicked cigar smoker." Rather suddenly in March, he became ill and was rushed back to Chicago. At first he seemed to hold up well, but in late April, his health began to seriously fail, and there was little that the physicians could do for an eighty-three-year-old patient with a weakening heart and liver. He knew the end was near, and he began giving things away, including a set of ten volumes on Irish literature to William L. Sullivan. On 24 May 1937, he went into a coma, and twelve hours later, on the eve of the anniversary of his wife's passing, he died in the presence of his three children. His last words before the coma were reported as "I am satisfied and peaceful." His personal estate was estimated to be worth just $4,000.[49]

The funeral was not official. Nonetheless, it was the most publicized burial since 1933, which was given for assassinated Mayor Anton Cermak. It was held on 26 May at St. Mary of the Lake Church with a final service at the grave site at Calvary Cemetery. More than fifteen hundred people attended, causing a local traffic jam. Among those present were Governor Henry Horner; Mayor Edward J. Kelly; Senator J. Hamilton Lewis; Carter Harrison; Patrick Nash, Democratic chairman for Cook County; Cook County Sheriff John Toman; Clayton Smith, president of the Cook County Board of Commissioners; Daniel J. McGrath, Irish consul in Chicago; and large delegations of the city's policemen and firemen. The city council adjourned in his honor, as did the city's courts and the state legislature, which had passed a resolution honoring him.[50]

The newspapers were profuse in their praise for the man one called "an exemplar to those who are to assume the responsibilities of society and government." The *Illinois State Journal*, Springfield's Republican paper, for example, noted his "achievements . . . the nobility of his private life, his genial disposition, and his freedom from all that was petty and mean." Hearst's *Herald and Examiner* in Chicago went further and proclaimed that in his death "Illinois loses her most beloved 'elder statesman' . . . his many years of public service were conspicuous for honesty and courage. And at a time when honesty in public office was like a candle shining in the night . . . He leaves no large estate . . . He leaves a heritage of affection." Clearly the death of Dunne had touched the heart of political Illinois.[51]

In the final analysis, Edward F. Dunne emerges as the most important and effective reformer in Illinois during the Progressive Era. His political career that included victories in 1905 and 1912—the only elections during the period that turned on reformist issues—was directly reflective of the contours of the reform movement in Chicago and the state, and he was the only elected official to bring directly into government the influence of Chicago's well-known progressive circles. Moreover, although showing some ideological flexibility as governor, he retained throughout his life his social reformist vision and priorities. It is significant that his last true political act was to rise from his sickbed in 1929 to appear before a legislative committee in opposition to a traction settlement that did not include the social reformist icon, immediate municipal ownership. Finally, Dunne compiled a record of progressive legislation that at the least equaled, if not exceeded, that of any other elected official in the state during this time. However, just as the career of Edward F. Dunne was directly entwined with the achievements of the reform movement, so it also speaks to the limits of reform in the city and the state. It is an undeniable fact that for all the energy expended upon reform in Illinois, it failed to affect meaningfully the state's political culture or the manner in which it was governed.

There were several sources for this failure, not the least of which was the very strength of the existing political order. Indeed, it is one of the central paradoxes of the period that it was while the greatest reformist agitation was occurring that real power was being consolidated in both major parties in the machines of Roger Sullivan and William Hale Thompson. In the end, the professionals simply proved to be better politicians than the reformers. They showed great skill either in absorbing progressive issues, as illustrated by "Hinky Dink" Kenna's support of municipal ownership, or in quietly sabotaging genuinely threatening reform, as the evidence suggests happened with the initiative and referendum.

The professionals were greatly aided in fending off reform by the fact that the reformers were so fragmented and ephemeral as to be self-defeating. There was, of course, the division between the social and structural reforms, a division that directly led to the fall of Chicago's first truly reformist administration and the rise of the corrupt regime of Fred Busse in 1907. There was also the egoism and self-absorption of many of the leading reformers themselves. Clarence Darrow, for example, a man of immense popularity and political potential, not only could not endure the tedium of a legislative seat, from which he quickly resigned, but abandoned Dunne and the fight for municipal ownership at the first major setback. The reformers may have been skilled at writing articles, organizing meetings, giving speeches, and even occasionally stirring the passions of the voters, but as a group they showed little aptitude for politics and the responsibilities of power. The activities of Dunne's appointees to the Chicago Board of Education were a case in point. Unprepared, befuddled, and at times just inept, the board, which included some of the best-known luminaries of the progressive movement, became a liability for Dunne and the cause of reform.

The cumulative effect of the political incompetence of the reformers was manifold. First, it resulted in the transfer of the responsibility for actually implementing reform to professional politicians, which made compromise inevitable. Second, it allowed those professional politicians who were sympathetic, or at least responsive to reform, the luxury of choosing their own fights and of not being forced to confront entrenched leaders. Last, the conflicting visions and ineffectiveness of the reformers so clouded the progressive agenda and the perception of reform that even a man like Roger Sullivan could successfully present himself to the Democratic voters in 1914 as a progressive.

The electorate itself was the third, and ultimately most important, source of the relative failure of progressivism in Illinois. Whether in the ethnic wards of Chicago or in the Republican counties of the downstate, the voters never showed a consistent commitment to broad reform. They might support specific issues, they might on occasion rise up against their political leaders (as happened in 1905 and 1912), but in the end they proved themselves to be fundamentally conservative and content with the existing state of affairs. That was, of course, a tribute to the skills of the professionals, but it also underscored the progressives' inability to offer a viable alternative. Had they as a body resolved their ideological and personal conflicts and presented a united front (and agenda), this might not have been the case.

The career of Edward F. Dunne may be best understood in the context of the weakness of the reform movement in Illinois. He came into the mayor's office in 1905, naively believing in the irresistibility of his popular mandate and in the political abilities of his social reformist allies. By the end of the year, neither belief had been upheld; the professionals and structural reformers had shown themselves to be entirely willing to disregard the explicitly stated will of the people, and Dunne's reformist advisers had shown little political expertise.

In his second year of office, as a result, he began to transform himself into a more effective politician, relying now upon the counsel of William O'Connell, a professional political operative. Accordingly, he reached out to the structural reformers through the appointment of Walter L. Fisher as special traction counsel and through the Werno letter to create a more effective reform coalition. It was a good strategy, and one that could have ensured his own reelection and perhaps the inauguration of new era of government for Chicago. Unfortunately, his own social reformist allies forced him away from compromise on the traction issue, directly resulting in his 1907 defeat. In retrospect, it is clear that Dunne was Chicago's best and last hope for meaningful progressive government. He seemed to recognize this in his repeated calls for support from the entire reform community. Sadly, the call went unanswered.

After 1907, Dunne never again allowed himself to become politically dependent upon the Chicago progressives. He continued to solicit their support, of course, and he remained a social reformer in orientation, but he managed his career not as a representative of a specific set of ideological beliefs but as more simply a reform politician. That was evident in his campaign for the mayoral nomination in 1911 and in his run for the governorship in the following year. In both, he sought a broader base through more general and less controversial platforms, while his campaign workers tended now to be more political than reformist in their backgrounds.

In the governor's office the transformation was completed. None of his appointments included the Chicago progressives, and his program for the Forty-eighth General Assembly was consistent with the moderate tradition of reform found in previous sessions of the legislature. Although still unquestionably a social reformer, he was now willing, albeit without much enthusiasm, to back such structural reforms as the Efficiency and Economy Commission as a means to draw support on other issues.

In the legislature he was confronted with a body divided among three major parties and filled with men with widely varying interests—not one of whom was politically dependent upon him. Accordingly, he could only cajole and persuade, and occasionally use his patronage, to bring about results. He came under considerable criticism from some reformers for not using more strong-armed tactics, especially regarding the initiative and referendum. However, the truth was that he did not have the power to force a single vote. That fact was subsequently emphasized by his inability to bring about the defeat of Hubert Kilens, the legislator who changed his vote and ensured the failure of the initiative and referendum. Looking back, it would appear unfair to fault Dunne for not succeeding where Charles Deneen, a man of vastly greater political experience and power, had also failed. On the whole, Dunne's politically pragmatic approach to the Forty-eighth General Assembly brought results that if not spectacular were at least highly substantial. Had he, as he had done as mayor, ignored the political game and attempted to force reform, even that would not have been possible.

Following the 1913 session of the legislature, reform was a declining force in Illinois politics. Each following election only made that point clearer. Under those circumstances and without any prospect of a united reform front emerging, Dunne resigned himself to becoming just a good administrator. In this, he proved his ability by shepherding the state through the constitutional crisis created by the Fergus suits and the preparedness campaign.

In 1916, he attempted to use reform as an issue to turn back the jugger-naut of a reunited and confident Republican Party. However, reform was a hollow issue in a year that saw a very progressive platform cynically approved by Sullivan-dominated state Democratic convention, and witnessed a will-ingness for some progressives (including President Woodrow Wilson) to ally themselves with the Sullivan organization in a harebrained scheme to replace Dunne as the gubernatorial nominee with Raymond Robins.

Not surprisingly, Dunne left office disillusioned with politics and the reform movement. Ironically, while he retired from the governorship scorned by some reformers as having been ineffective, this was not the case with the general political community and with those reformers who were in close con-tact with the realities of politics. For example, John H. Walker, an important labor leader, wrote privately, just months before the election, of Dunne's "un-failing devotion to a square deal and the cause of right and justice, we testify that we have made magnificent progress and this to your everlasting credit."[52]

He only returned to political life to any significant degree after his friends and relatives forced him to go to Irish Race Convention in 1919, resulting in his trip to Europe on behalf of the cause of Irish independence. The pleasures of that experience motivated him to a limited political participation in the years that followed; they did not, however, inspire him to resume close rela-tions (with the minor exception Clarence Darrow in 1922) with the Chicago progressives. Nonetheless, he was not a bitter person, and he never discarded his social reformist vision of government, which happily for him, seemed at last fulfilled in the New Deal. He never ceased to be an advocate of justice and humanity.

NOTES

BIBLIOGRAPHY

INDEX

NOTES

Preface

1. *Edward F. Dunne Memorial Service*, 21 May 1938, 10–11, copy in Edward F. Dunne Scrapbooks and Papers, Illinois Historical Survey, University of Illinois Library, Urbana-Champaign.

2. Robert P. Howard, *Mostly Good and Competent Men: Illinois Governors, 1818–1988* (Springfield, Ill.: Sangamon State University and the Illinois State Historical Society, 1988), 219.

3. Perry R. Duis, *The Saloon: Public Drinking in Chicago and Boston, 1880–1920* (Champaign: University of Illinois Press, 1983), 255.

4. Melvin G. Holli, *Reform in Detroit: Hazeen Pingree and Urban Politics* (New York: Oxford University Press, 1969).

5. John D. Buenker, "Edward F. Dunne: The Urban New Stock Democrat as Progressive," *Mid-American* 50 (1968): 3–21; Richard D. Becker, "Edward Dunne, Reform Mayor of Chicago, 1905–07" (Ph.D. diss., University of Chicago, 1971); Richard Allen Morton, "Edward F. Dunne: Illinois' Most Progressive Governor," *Illinois Historical Journal* 83 (winter 1990): 218–234; Paul M. Green and Melvin G. Holli, eds., *The Mayors: The Chicago Political Tradition* (Carbondale: Southern Illinois University Press, 1987), 33–49; Robert P. Howard, *Mostly Good and Competent Men*, 219–25.

6. William T. Hutchinson, *Lowden of Illinois: The Life of Frank O. Lowden*, 2 vols. (Chicago: University of Chicago Press, 1957).

1. Origins of a Social Reformer

1. Charles C. Tansill, *America and the Fight for Irish Freedom, 1866–1922* (New York: Devin Adair, 1957), 26; Obituary, *Oak Leaves* (Oak Park, Ill.), 16 April 1921.

2. Eileen Dunne Corboy, "A Christmas Letter to My Three Lovely Grandchildren" (author's collection), December 1953, 1; *Chicago American*, 12 October 1935; Obituary, *Oak Leaves*, 16 April 1921.

3. James Cunningham, comp., *The City Charter and Revised Ordinances of the City of Peoria* (Peoria, Ill.: N. C. Nason, 1869), xxii.

4. Edward Dunne Corboy, Dunne's grandson, telephone interview with author, 24 March 1984.

5. Peoria Public School District 150 to author, 21 February 1984; *Peoria (Ill.) Daily Record*, 30 June 1941.

6. *Chicago American*, 12 October 1935; *Dublin University Calendar*, 1874, 218–20; ibid., 1875, 229.

7. *Chicago American*, 12 October 1935, 26 February 1905; Obituary, *Oak Leaves*, 16 April 1921, 32.

8. Walter A. Townsend, *Illinois Democracy*, 2 vols. (Springfield: Democratic Historical Association, 1935), 2:6.

9. Ibid.

10. Ibid.

11. Edward F. Dunne, *Illinois, the Heart of the Nation*, 5 vols. (Chicago: Lewis Publishing, 1933), 2:189.

12. Harvey Wish, "Governor Altgeld Pardons the Anarchists," *Journal of the Illinois State Historical Society* 31 (December 1938): 428.

13. *Chicago Tribune*, 20 March 1892, 16 August 1892; *Chicago Journal*, 22 August 1892; *Chicago Daily News*, 20 August 1892, 22 August 1892.

14. Fremont O. Bennett, comp., *Politics and Politicians of Chicago* (Chicago: Blakely Printing, 1886), 547; John W. Leonard, ed., *The Book of Chicagoans, 1905* (Chicago: A. N. Marquis, 1905), 577; *Chicago American*, 25 February 1905.

15. *Chicago American*, 12 October 1935.

16. Dunne, *Illinois*, 2:189.

17. Edward F. Dunne, *Judge, Mayor, Governor*, ed. William L. Sullivan (Chicago: Windermere Press, 1916), 162.

18. Ibid, 68–75; Arthur Weinberg and Lila Weinberg, *Clarence Darrow: A Sentimental Rebel* (New York: G. P. Putnam's Sons), 82.

19. *New York Irish-American*, 14 June 1895, Edward F. Dunne Scrapbooks and Papers, Scrapbook 1:65, Illinois Historical Survey, University of Illinois Library, Urbana-Champaign; unattributed and undated newspaper article, Edward F. Dunne Scrapbooks and Papers, Scrapbook 3:13

20. Democratic Publishing Company, *Prominent Democrats of Illinois: A Brief History of the Rise and Progress of the Democratic Party of Illinois* (Chicago, 1899), 334.

21. Dunne, *Judge, Mayor, Governor*, 91; *Chicago Tribune*, 20 February 1898.

22. Democratic Publishing Company, *Prominent Democrats*, 334.

23. See Arthur W. Thurner, "The Impact of Ethnic Groups on the Democratic Party in Chicago, 1920–1928" (Ph.D. diss., University of Chicago, 1966).

24. Charles E. Merriam, *Chicago: A More Intimate View of Urban Politics* (New York: Macmillan, 1929), 90–91.

25. Ralph R. Tingley, "From Carter Harrison II to Fred Busse: A Study of Chicago Political Parties and Personages from 1896 to 1902" (Ph.D. diss., University of Chicago, 1950).

26. Carter Harrison was actually the fourth of that name in succession in his family, but because of the prominence of his father, he was known as Carter Harrison II or Junior. Paul Michael Green, "The Chicago Democratic Party, 1840–1920: From Factionalism to Political Organization" (Ph.D. diss., University of Chicago, 1975), 77–84.

27. George A. Schilling, public statement, 10 October 1914, Correspondences, box 2, George A. Schilling Papers, Illinois State Historical Library, Springfield.

28. Melvin Holli, *Reform in Detroit: Hazen S. Pingree and Urban Politics* (New York: Oxford University Press, 1969).

29. See Sidney I. Roberts, "The Municipal Voters League and Chicago Boodlers," *Journal of the Illinois State Historical Society* 53 (Summer 1960): 117–40; Michael McCarthy, "Businessmen and Professionals in Municipal Reform: the Chicago Experience, 1867–1920" (Ph.D. diss., Northwestern University, 1970).

30. Dunne, *Judge, Mayor, Governor*, 93.

31. *Chautauguan* 33 (May 1905): 196.

32. Hugo S. Grossner, "The Movement for Municipal Ownership in Chicago," *Annals of the American Academy of Political and Social Sciences* 27 (January–May 1906): 75.

33. Ibid.; Harry P. Weber, *Outline History of Chicago Traction* (Chicago: n.p., 1936), 5–14.

34. Ibid.; Dunne, *Illinois*, 2:221.

35. *American Street Railway Investments* 8 (1901): 58–64; *Street Railway Journal* 15 (1899): 77.

36. Weber *Outline History of Chicago Traction*, 26–287; Dunne, *Illinois*, 2:221; Weber, *Outline History of Chicago Traction*, 26–28.

37. Weber, *Outline History of Chicago Traction*, 38.

38. Walter L. Fisher, "Autobiographical Sketch" (unpublished, 1932?), Illinois Historical Survey, University of Illinois Library, Urbana-Champaign.

39. Dunne, *Judge, Mayor, Governor*, 92, 137–38. *Chicago Tribune*, 13 May 1902, 4 December 1902, 7 December 1902; Board of Aldermen, Chicago, *Proceedings for the Municipal Year, 1902–1903* (Chicago: John F. Higgins, 1903), 1573–88, 1819–25, 1893–95, 2098–2102, 2195–96.

40. James Langland, comp., *The Daily News Almanac and Year-Book for 1904* (Chicago Daily News, 1903), 355–56 (hereafter references to yearly editions will be cited as *Daily News Almanac*).

41. *Chicago Tribune*, 22 April 1902, 28 March 1903, 30 March 1903, 1 April 1903; llinois House of Representatives, *Journal of the House of Representatives of the Forty-Third General Assembly of the State of Illinois* (Springfield: Phillips Brothers, 1903), 652, 965, 967, 987, 1044 (hereafter references to House journals of the Forty-third, Forty-eighth, and Forty-ninth General Assembly sessions will be cited as *House Journal*); Illinois Senate, *Journal of the Senate of the Forty-Third General Assembly of the State of Illinois* (Springfield: Phillips Brothers, 1903), 76, 497, 616, 636, 664, 659, 952, 1023 (hereafter references to Senate journals of the Forty-third,

Forty-eighth, and Forty-ninth General Assembly sessions will be cited as *Senate Journal*).

42."Minutes of the Public Ownership Party," Chicago, 15 May–September 1902, "George A. Schilling Papers," box 4, Illinois State Historical Library, Springfield; George S. Schilling to Samuel M. Jones, 21 October 1902, Samuel Milton Jones Papers, Toledo-Lucas County Public Library, Toledo, Ohio (microfilm ed., reel 11); *Chicago Tribune*, 5–6 November 1902, 20–21 January 1903, 5 February 1903, 14 February 1903, 24–25 February 1903, 5 September 1904; Caro Lloyd, *Henry Demarest Lloyd, 1847–1903: A Biography* (New York: G. P. Putnam's Sons, Knickerbocker Press, 1912), 2:281–310; Chester McArthur Destler, *Henry Demarest Lloyd and the Empire of Reform* (Philadelphia: University of Pennsylvania Press, 1963), 525–26; Weber, *Outline History of Chicago Traction*, 50; ibid.

43. *Chicago Tribune*, 5 September 1904.

44. Lloyd, *Henry Demarest Lloyd*, 308; Destler, *Empire of Reform*, 525–26.

45. *Chicago Tribune*, 26 August 1904, 29 August 1904; Board of Aldermen, Chicago, *Proceedings, Being from April 11, 1904, to April 6, 1905, Inclusive* (Chicago: John F. Higgins, 1905), 1164, 1786, 3053, 3332; Weber, *Outline History of Chicago Traction*, 43–44.

47. *Chicago Record-Herald*, 5 September 1904; *Chicago Tribune*, 5 September 1904, 6 November 1904.

48. *Chicago Record-Herald*, 6 September 1904; Tingley, "From Carter Harrison II," 155; Green, "The Chicago Democratic Party," 99–108; *Chicago Tribune*, November 1904, 5 December 1904; *Chicago Record-Herald*, 12 November 1904, 16 January 1905, 17 January 1905, 28 January 1905.

49. Ibid., 8 February 1905, 24 January 1905.

50. Ibid., 24 January 1905, 30–31 January 1905, 5 February 1905, 13 February 1905, 24 February 1905.

51. Ibid., 12 February 1905, 26 February 1905; *Chicago American*, 26 February 1905.

52. *Chicago Tribune*, 16 February 1905.

53. Ibid., 11–12 March 1905, 23 March 1905, 25 March 1905, 29 March 1905.

54. *Chicago American*, 13 March 1905, 26 March 1905, 1 April 1905, *Chicago Tribune*, 2 April 1905.

55. *Chicago American*, 1 April 1905; *Chicago Tribune*, 4 April 1905; *Daily News Almanac* (1906), 290; Green, "The Chicago Democratic Party," 116.

56. *Daily News Almanac* (1906), 289; Weber, *Outline History of Chicago Traction*, 50.

57. *Chicago American*, 5 April 1905; *Chicago Tribune*, 14 April 1905.

2. "I Shall Not Resign"

1. Perry R. Duis, *The Saloon: Public Drinking in Chicago and Boston, 1880–1920* (Champaign: University of Illinois Press, 1983), 255.

2. Board of Aldermen, Chicago, *Proceedings, Being from April 10, 1905, to April 7, 1906, Inclusive* (Chicago: John F. Higgins, Printer, 1906), 53–54 (hereafter cited as *Council Proceedings*).

3. *Chicago American*, 13 April 1905; *Biographical Directory of the American Congress, 1774–1961* (Washington, D.C.: U.S. Government Printing Office, 1961), 1216.

4. *Daily News Almanac* (1906), 407–9.

5. Stanley Powers, "Chicago's Strike Ordeal," *World's Work* 10 (July 1905): 6378–846; *Chicago American*, 10 April 1905, 13 April 1905, 16–18 April 1905, 30 April 1905; *Chicago Tribune*, 28 April 1905, 30 April 1905, 1 May 1905.

6. *Chicago Tribune*, 6 May 1905, 11 May 1905; *Chicago American*, 29–30 April 1905, 20–21 July 1905, 24 July 1905, 27 July 1905.

7. *Chicago Tribune*, 29 April 1905.

8. *Cleveland Plain Dealer*, 2–3 June 1905; *Chicago Tribune*, 3–4 June 1905.

9. *Cleveland Plain Dealer*, 4 June 1905; *Chicago Tribune*, 10 June 1905, 13 June 1905; "Interview with Mr. Dalrymple," *Street Railway Journal* 26 (5 August 1905): 22-24.

10. *Cleveland Plain Dealer*, 19 June 1905, 30 June 1905; *Chicago Tribune*; 10 June 1905, 17–18 June 1905, 30 June 1905. Dunne was so impressed with DuPont that he named him his special traction engineer.

11. *Council Proceedings* (1905–6), 730–42; Ida Tarbell, "How Chicago Is Finding Itself," pt. 2, *American Magazine* 67 (December 1908): 126.

12. Ibid.; "Immediate Municipal Ownership a Year After," *American Monthly Review of the Reviews*," 33 (May 1906): 549–54.

13. *Chicago American*, 26 July 1905, 5–7 August 1905, 10 November 1906; *Chicago Tribune*, 10 August 1905.

14. *Chicago Tribune*, 2 June 1905.

15. Melvin G. Holli, *Reform in Detroit: Hazen S. Pingree and Urban Politics* (New York: Oxford University Press, 1969), 158; *Chicago Tribune*, 7 September 1905.

16. *Chicago Tribune*, 14 March 1905, 7 September 1905.

17. Ibid., 19 September 1905, 24 October 1905.

18. Tarbell, "How Chicago Is Finding Itself," pt. 2: 125.

19. *Chicago Tribune*, 17 August 1905.

20. Ibid., 17 August 1905, 12 September 1905; *Chicago American*, 12 September 1905.

21. *Chicago Tribune*, 13 September 1905; *Chicago American*, 13 September 1905.

22. *Chicago Tribune*, 13–14 September 1905.

23. *Chicago Tribune*, 16 September 1905; *Chicago American*, 5 September 1905.

24. *Chicago Tribune*, 22–23 September 1905, 9 October 1905, 17 October 1905, 28 October 1905.

25. *Council Proceedings* (1905–6), 1273–74, 1363–64, 1379–81.

26. Ibid., 1340–41, 1354, 1403.

27. *Chicago American*, 7 November 1905.

28. Tarbell, "How Chicago Is Finding Itself," pt. 2: 125; *Chicago Record-Herald*, 8 November 1905.

29. Edward F. Dunne, *Illinois, the Heart of the Nation*, 5 vols. (Chicago: Lewis Publishing, 1933), 2:278. Clarence S. Darrow, *The Story of My Life* (New York: Scribner's, 1960).

30. *Chicago Tribune*, 12 January 1906.

31. *Chicago American*, 2 March 1906.

32. *Council Proceedings* (1905–6), 1419–22; *Chicago American*, 15 November 1905, 12 December 1905, 27 December 1905; *Chicago Tribune*, 24 November 1905.

33. *Council Proceedings* (1905–6); *Chicago American*, 27 December 1905, 28 December 1905, 26 January 1906, 5 February 1906, 7 February 1906; *Chicago Tribune*, 8 December 1905.

34. *Council Proceedings* (1905–6), 2626–33, 2635–43; *Chicago American*, 15 February 1906; *Chicago Tribune*, 14 February 1906.

35. *Chicago American*, 24–27 December 1905.

36. *Denver Post*, 12 January 1906; *Chicago Tribune*, 12 January 1906.

37. *Council Proceedings* (1905–6), 2206–22; *Chicago Tribune*, 19 January 1906; *Chicago American*, 26 January 1906.

38. *Chicago American*, 10 February 1906; *Illinois Issue*, 13 April 1906; *Chicago Tribune*, 27 February 1906.

39. *Daily News Almanac* (1906), 69.

40. See Duis, *The Saloon*.

41. *Chicago Tribune*, 3 February 1906, 16 February 1906, 6 March 1906; *Council Proceedings* (1905–6), 2687–88; 2789–91.

42. *Chicago Tribune*, 19 May 1906.

43. *Blair v City of Chicago*, 201 U.S. 400 (1906); *Daily News Almanac* (1907), 336, 441.

44. *Chicago American*, 12 March 1906.

45. Ibid.

46. *Chicago Tribune*, 1 February 1906.

47. Ibid., 2 April 1906.

48. *Daily News Almanac* (1907), 362; *Chicago Tribune*, 4 April 1906.

49. *Chicago American*, 4 April 1906.

3. Chicago's Radical Mayor

1. *Chicago Tribune*, 2 May 1906.

2. Walter L. Fisher, "Autobiographical Sketch" (unpublished, 1932?), Illinois Historical Survey, University of Illinois Library, Urbana-Champaign; Alan B. Gould, "Walter L. Fisher: Profile of an Urban Reformer, 1880–1910," *Mid-America* 57 (July 1975): 151–72; Richard W. Callender, "Walter L. Fisher, 1862–1935: The Regulation of Public Utilities" (master's thesis, University of Illinois at Urbana-Champaign, 1959).

3. *Chicago American*, 4 December, 1905.

4. *Chicago Tribune*, 11 April 1906; *Outlook* 83 (19 May 1906): 97.

5. *Chicago Tribune*, 13 April 1906; *Chicago American*, 11 April 1906.

6. Board of Aldermen, Chicago, *Proceedings of the City Council of the City of Chicago for the Municipal Year 1906–1907, Being from April 7, 1906, to April 11, 1907, Inclusive* (Chicago: John F. Higgins, 1907), 2562 (hereafter cited as *Council Proceedings*); *Outlook* 83 (19 May 1906): 98.

7. Ibid.

8. *Chicago Daily News*, 12 April 1906, 29 April 1906; *Chicago Tribune*, 29 April 1906.

9. Edward F. Dunne, *Illinois, the Heart of the Nation*, 5 vols. (Chicago: Lewis Publishing, 1933), 2:279.

10. *Chicago Tribune*, 26 May 1906.

11. Ibid, 25 May 1906; Alan R. Lind, *Chicago Surface Lines: An Illustrated History* (Park Forest, Ill.: Transport History Press, 1975), 210–17; *Council Proceedings* (1906–7), 521, 786, 836.

12. *Council Proceedings* (1906–7), 253, 302, 1420, 3755.

13. Mary J. Herrick, *The Chicago Schools: A Social and Political History* (Beverly Hills, Calif.: Sage Publications, 1971), 97.

14. George S. Counts, *School and Society in Chicago* (New York: Harcourt Brace, 1928), 90; Herrick, *Chicago Schools*, 96; Marjorie Murphy, "Taxation and Social Conflict: Teacher Unionism and Public School Finance in Chicago, 1893–1934," *Journal of the Ilinois State Historical Society* 74 (winter 1981): 242–60; Herrick, *Chicago Schools*, 102–9.

15. Counts, *Schools and Society*, 66, 96.

16. John W. Leonard, ed., *The Book of Chicagoans, 1905* (Chicago: A. N. Marquis, 1905), 136; *Outlook* 22 (15 July 1905): 733; *Forum* 38 (June–July 1906): 362.

17. Counts, *School and Society*, 109.

18. Herrick, *Chicago Schools*, 127; *School Review* 15 (1907): 162–63.

19. Margaret A. Haley, *Battleground: The Autobiography of Margaret A. Haley*, ed. Robert Reid (Champaign: University of Illinois Press, 1982), 105.

20. *The Public* 9 (14 July 1906): 347.

21. *Chicago Tribune*, 20 June 1905.

22. Haley, *Battleground*, 105–6. Raymond Robins to Edward F. Dunne, 8 May 1905, box 2, Raymond Robins Papers, Wisconsin Historical Society, Madison; *Chicago Tribune*, 10 July 1906.

23. *Chicago Tribune*, 10 July 1906.

24. Ibid., 11 July 1906.

25. Ibid., 6 July 1906.

26. Ibid., 19 July 1906, 30 August 1906; Richard T. Ely to Jane Addams, 6 January 1906, Jane Addams Papers (microfilm ed., reel 4), Manuscript Division, Library of Congress, Washington, D.C.; Addams's position may have been compromised by the fact that Macmillan was her own publisher.

27. Ibid., 31 August 1906, 30 August 1906.

28. Manuscript, "Living a Long Life Over Again," 294, Louis Freeland Post Papers, Manuscript Division, Library of Congress, Washington, D.C.; *Chicago Tribune*, 28 September 1906.

29. *Chicago Tribune*, 29 August 1906, 20 October 1906.

30. Ibid., 10 October 1906. Dunne sued over the use of the term "boodler." He won five hundred dollars and a printed retraction in the 13 November 1908 edition of the newspaper.

31. Ibid., 13 October 1906, 26 October 1906.

32. Edwin G. Cooley to Samuel S. Alschuler, 7 July 1908, box 1, Samuel J. Alschuler Papers, Illinois State Historical Society, Springfield.

33. *Chicago Tribune*, 31 October 1906.

34. Ibid., 10 December 1906.

35. Ibid., 13–14 November 1906, 6 December 1906.

36. Ibid., 17 August 1906.

37. Ibid., 11 August 1906.

38. Ibid., 25 September 1906.

39. Ibid., 11 October 1906, 24 November 1906.

40. Ibid., 18 November 1906, 26 May 1906.

41. Tom L. Johnson to George A. Schilling, 28 March 1901, box 2, George A. Schilling Papers, Illinois State Historical Library, Springfield.

42. *Chicago American*, 11 September 1906.

43. Ibid., 20 September 1906, 5 October 1906.

44. Ibid., 13 October 1906, 7 November 1906.

45. *Railway Age* 39 (21 December 1906): 787.

46. *Chicago Daily News*, 19 December 1906; Ida Tarbell, "How Chicago is Finding Itself," pt. 2, *American Magazine* 67 December 1908): 124–37.

47. *Chicago Tribune*, 8 January 1907, 13 January 1907; *Chicago American*, 8 January 1907.

48. *Council Proceedings* (1906–7), 3078; *Chicago Tribune* 12 February 1907.

49. *Chicago Tribune*, 5 February 1907, 12 February 1907; *Chicago American*, 15 January 1907; Edward F. Dunne to Walter L. Fisher, 6 February 1907, Walter L. Fisher Papers, Manuscript Division, Library of Congress, Washington, D.C.

50. *Chicago Tribune*, 8 January 1907, 12 January 1907, 15 January 1907, sec. 1, 3 February 1907, sec. 1.

51. Ibid., 15 January 1907; Dunne, *Illinois*, 2:501–2. *Chicago American*, 16 February 1907, 18 February 1907, 21–22 February 1907.

52. *Chicago Tribune*, 23 February 1907, 24 February 1907, sec. 1.

53. Ibid., 26 February 1907.

54. Ralph R. Tingley, "From Carter Harrison II to Fred Busse: A Study of Chicago Political Parties and Personages from 1896 to 1907" (Ph.D. diss., University of Chicago, 1950), 207; *Chicago Tribune*, 23 February 1907, 3 March 1907.

55. *Chicago Tribune*, 3–4 March 1907, 22 March 1907, 28–29 March 1907;

Guy Cramer to Raymond Robins, 9 March 1906, box 2, Raymond Robins Papers, Wisconsin Historical Society, Madison. In fact, Dunne's record of pardons were "about the same in number" as those of his predecessor. They did, however, receive much more publicity.

56. Ibid., 28 March 1907.

57. Ibid., 31 March 1907, 1 April 1907.

58. Ibid., 22 March 1907; Municipal Ownership Central Committee to Raymond Robins, 19 March 1907, Margaret A. Haley to Raymond Robins, 21 March 1907, Chicago Federation of Labor Circular, 18 March 1907, box 2, Raymond Robins Papers, Wisconsin Historical Society, Madison.

59. *Chicago Tribune*, 11–12 March 1907.

60. Ibid., 6–8 March 1907, 24 March 1907, 30 March 1907.

61. Ibid., 28 March 1907; *Chicago American*, 27 March 1907.

62. *Chicago Tribune*, 9 March 1907.

63. Ibid., 27 March 1907; Tingley, "From Carter Harrison II to Fred Busse," 218.

64. *Chicago Tribune*, 23 March 1907, 31 March 1907, 3 April 1907; *Chicago American*, 30 March 1907.

65. Dunne, *Illinois*, 2:295.

66. *Chicago Tribune*, 3 April 1907.

67. Compiled from U.S. Department of the Interior, Census Office, *Report of the Vital and Social Statistics in the United States at the Eleventh Census, 1890*, pt. 2 (Washington, D.C.: Government Printing Office, 1894), 161–81; U.S. Department of Commerce, Bureau of the Census, *Thirteenth Census of the United States Taken in the Year 1910*, Population, vol. 2 (Washington, D.C.: Government Printing Office, 1913); *Daily News Almanac* (1908), 316–21.

68. *Chicago Tribune*, 23 April 1907.

69. Ibid., 16 April 1907; *Chicago Record-Herald*, 16 April 1907.

70. Ibid.

4. Toward the Governorship

1. Quoted in Robert P. Howard, *Mostly Good and Competent Men: Illinois Governors, 1818 to 1988* (Springfield, Ill.: Illinois Issue, Sangamon State University and Illinois State Historical Society, 1988), 221.

2. Edward F. Dunne, *Illinois, the Heart of the Nation*, 5 vols. (Chicago: Lewis Publishing, 1933), 2:382.

3. *Chicago Tribune*, 2 June 1907.

4. *Daily News Almanac* (1906), 296, 379. For the full account of charter reform in Chicago during this period, see Maureen Flanagan, *Charter Reform in Chicago* (Carbondale: Southern Illinois University Press, 1987).

5. *People ex rel. Louis Post v. Healey*, 231 Ill. 629; Dominic Candeloro, "The School Board Crisis of 1907," *Journal of Illinois State Historical Society* 68 (No-

vember 1975): 396–406.

6. *Edwin L. Lobdell et al. v. City of Chicago et al.*, 227 Ill. 218; *Daily News Almanac* (1908), 411.

7. *Norfolk Virginia-Pilot*, 19 September 1907.

8. *Inter-Ocean* (Chicago), 7 December 1907.

9. Ibid., 2 January 1908.

10. *Chicago Tribune*, 11 July 1908.

11. *Chicago Socialist*, 1 December, 1908.

12. *Chicago Daily News*, 6 March 1909; *Chicago Record-Herald*, 24 April 1909.

13. *Rockford Morning Star*, 8 January 1909; *Galesburg Daily Republican Register*, 13 February 1909; *Kansas City Times*, 28 May 1909; *Chicago Examiner*, 1 October 1909; *Chicago Daily News*, 30 January 1909.

14. See Joel Tarr, *A Study in Boss Politics: William Lorimer of Chicago* (Champaign: University of Illinois Press, 1971).

15. William Bayard Hale, "Chicago, Its Struggle and Its Dream," *World's Work* 19 (April 1910): 12792–805.

16. *Chicago Tribune*, 7–9 July 1910.

17. Sophie J. Eisenstein, "The Election of 1912 in Chicago" (master's thesis, University of Chicago, 1947), 9; Carter H. Harrison to William Randolph Hearst, 5 December 1910, box 1, Carter H. Harrison IV Papers, Newberry Library, Chicago; *Chicago Tribune*, 25 November 1910, 10 December 1910, 12 January 1911.

18. *Chicago Tribune*, 20–21 November 1910.

19. Ibid., 13 January 1911, 22 January 1911; 19 February 1911.

20. Ibid., 17 January 1911, 30–31 January 1911, 19 February 1911; *Chicago Daily News*, 20 March 1911; *Chicago Record-Herald*, 26 March 1911.

21. *Chicago Record-Herald*, 21 January 1911, 30 January 1911; see Barry D. Karl, *Charles S. Merriam and the Study of Politics* (Chicago: University of Chicago Press, 1974); *Chicago Tribune*, 26 January 1911, 7 February 1911, 10–11 February 1911.

22. *Chicago Tribune*, 4 February 1911.

23. Ibid., 13 January 1911, 1–2 February 1911, 5 February 1911, 7 February 1911, 11 February 1911, 19 February 1911.

24. *Chicago American*, 25 February 1911.

25. Ibid., 28 February 1911.

26. Ibid., 27–28 February 1911.

27. *Chicago Tribune*, 3 February 1911, 1 March 1911, 12 March 1911, 14 March 1911; *Chicago American*, 1–3 March 1911.

28. *Daily News Almanac* (1912), 461–62.

29. For more on the tension between Chicago and downstate, see William Booth Philip, "Chicago and Downstate: A Study of Their Conflict, 1870–1934" (Ph.D. diss., University of Chicago, 1940).

30. *Chicago Tribune*, 11 June 1911; *Chicago Record-Herald*, 11 June 1911; *Chicago Examiner*, 11 June 1911.

31. *Daily News Almanac* (1911), 45–51, 463. After three attempts, Illinois passed a primary law that was acceptable to the United States Supreme Court. It established a binding primary for all offices except for trustees for the University of Illinois and school and township board members. A nonbinding presidential primary was subsequently added; 1912 was the first major election year in which any binding primary was in force.

32. *Illinois State Register*, 5 October 1905. (The *Illinois State Register* was published in Springfield.)

33. Edward F. Dunne to Samuel S. Alschuler, 22 January 1912, box 1, Samuel J. Alschuler Papers, Illinois State Historical Library, Springfield; Carter Harrison Jr., *Stormy Years* (Indianapolis: Bobbs-Merrill, 1935), 318–19; Carter Harrison to Daniel Keegan, 8 April 1912, box 1, Carter Harrison IV Papers; Dunne, *Illinois*, 2:312.

34. Dunne, *Illinois*, 2:312; Eisenstein, "The Election of 1912 in Chicago," 34; *Chicago Tribune*, 10 March 1912.

35. *Chicago Tribune*, 22 February 1912.

36. Ibid., 4 February 1912, 18 February 1912.

37. Ibid., 16–17 March 1912.

38. *Charleston Daily Courier*, 15 March 1912; *East St. Louis Journal*, 1 April 1912.

39. *Chicago Tribune*, 19 March 1912, 28 March 1912.

40. Ibid., 11 April 1912; *Daily News Almanac* (1913), 485.

41. *Mason County Democrat*, 12 April 1912.

42. *Chicago Tribune*, 16 April 1912; *Chicago Daily News*, 15–16 April 1912; Harrison, *Stormy Years*, 319–25.

43. *Chicago Tribune*, 20 April 1912; Democratic National Convention, *Official Report of the Democratic National Convention, Baltimore, 1912* (Chicago: Peterson Lino-Typing, 1912), 78, 100–101; Arthur S. Link, *Wilson: The Road to the White House*, 1st pbk. ed. (Princeton: Princeton University Press, 1968), 409, 440–41, 459–60.

44. *Chicago Tribune*, 7–8 September 1912, 19 October 1912.

45. Charles S. Merriam, *Chicago: A More Intimate View of Urban Politics* (New York: Macmillan, 1929), 181; Dunne, *Illinois*, 2:176–79; Roy O. West and William C. Walton, "Charles S. Deneen, 1863–1940," *Journal of the Illinois State Historical Society* 34 (1941): 12–25.

46. Charles A. Church, *History of the Republican Party in Illinois, 1854–1912* (Rockford, Ill.: Wilson Brothers, 1912), 222; Ralph Arthur Straetz, "The Progressive Movement in Illinois, 1910–1916" (Ph.D. diss., University of Illinois, 1951), 152–330.

47. *Chicago Tribune*, 23 July 1912, 11–12 October 1912, 14 October 1912, 30 October 1912; *Mason County Democrat*, 25 October 1912.

48. *Chicago Tribune*, 11 September 1912; 16 September 1912; 9 October 1912; 13 October 1912.

49. Ibid., 12 September 1912.

50. Ibid., 21 September 1912.

51. Ibid., 3 September 1912.

52. Ibid., 12–13 October 1912; 15 October 1912.

53. Ibid., 28 October 1912.

54. *Nashville Journal*, 26 September 1912.

55. *Chicago Tribune*, 22 October 1912; Samuel S. Alschuler to M. T. Healey, 2 May 1912, Personal Letters of Samuel Alschuler, 290, Samuel J. Alschuler Papers.

56. *Chicago Tribune*, 22–23 September 1912, 30 September 1912.

57. *Daily News Almanac* (1912), 507; ibid., (1913), 437, 519. Dunne received 443,120 votes, or 38.01 percent of the total; Deneen took 318,469 votes, or 27.39 percent; and Funk 303,401 votes, or 26.09 percent. In the presidential contest, Wilson carried Illinois with 405,048 votes, or 35.34 percent; Roosevelt came in second with 386,478, or 33.07 percent; and Taft was last with 253,593 votes, or 22.12 percent.

5. Consensus for Reform: The Forty-Eighth General Assembly

1. *Chicago Tribune*, 10 November 1912.

2. Ibid., 7 January 1913.

3. Ibid., 15 January 1913; Charles Karch to Woodrow Wilson, 22 January 1913, *Thomas Woodrow Wilson Papers*, (microfilm ed., series 2, reel 41).

4. *Chicago Tribune*, 16 January 1913; 26 January 1913.

5. Ibid., 21–24 January 1913.

6. Ibid., 29 January 1913.

7. Ibid., 8 January 1913, 30 January 1913; *Illinois State Register*, 30 January 1913; *Ilinois State Journal*, 30 January 1913 (the *Illinois State Journal* was published in Springfield); *House Journal* (1913), 105.

8. *Chicago Tribune*, 4 February 1913; *House Journal* (1913), 197–208.

9. Edward F. Dunne, *Illinois, the Heart of the Nation*, 5 vols. (Chicago: Lewis Publishing, 1933), 2:317–18.

10. *Chicago Tribune*, 5 February 1913, 11 February 1913.

11. Ibid., 19–20 February 1913; *Illinois State Journal*, 19 February 1913.

12. *Chicago Tribune*, 20 February 1913.

13. Ibid., 17 February 1913; *Illinois State Journal*, 27 February 1913.

14. *Chicago Tribune*, 5 March 1913.

15. Ibid., 8 March 1913; *Washington Post*, 5–6 March 1913.

16. *Chicago Tribune*, 18–19 March 1913; *House Journal* (1913), 347–54; Paolo E. Colletta, *William Jennings Bryan*, 3 vols. (Lincoln: University of Nebraska Press, 1969), vol. 2, *Progressive Politician and Moral Statesman, 1909–1915*, 98.

17. *House Journal* (1913), 416–19; *Chicago Tribune*, 26 March 1913; *Illinois State Journal*, 28 March 1913; *Illinois State Register*, 28 March 1913.

18. *Chicago Tribune*, 14 April 1913.

19. Edwin Bacon and Morrill Wyman, *Direct Elections and Law-Making by Popular Vote* (Boston: Houghton Mifflin, 1912), 1–19; Ellis Paxson Oberholtzer, *The*

Referendum in America (New York: Scribner's, 1911), 100, 169.

20. *Daily News Almanac* (1912), 92, 424. Illinois had limited forms of recall in cities with the commission form of government and the initiative in its larger cities. Illinois Reference Bureau, *Constitutional Conventions in Illinois* (Springfield: Illinois State Journal Co., 1919), 103; *House Journal* (1911), 941; *Illinois State Register*, 28 March 1913.

21. *Illinois State Journal*, 14 May 1913; *Illinois State Register*, 10 April 1913, 6 May 1913; Civic Federation of Chicago, *Fifty Years on the Civic Front, 1893–1943: A Report on the Achievement of the Civic Federation, Chicago* (Chicago, 1943), 4–7; id., *Legislative Report of the Civic Federation of Chicago, Covering the Regular Session of the Forty-Seventh General Assembly of Illinois*, Bulletin 5 (Chicago, 1911), 8.

22. Civic Federation of Chicago, *Dangers of the Initiative and Referendum*, Bulletin 3 (Chicago, 1911), 8; *Illinois State Register*, 4–5 April 1913, 10 April 1913, 17–18 April 1913.

23. *Senate Journal* (1913), 417–18, 817–20; *Illinois State Journal*, 9 April 1913; *Illinois State Register*, 30 April 1913; *Chicago Tribune*, 13 April 1913.

24. *Illinois State Register*, 7 May 1913.

25. Ibid., 7 May 1913, 13 May 1913.

26. Ibid., 11 May 1913, 13–14 May 1913.

27. *Senate Journal* (1913), 817–20; *House Journal* (1913), 939–40. This was also the method used in constitutional referenda.

28. *Illinois State Journal*, 14 May 1913; *Illinois State Register*, 14 May 1913; *Chicago Tribune*, 14 May 1913; *House Journal*, (1913); 939–48.

29. Ibid.

30. *Illinois State Register*, 21 May 1913, 28 May 1913; *House Journal* (1913) 1114–15.

31. Ibid.; unsigned to Carl Vrooman, 17 July 1916, box 11, Raymond Robins Papers, Wisconsin Historical Society, Madison.

32. *House Journal* (1913), 1302–5; *Illinois State Register*, 6 June 1913; *Illinois State Journal*, 6 June 1913; *Chicago Tribune*, 6 June 1913.

33. *Chicago Tribune*, 22 June 1913.

34. *House Journal* (1913), 1565–66, 1722–25; *Senate Journal* (1913), 1722, 1725; *Daily News Almanac* (1912), 90, 512; *Illinois State Register*, 11 June 1913, 13 June 1913, 19 June 1913.

35. *House Journal* (1913), 1388, 1876–77; *Illinois State Register*, 17 June 1913.

36. Dunne, *Illinois*, 2:324.

37. John A. Fairlie, "The Illinois Legislation of 1913," *Journal of Political Economics* 21 (July 1913): 933.

38. *House Journal* (1913), 1455–56; *Senate Journal* (1913), 2216; *Chicago Tribune*, 13 June 1913, 22 June 1913, 24 June 1913, 26 June 1913, 1 July 1913.

39. *House Journal* (1913), 1409–10, 1834–35; *Senate Journal* (1913), 2110–12; David R. Wrone, "Illinois Pulls Out of the Mud, *Journal of the Illinois State Historical Society*, 58 (1965): 54–76; Illinois Highway Improvement Association, *Illinois*

Highway Improvement (Chicago: The Association, 1919), 29, 31, 37, 45, 47.

40. *Senate Journal* (1913), 669, 1117; *House Journal* (1913), 437–38, 1838, 2167; Edward A. Fitzpatrick, *McCarthy of Wisconsin* (New York: Columbia University Press, 1944).

41. *House Journal* (1913), 1384, 1437; *Senate Journal* (1913), 1755, 2195; *Chicago Tribune*, 11 June 1913; Earl A. Becker, *A History of Labor Legislation in Illinois* (Chicago: University of Chicago Press, 1929), 463.

42. Dunne to James, 18 October 1913, box 43, Edmund Janes James Papers, University Archives, University of Illinois, Urbana-Champaign.

43. *Senate Journal* (1913), 1202–3; *House Journal* (1913), 1414; Grace Wilbur Trout, "Side Lights on Illinois Suffrage History," *Journal of the Illinois State Historical Society*, 13 (1920): 145–79; National-American Woman Suffrage Association, *Forty-Fifth Annual Report, Given at Convention Held in Washington D.C., November 9 to December 5, 1913* (New York: The Association, 1913), 80–83; Eleanor Flexner, *Century of Struggle: The Woman's Rights Movement in the United States* (Cambridge, Mass.: Harvard University Press, Belknap Press, 1975), 268–70; Carrie Chapman Catt and Netti Rogers Shuler, *Woman Suffrage and Politics: The Inner Story of the Suffrage Movement* (Seattle: University of Washington Press, 1969), 189–95; "Suffrage Conquest of Illinois," *Literary Digest* 46 (1913), 1409–11; Gertrude May Beldon, "A History of the Woman Suffrage Movement in Illinois" (master's thesis, University of Chicago, 1913.

44. *Chicago Tribune*, 27 June 1913; *Illinois State Register, 27 June 1913; Illinois State Journal*, 27 June 1913.

45. Catt and Shuler, *Woman Suffrage and Politics*, 192.

46. *Senate Journal* (1913), 2290–98; *House Journal* (1913), 2156–67; *Illinois State Register*, 9 April 1913; *Chicago Tribune*, 1 July 1913; *Illinois State Journal*, 29–30 June 1913.

47. Fairlie, "The Illinois Legislation of 1913," 931–32, 937.

48. Author's interview with Edward Dunne Corboy, Dunne's grandson, 24 March 1984.

49. *Illinois State Journal*, 23–24 September 1913, 29 September 1913.

50. Ibid., 27 October, 1913.

51. Edward F. Dunne, *Judge, Mayor, Governor*, ed. William L. Sullivan (Chicago: Windermere Press, 1916), 522–23; *Chicago Tribune*, 6 November 1913; Illinois State Reformatory, *Twelfth Biennial Report, from July 1, 1912, to June 30, 1914* (Pontiac: Illinois State Reformatory Printers, 1914), 43–44; State Board of Prison Industries, *Annual Report, January 1, 1913, to December 30, 1914* (Springfield: Schnepp and Barnes, 1915), 5.

52. Dunne, *Judge, Mayor, Governor*, 647; David Rothman, *Conscience and Convenience: The Asylum and Its Alternatives in Progressive America* (Boston: Little, Brown, 1980).

53. *Chicago Tribune*, 21 June 1915; Southern Illinois Penitentiary (Chester), *Report for the Two Years Ending September 30, 1914* (Springfield: Schnepp and Barnes,

1915), 15; State Board of Prison Industries, *Annual Report, January 1, 1913, to December 30, 1914*, 5–11; Illinois State Penitentiary (Joliet), *Report for the Two Years Ending September 30, 1914* (Springfield: Schnepp and Barnes, 1915), 7–13.

54. Dunne, *Judge, Mayor, Governor*, 456.

55. *Illinois State Register*, 24 November 1913; *Chicago Tribune*, 19 January 1914.

6. Governor of Illinois

1. Harold Zink, *City Bosses in the United States: A Study of Twenty Municipal Bosses* (Durham, N.C.: Duke University Press, 1930), 291.

2. Samuel Alvin Lilly, "The Political Career of Roger Sullivan" (master's thesis, Eastern Illinois University, 1964), 13–14.

3. Ibid., 27–35.

4. Ibid., 4.

5. *Chicago Tribune*, 1 February 1914, 8 February 1914, 10 February 1914; *Illinois State Register*, 19 February 1914.

6. *Chicago Tribune*, 20 February 1914, 26 February 1914.

7. Carter Harrison to William Jennings Bryan, 11 May 1914, Outgoing Letters, Carter H. Harrison IV Papers, Newberry Library, Chicago,; Edward F. Dunne to William Jennings Bryan (with handwritten note by Bryan on reverse), 12 June 1914, General Correspondence, box 30, William Jennings Bryan Papers, Manuscript Division, Library of Congress, Washington, D.C.

8. Edward F. Dunne to William Jennings Bryan, 25 May 1914, 12 June 1914, General Correspondence, box 30, William Jennings Bryan Papers.

9. Carl Vrooman to William Jennings Bryan, 14 June 1914, General Correspondence, box 30, William Jennings Bryan Papers; Carter Harrison to William Jennings Bryan, 15 June 1914, General Correspondence, box 30, William Jennings Bryan Papers; Edward F. Dunne to William Jennings Bryan, General Correspondence, box 30, William Jennings Bryan Papers; *Illinois State Register*, 1 March 1914.

10. Carter Harrison to William Jennings Bryan, 11 May 1914, Outgoing Papers, Carter H. Harrison IV Papers; Edward F. Dunne to William Jennings Bryan, 25 May 1914, 12 June 1914, General Correspondence, box 30, William Jennings Bryan Papers; Carter Harrison to William Jennings Bryan, 15 June 1914, General Correspondence, box 30, William Jennings Bryan Papers; *Illinois State Register*, 2 June 1914, 20 June 1914, 16 July 1914, 19 July 1914; *Chicago Tribune*, 15–16 July 1914, 22 July 1914.

11. *Chicago Tribune*, 20 July 1914.

12. Ibid., 28–29 August 1914, 3–4 September 1914, 6 September 1914, 8 September 1914.

13. Ibid., 12 May 1914, 29 June 1914, 19 July 1914, 4 September 1914, 7 September 1914; *Illinois State Register*, 16 August 1914; Lilly, "Roger Sullivan," 49–53.

14. *Illinois State Register*, 16 July 1914; *Chicago Tribune*, 30 August 1914.

15. *Daily News Almanac* (1915), 522; *Illinois State Register* 19 September 1914.

16. *Chicago Tribune*, 23–24 July 1914, 4 September 1914, 25 September 1914, 27 September 1914, 22–23 October 1914, 29–30 October 1914.

17. Ibid.

18. *Illinois State Register*, 21 October 1914, 22 October 1914; *Chicago Tribune*, 23 October 1914; Carter Harrison, *Stormy Years: The Autobiography of Carter H. Harrison, Five Times Mayor of Chicago* (Indianapolis: Bobbs-Merrill, 1935), 329–30.

19. *Daily News Almanac* (1915), 476–78.

20. Ibid.

21. Ibid, 478.

22. *Chicago Tribune*, 1–2 January 1915; *Illinois State Register*, 1 January 1915.

23. James H. Timberlake, *Prohibition and the Progressive Movement, 1900–1922* (New York: Atheneum Press, 1970).

24. Anti-Saloon League of American, *The Anti-Saloon League Yearbook, 1910* (Westerville, Ohio: The League, 1910), 19; Anti-Saloon League of American, *The Anti-Saloon League Year Book, 1909*, 29–30; John Buenker, "The Illinois Legislature and Prohibition, 1907–1909," *Journal of the Illinois State Historical Society* 62 (winter 1969): 374; *Chicago Tribune*, 22 June 1913, 24 June 1913.

25. Ibid., 7 April 1915, 11 April 1915; Edward F. Dunne, *Illinois, the Heart of the Nation*, 5 vols. (Chicago: Lewis Publishing, 1933), 2:370, 529.

26. *Chicago Tribune*, 6 January 1915, 10 February 1915.

27. Ibid., 6–9 January 1915, 21 January 1915, 31 January 1915.

28. Ibid., 13 January 1915, 5 February 1915, 11 February 1915; *Illinois State Register*, 10 February 1915.

29. *Chicago Tribune*, 4 February 1915.

30. Ibid., 16–17 February 1915; *Illinois State Register*, 17 February 1915; *House Journal* (1915), 106–7; *Senate Journal* (1915), 167–68. The Senate, too, had its share of controversy. At issue were two seats. The Democrats managed to win, giving the body twenty-five Democrats, twenty-five Republicans, and one Progressive. A Democrat, Stephen D. Canady (Montgomery County-D) was elected president pro tempore.

31. *Chicago Tribune*, 16–17 February 1915.

32. Edward F. Dunne, *Judge, Mayor, Governor*, ed. William L. Sullivan (Chicago: Windermere Press, 1916), 658–87.

33. Robert A. Waller, *Rainey of Illinois: A Political Biography, 1903–1934*, Illinois Studies in Social Sciences, no. 60 (Champaign: University of Illinois Press), 56; id., "The Illinois Waterway from Conception to Completion, 1908–1913," *Journal of the Illinois State Historical Society* 65 (summer 1972): 121–30; Mildred Cecilia Warner, "The History of the Deep Waterway in the State of Illinois" (master's thesis, University of Illinois at Urbana-Champaign, 1947), 28.

34. Waller, "The Illinois Waterway," 126–30.

35. *Illinois State Register*, 4 December 1914; Dunne, *Judge, Mayor, Governor*, 592–99, 658.

36. *Illinois State Register,* 7 February 1915, 10 April 1915; *Chicago Tribune,* 7 February 1915, 5 March 1915, 25 April 1915, 20 May 1915; *House Journal* (1915), 826–28; *State Journal,* (1915), 1039–66.

37. *Senate Journal* (1915), 1040–44.

38. Dunne, *Judge, Mayor, Governor,* 721; Waller, *Rainey of Illinois,* 64.

39. George C. Sikes, "Why Edward F. Dunne Should Be Eliminated as a Candidate for Governor" (August 1916), 5, Robert Jerome Dunne Papers, Chicago Historical Society, Chicago.

40. *Chicago Tribune,* 16 February 1915.

41. Ibid., 14 February 1915.

42. *Daily News Almanac* (1916), 561; *Chicago Tribune,* 17 March 1915.

43. Lloyd Wendt and Herman Kogan, *Big Bill of Chicago* (Indianapolis: Bobbs-Merrill, n.d.), 13–14, 51; John Bright, *Hizzoner Big Bill Thompson* (New York: Jonathan Caper and Harrison Smith, 1930), 34; Douglas Bukowski, "Big Bill Thompson: The 'Model' Politician," in Paul M. Green and Melvin G. Holli, eds., *The Mayors: The Chicago Political Tradition* (Carbondale: Southern Illinois University Press, 1987), 61–65.

44. Wendt and Kogan, *Big Bill,* 94, 114; William L. Chenery, "The Fall of a Mayor," *New Republic,* 13 May 1915, 36; "Republican Victory in Chicago," *Literary Digest,* 17 April 1915, 863–64; *Daily News Almanac* (1916), 507.

45. Dunne, *Judge, Mayor, Governor,* 704–5, 714. The governor lost two "warm friends" on the *Lusitania.*

46. *Illinois State Register,* 9 June 1915.

47. *Chicago Tribune,* 3 March 1915, 19 June 1915; *Illinois State Register,* 20 June 1915; *Daily News Almanac* (1916), 660–61.

48. *House Journal* (1915), 1383–88; Dunne, *Illinois,* 2:371; *Chicago Tribune,* 30 June 1915; *Illinois State Register,* 1 July 1915.

49. *Daily News Almanac* (1916), 279; *Journal of the Illinois State Historical Society* 8 (April 1915–January 1916), 351.

50. *Illinois State Register,* 15 April 1915, 22–23 April 1915; *House Journal* (1915), 988, 1059, 1072; *Senate Journal* (1915), 1504–5; Dunne, *Judge, Mayor, Governor,* 495, 535, 809, 815.

51. *Chicago Tribune,* 7 August 1915, 28 November 1915; Dunne, *Judge, Mayor, Governor,* 734–42. The governor was on the record against capital punishment as early as 1904.

52. *Chicago Tribune,* 2 July 1915, 15 October 1915, 17 November 1915; Waller, *Rainey of Illinois,* 68.

53. A. D. Melvin, "The 1908 Outbreak of Foot-and-Mouth Disease in the United States," in the U.S. Department of Agriculture, *25th Annual Report of the Bureau of Animal Industry for the Year 1908* (Washington, D.C.: Government Printing Office, 1910), 379–92; id., *Report of the Chief of the Bureau of Animal Industry* (Washington, D.C.: Government Printing Office, 1915), 6.

54. Secretary of State (Illinois) Lewis G. Stevenson, *The Foot and Mouth Dis-*

ease in Illinois: Its Cause, Character, Cost, and Irradication by American Experts in Veterinary Medicine and Animal Husbandry before the Illinois General Assembly on January 19, 1915 (Springfield: Illinois State Journal Co., 1915), 3; *Chicago Tribune*, 31 October 1915.

55. *Chicago Tribune*, 23 October 1915, 25 October 1915; Dunne, *Judge, Mayor, Governor*, 768–69.

56. *Chicago Tribune*, 25 October 1915.

57. *Illinois State Register*, 11 July 1915.

58. Citizens Association of Chicago, *Forty-Second Annual Report* (Chicago: The Association, 1916), 9.

59. *Chicago Tribune*, 29 August 1915; *Illinois State Register*, 29 August 1915.

60. *J. B. Fergus v. Andrew Russel, et al.*, 270 Ill. 304–72, 626–33; Citizens Association of Chicago, *Results of the Legislative Injunction Suit*, Bulletin 34 (Chicago, 1916), 1–8.

61. *Daily News Almanac* (1916), 662; *Chicago Tribune*, 23 November 1915, 4 December 1915.

7. Illinois Returns to "Normalcy": The Elections of 1916

1. *Chicago Tribune*, 28 March 1915, 4 July 1915, 9 July 1915, 13 July 1915, 1 September 1915, 24 September 1915, 23 December 1915; *Illinois State Register*, 5 January 1916, 21 January 1916; Edward F. Dunne, *Judge, Mayor, Governor*, ed. William L. Sullivan (Chicago: Windermere Press, 1916), 790.

2. *Washington Post*, 4 January 1916, 7 January 1916, 12 January 1916, 29 January 1916; Henry F. Pringle, *The Life and Times of William Howard Taft*, 2 vols. (New York: Farrar and Rhinehart, 1939), 2:951–53; A. L. Todd, *Justice on Trial: The Case of Louis D. Brandeis* (New York: McGraw-Hill, 1964), 30.

3. Illinois Senate, *Journal of the Second Special Session of the Forty-Ninth General Assembly of the State of Illinois* (Springfield: Illinois State Journal Co., 1916), 121; Illinois House of Representatives, *Journal of the First Special Session of the House of Representatives of the Forty-Ninth General Assembly of the State of Illinois* (Springfield: Illinois State Journal Co., 1916), 117 (hereafter cited as Illinois House, *Journal of the First Special Session); Illinois State Register*, 8 January 1916).

4. Illinois House, *Journal of the First Special Session*, 112–22.

5. *Illinois State Register*, 30 January 1916, 28 February 1916; Department of Public Works and Building, Division of Waterways, *First Annual Report* (Springfield: Illinois State Journal Co., 1918), 12–14.

6. *Chicago Tribune*, 15–16 January 1916.

7. Ibid., 17 January 1916, 27 January 1916; Burton A. Boxerman, "Adolph Joachim Sabath in Congress: The Early Years, 1907–1932," *Journal of the Illinois State Historical Society* 66 (autumn 1973): 327–40.

8. *Chicago Tribune*, 4 February 1916, 16 February 1916, 20 February 1916.

9. Ibid., 16 March 1916; *Daily News Almanac* (1917), 581.

10. *Chicago Tribune*, 29 February 1916, 12 April 1916.

11. Ibid., 13–14 April 1916.

12. Ibid., 20–21 April 1916; 13 May 1916; *Daily News Almanac* (1917), 576–77.

13. *Chicago Tribune*, 12–16 June 1916; *Illinois State Register*, 12 June 1916, 16 June 1916.

14. *Illinois State Register*, 20 June 1916.

15. Ibid., 23 February 1916, 4 June 1916; *Chicago Tribune*, 15 May 1916, 3 June 1916; Dunne, *Judge, Mayor, Governor*, 743–48, 804–8; Paolo E. Coletta, *William Jennings Bryan*, 3 vols. (Lincoln: University of Nebraska Press, 1969), vol. 3, *Political Puritan, 1915–1925*, 1–19.

16. *Chicago Tribune*, 10 March 1916, 19–20 June 1916.

17. Ibid., 27 June 1916; 3 July 1916; *Daily News Almanac* (1917), 253; Ralph Arthur Straetz, "The Progressive Movement in Illinois, 1910–1916" (Ph.D. diss., University of Illinois, 1951), 537–39.

18. Noram Harper to Raymond Robins, 8 July 1916, box 11, Raymond Robins Papers, Wisconsin Historical Society, Madison.

19. Jesse Heylin to Raymond Robins, 21 July 1916, box 11, Raymond Robins Papers; unsigned to Carl Vrooman, 17 July 1916, box 11, Raymond Robins Papers; William H. Stephens to Raymond Robins, 3 July 1960, box 11, Raymond Robins Papers.

20. *Chicago Tribune*, 27 June 1916; *Illinois State Register*, 11 July 1916.

21. *Chicago Tribune*, 13 July 1916, 17 July 1916, 19 July 1916; *Illinois State Register*, 11 July 1916; "The Progressive Vote and the Results in November," *Nation*, 6 July 1916, 7.

22. Josephus Daniels to William Jennings Bryan, 17 July 1916, box 31, Josephus Daniels Papers, Manuscript Division, Library of Congress, Washington, D.C.

23. *Chicago Tribune*, 16–17 July 1916, 19 July 1916.

24. Ibid., 6 August 1916; Alan R. Havig, "The Raymond Robins Case for Progressive Republicanism," *Journal of the Illinois State Historical Society* 64 (winter 1971): 401–18.

25. *Chicago Tribune*, 6 August 1916.

26. Ibid., 19 July 1916; *Illinois State Register*, 2 August 1916.

27. *Illinois State Register*, 30 July 1916. The decision was won on appeal before the Illinois Supreme Court, too late to help Dunne win reelection.

28. Ibid., 11 July 1916, 12 August 1916, 18 August 1916, 20 August 1916, 27 August 1916; *Chicago Tribune*, 14 August 1916, 16 August 1916, 20 August 1916.

29. *Chicago Tribune*, 1 September 1916.

30. Ibid., 9 September 1916.

31. Ibid., 27 September 1916; *Illinois State Register*, 1 November 1916.

32. *Daily News Almanac* (1917), 432.

33. James D. Nowland, comp., *Illinois Major Party Platforms: 1900–1964*, Institute of Government and Public Affairs (Champaign: University of Illinois Press,

1966), 115–22.

34. Ibid., 120; *Chicago Tribune*, 27 September 1916; *Illinois State Register*, 27 September 1916.

35. *Chicago Tribune*, 6 June 1916; Straetz, "Progressive movement," 558–59.

36. William T. Hutchinson, *Lowden of Illinois: The Life of Frank O. Lowden*, 2 vols. (Chicago: University of Chicago Press, 1957), vol. 1, *City and State*, 265–82.

37. Ibid., 12–14, 54–57.

38. Ibid.

39. Ibid., 250, 265.

40. Ibid.; *Chicago Tribune*, 25 September 1916, 30 September 1916, 3 October 1916, 12 October 1916; *Illinois State Register*, 19 October 1916.

41. *Chicago Tribune*, 17 October 1916.

42. Ibid., 27 October 1916, 29 October 1916; *Illinois State Register*, 29 October 1916; Coletta, *Political Puritan*, 40–41.

43. *Illinois State Register*, 9 August 1916, 4 October 1916, 7 October 1916, 4 November 1916; *Chicago Tribune*, 20 October 1916.

44. *Illinois State Register*, 29 October 1916, 5–6 November 1916; Walker to Dunne, 9 May 1916; John Hunter Walker Papers, Illinois Historical Survey, University of Illinois Library, Urbana-Champaign.

45. *Chicago Tribune*, 6 October 1916, 14–15 October 1916, 17–18 October 1916, 20 October 1916; Hutchinson, *City and State*, 286–87.

46. *Chicago Tribune*, 2 November 1916.

47. Ibid., 5 November 1916.

48. Ibid., 9 November 1916; *Daily News Almanac* (1917), 432, 591.

49. *Chicago Tribune*, 9 November 1916.

50. *St. Louis Globe-Democrat*, 10 November 1916.

51. The durability of this return to "normalcy" was underscored by the fact that with Lowden was elected, in effect, a state administration that was to endure for sixteen years; serving as treasurer was Len Small, who followed Lowden into the governor's office for two terms, to be followed in turn by Louis Emerson, secretary of state under Lowden.

52. *Illinois State Register*, 5 December 1916, 17 December 1916.

53. Ibid., 7 January 1917.

54. Ibid., 9 January 1917; *Illinois State Journal*, 9 January 1917; *Chicago Tribune*, 9 January 1917.

8. Final Years

1. Dunne to Bryan, 11 November 1916, General Correspondence, box 31, William Jennings Bryan Papers, Manuscript Division, Library of Congress, Washington, D.C.

2. *Chicago Tribune*, 19 July 1918.

3. Author's interview with Edward Dunne Corboy, Dunne's grandson, 23

January 1984.

4. *Chicago Tribune*, 23 April 1917, 26 November 1917, 22 January 1919; *Illinois State Register*, 8 May 1917; unattributed and undated newspaper article, Edward F. Dunne Scrapbooks and Letters, Scrapbook 7:134, Illinois Historical Survey, University of Illinois Library, Urbana-Champaign.

5. *Chicago Tribune*, 24 August 1918, 26 August 1918, 29 August 1918, 12 September 1918.

6. Ibid., 1 August 1918, 12 August 1918, 12 September 1918, 3 November 1918, 6 November 1918, 26 November 1918.

7. Ibid., 28 April 1917, 10 June 1917, 27 November 1918, 8–9 December 1918, 12 December 1918, 15 December 1918, 17 December 1918, 25 December 1918, 8 January 1919, 22 January 1919; Alan J. Ward, *Ireland and Anglo-American Relations, 1899–1921* (Toronto: University of Toronto Press, 1969), 177.

8. Charles C. Tansill, *America and the Fight for Irish Freedom, 1866–1922* (New York: Devin-Adair, 1957), 296; Ward, *Ireland*, 126, 164.

9. Thomas H. Pendergast to Dever, 20(?) September 1920, box 1, William E. Dever Papers, Chicago Historical Society, Chicago.

10. *Chicago Tribune*, 23–24 February 1919; *Philadelphia Evening Bulletin*, 22 February 1919, 24 February 1919; *Chicago Herald and Examiner*, 24 February 1919.

11. *Chicago Tribune*, 2 March 1919; *New York Times*, 5 March 1919; 29 March 1919; Ward, *Ireland*, 137.

12. *New York Times*, 9 March 1919; Tansill, *America*, 302; Ward, *Ireland*, 174; Arthur Walworth, *Wilson and His Peacemakers: American Diplomacy at the Paris Peace Conference, 1919* (New York: W. W. Norton, 1986), 468.

13. Tansill, *America*, 306–7.

14. *New York Times*, 1–2 April 1919, 12 April 1919; Tansill, *America*, 312–13; Ward, *Ireland*, 177.

15. Ibid.; Thomas E. Hachey, *Britain and Irish Separatism: From Fenians to the Irish Free State, 1867–1922* (Washington, D.C.: Catholic University of America, 1977, 1984), 227.

16. *New York Times*, 5 May 1919, 7 May 1919, 11 May 1919; *Times* (London), 5–9 May 1919, 12 May 1919; Ward, *Ireland*, 179; Hachey, *Britain*, 226.

17. *New York Times*, 12–13 May 1919; *Times* (London), 12–13 May 1919; 13 June 1919.

18. *Times* (London), 14–15 May 1919; Walworth, *Wilson*, 470; Hachey, *Britain*, 227; Ward, *Ireland*, 180–81.

19. *Times* (London), 13 June 1919; *Chicago Daily News*, 16 May 1919; *New York Times*, 16 June 1919; Ward, *Ireland*, 181; Hachey, *Britain*, 230. The report appeared over Walsh's and Dunne's names; Ryan, believing his fellow delegates were too radical, left early for the United States.

20. *New York Times*, 11–12 June 1919; 18 June 1919; Ward, *Ireland*, 184; Walworth, *Wilson*, 471, 477.

21. *New York Times*, 9 July 1919; *Chicago Herald and Examiner*, 13 July 1919.

22. *Chicago Tribune*, 13 July 1919; *Chicago Herald and Examiner*, 12–13 July 1919; *New York Times*, 12 July 1919; 31 August 1919. Murphy had been appointed to replace Ryan in Paris. He arrived too late to make a real contribution.

23. *Chicago Tribune*, 11 May 1920; 27 June 1929; 30 June 1920; 2 July 1920. Roger Sullivan had died on 14 April 1920.

24. Ibid., 27 June 1920, 30 June 1929, 25 October 1920.

25. Richard Allen Morton, "Descent into History: Chicago, Ideologies and Repression, 1917–1918" (master's thesis, Eastern Illinois University, 1975), 185–217.

26. *Daily News Almanac* (1923), 676.

27. Edward F. Dunne, *Illinois, the Heart of the Nation*, 5 vols. (Chicago: Lewis Publishing, 1933), 2:427.

28. Ibid., 2:432; *Chicago Tribune*, 31 October 1922.

29. Dunne, *Illinois*, 2:432; William H. Stewart, *The Twenty Incredible Years* (Chicago: M. A. Donohue, 1937), 180.

30. *Chicago Tribune*, 13 November 1922, 26–27 November 1922; 8 December 1922; *Chicago American*, 19 October 1922, 14 November 1922, 17–18 November 1922, 22 November 1922, Dunne, *Illinois*, 2:432–54.

31. *Chicago Tribune*, 19 November 1922, 25 November 1922, 29–30 November 1922, 2 December 1922, 10 December 1922; Eugene Staley, *History of the Illinois Federation of Labor* (Chicago: University of Chicago Press, 1930), 427–48.

32. Stuart, *Incredible Years*, 81.

33. *Chicago Tribune*, 22 October 1922, 21 March 1923, 23 March 1923, 25 March 1923; *Chicago American*, 5 February 1923, 9 February 1923, 19 March 1923, 28 March 1923, 5 April 1923; Stuart, *Incredible Years*, 187. For more on Dever, see John R. Schmidt, *"The Mayor Who Cleaned Up Chicago": A Political Biography of William E. Dever* (DeKalb: Northern Illinois University Press, 1989).

34. *Chicago Tribune*, 6 April 1924, 9 April 1924; *Chicago American*, 5 April 1923.

35. *Chicago Tribune*, 20 February 1925, 5 April 1925; *Chicago American*, 2 February 1923, 8 February 1923.

36. Ibid., 1 April 1925, 5–6 April 1925; Stuart, *Incredible Years*, 224. Dunne served as chairman, and William O'Connell as treasurer.

37. *Chicago Tribune*, 10 January 1926, 24–25 February 1926; Carroll Hill Woody, *The Chicago Primary of 1926: A Study in Election Methods* (Chicago: University of Chicago Press, 1926), 33–34.

38. *Chicago Tribune*, 14 April 1926; *Daily News Almanac* (1927), 727–38; Woody, *Chicago Primary*, 54.

39. Dunne, *Illinois*, 2:530–43; Harry P. Weber, *Outline History of Chicago Traction* (Chicago: n.p., 1936), 274–383; Linda J. Lear, *Harold L. Ickes: The Aggressive Progressive, 1874–1933* (New York: Garland, 1981), 333–37.

40. *Chicago Tribune*, 24 April 1929; *Chicago Herald and Examiner*, 24 April 1929; *Illinois State Journal*, 24 April 1929; Harry P. Weber, *Chicago Traction*, 352; Chicago Transit Authority, *Chicago's Mass Transportation System* (Chicago: Chi-

cago Transit Authority, 1959), 5.

41. *Illinois State Register*, 22 April 1932, 24 April 1932; handwritten comment on Dunne by Harrison inside "Program for the Illinois Delegates to the Democratic National Convention, Chicago, June 27, 1932," folio: Political Mementos of His Life, Carter H. Harrison IV Papers, Newberry Library, Chicago; Kristie Miller, "Ruth Hanna McCormick and the Senatorial Election of 1930," *Illinois Historical Journal* 63 (Autumn 1988): 191–210.

42. Author's interview with Edward Dunne Corboy, Dunne's grandson, 23 January 1987; Walter A. Townsend, *Illinois Democracy: A History of the Party and Its Representative Members, Past and Present*, 2 vols. (Springfield: Democratic Historical Association, 1933), 2:8; Lenox R. Lohr, *Fair Management: The Story of a Century of Progress Exposition* (Chicago: Cuneo Press, 1952), 148.

43. *Chicago Tribune*, 11 April 1921, 26 May 1928; *Chicago Daily News*, 27 July 1925, 24 July 1936; *Chicago Herald and Examiner*, 27 July 1925.

44. Dunne, *Illinois,* 1:iii.

45. John A. Zventina, Review of *Illinois, the Heart of the Nation*, by Edward F. Dunne, *Mid-America* 16, n.s. 5 (April 1934): 246.

46. *Chicago Herald and Examiner*, 13 October 1933; *Chicago American*, 12 October 1935.

47. *New York Times*, 25 May 1937.

48. Ibid., 13 October 1935; author's interview with Edward Dunne Corboy, Dunne's grandson, 23 January 1987.

49. Dunne to William L. Sullivan, 5 March 1937, Edward F. Dunne Scrapbooks and Papers, Illinois Historical Survey, University of Illinois Library, Urbana-Champaign; Dunne to William L.Sullivan (?), 11 March 1937; Edward F. Dunne Scrapbooks and Papers; Dunne to William L. Sullivan (?), 4 May 1937, Edward F. Dunne Scrapbooks and Papers; *Illinois State Register*, 25 May 1937; *Chicago Daily News*, 24 May 1937.

50. *Chicago Tribune*, 27 May 1937.

51. *Illinois State Register*, 24 May 1937; *Illinois State Journal*, 25 May 1937; *Chicago Herald and Examiner*, 25 May 1937.

52. John H. Walker to Edward F. Dunne, 9 May 1916, John Hunter Walker Collection, Illinois Historical Survey, University of Illinois Library, Urbana-Champaign.

BIBLIOGRAPHY

Manuscript Collections

Addams, Jane. Papers (microfilm ed.). Manuscript Division, Library of Congress, Washington, D.C.

Alschuler, Samuel J. Papers. Illinois State Historical Library, Springfield, Illinois.

Baker, Newton D. Papers. Western Reserve Historical Society, Cleveland, Ohio.

Bryan, William Jennings. Papers. Manuscript Division, Library of Congress, Washington, D.C.

Darrow, Clarence S. Papers. Manuscript Division, Library of Congress, Washington, D.C.

Deneen, Charles S. Collection. Illinois State Historical Library, Springfield, Illinois.

Dever, William E. Papers. Chicago Historical Society, Chicago.

Dunne, Edward Fitzsimons. Collection. Illinois State Historical Library, Springfield.

———. Scrapbooks and Papers. Illinois Historical Survey, University of Illinois Library, Urbana-Champaign.

Dunne, Robert Jerome. Papers. Chicago Historical Society, Chicago.

Fisher, Walter L. Papers. Manuscript Division, Library of Congress, Washington, D.C.

Fitzpatrick, John J. Papers. Chicago Historical Society, Chicago.

Harrison IV, Carter H. Papers. Newberry Library, Chicago.

Humphrey, Otis J. Papers. Illinois State Historical Library, Springfield.

James, Edmund J. Papers. Archives, University of Illinois Library, Urbana-Champaign.

Johnson, Tom L. Papers. Western Reserve Historical Society, Cleveland, Ohio.

Jones, Samuel M. Papers (microfilm ed.). Toledo-Lucas County Public Library, Toledo, Ohio.

Robins, Raymond. Papers. Wisconsin Historical Society, Madison.

Schilling, George S. Papers. Illinois State Historical Library, Springfield.

Walker, John H. Papers. Illinois State Historical Library, Springfield.

Schwartz, Ulysses. Papers. Chicago Historical Society, Chicago.

Wilson, Thomas Woodrow. Papers (microfilm ed.). Manuscript Division, Library of Congress, Washington, D.C.

Government Publications

Board of Aldermen, Chicago. *Proceedings for the Municipal Year,1905–1906*. Chicago: John F. Higgins, 1906.

———. *Proceedings for the Municipal Year, 1906–1907*. Chicago: John F. Higgins, 1907.

Board of Prison Industries, Illinois. *Annual Report, January 1, to December 30, 1914*. Springfield: Schnepp and Barnes, 1915.

Cunningham, James, comp. *The City Charter and Revised Ordinances of the City of Peoria, Illinois*. Peoria: N. C. Nason, 1869.

Illinois General Assembly. House. *Journal of the House of Representatives of the Forty-Seventh General Assembly*. Springfield: Illinois State Journal Co., 1912.

———. House. *Journal of the House of Representatives of the Forty-Eighth General Assembly*. Springfield: Illinois State Journal Co., 1914.

———. House. *Journal of the House of Representatives of the Forty-Ninth General Assembly*. Springfield: Illinois State Journal Co., 1915.

———. House. *Journal of the House of Representatives of the First Special Session of the Forty-Ninth General Assembly*. Springfield: Illinois State Journal Co., 1915.

———. House. *Journal of the House of Representatives of the Second Special Session of the Forty-Ninth General Assembly*. Springfield: Illinois State Journal Co., 1916.

———. Senate. *Journal of the Senate of the Forty-Seventh General Assembly*. Springfield: Illinois State Journal Co., 1912.

———. Senate. *Journal of the Senate of the Forty-Eighth General Assembly*. Springfield: Illinois State Journal Co., 1914.

———. Senate. *Journal of the Senate of the Forty-Ninth General Assembly*. Springfield: Illinois State Journal Co., 1915.

———. Senate. *Journal of the Senate of the First Special Session of the Forty-Ninth General Assembly*. Springfield: Illinois State Journal Co., 1916.

———. Senate. *Journal of the Senate of the Second Special Session of the Forty-Ninth General Assembly*. Springfield: Illinois State Journal Co., 1916.

Illinois Legislative Reference Bureau. *Constitutional Conventions in Illinois*. Springfield: Illinois State Journal Co., 1916.

Illinois State Reformatory. *Twelfth Biennial Report*. Pontiac: Illinois State Reformatory Printers, 1914.

Southern Illinois Penitentiary. *Report for the Two Years Ending September 30, 1914*. Springfield: Schnepp and Barnes, 1915.

Stevenson, Lewis G., Illinois Secretary of State. *Blue Book of the State of Illinois, 1915–1916*. Danville: Illinois Printing Co., 1917.

———. *The Foot and Mouth Disease in Illinois*. Springfield: Illinois State Journal Co., 1915.

U.S. Department of Agriculture. *Report of the Chief of Animal Industry*. Washington,

D.C.: Government Printing Office, 1910.
————. *Twenty-Fifth Annual Report*. Washington, D.C.: Government Printing Office, 1910.
U.S. Department of Commerce. Bureau of the Census. *Thirteenth Census*. Vol. 2. Washington, D.C.: Government Printing Office, 1913.
U.S. Department of the Interior. Census Office. *Vital and Social Statistics of the Eleventh Census, 1890*. Pt. 2. Washington, D.C.: Government Printing Office, 1895.

Books

Bacon, Edwin, and Morrill Wyman. *Direct Elections and the Law-Making by Popular Vote*. Boston: Houghton Mifflin, 1912.
Becker, Earl L. *A History of Labor Legislation in Illinois*. Chicago: University of Chicago Press, 1929.
Bennett, Fremont, comp. *Politics and Politicians of Chicago, Cook County, and Illinois*. Chicago: Blakely Printing, 1886.
Blum, John M. *Joe Tumulty and the Wilson Era*. Boston: Houghton Mifflin, 1951.
Bright, John. *Hizzoner Big Bill Thompson*. New York: Jonathan Caper and Harrison Smith, 1930.
Catt, Carrie Chapman, and Nettie Rogers Shuler. *Women's Suffrage and Politics: The Inner Side of the Suffrage Movement*. Seattle: University of Washington Press, 1969.
Church, Charles A. *History of the Republican Party in Illinois, 1854–1912, with a Review of the Aggressions of the Slave-Power*. Rockford, Ill.: Wilson Brothers, 1912.
Coletta, Paola E. *William Jennings Bryan*. 3 vols. Lincoln: University of Nebraska Press, 1959.
Counts, George S. *School and Society in Chicago*. New York: Harcourt Brace, 1928.
Darrow, Clarence. *The Story of My Life*. New York: Scribner's, 1932.
Destler, Chester McArthur. *Henry Demarest Lloyd and the Empire of Reform*. Philadelphia: University of Pennsylvania Press, 1963.
DuBois, Ellen Carol. *Feminism and Suffrage: The Emergence of an Independent Women's Movement in America, 1848–1869*. Ithaca, N.Y.: Cornell University Press, 1978.
Duis, Perry R. *The Saloon: Public Drinking in Chicago and Boston, 1880–1920*. Champaign: University of Illinois Press, 1983.
Dunne, Edward F. *Illinois, the Heart of the Nation*. 5 vols. Chicago: Lewis Publishing, 1933.
————. *Judge, Mayor, Governor*. Edited by William L. Sullivan. Chicago: Windermere Press, 1916.
Fitzpatrick, Edward A. *McCarthy of Wisconsin*. New York: Columbia University Press, 1944.
Flanagan, Maureen A. *Charter Reform in Chicago*. Carbondale: Southern Illinois

University Press, 1987.

Flexner, Eleanor. *Century of Struggle: The Woman's Rights Movement in the United States.* Cambridge, Mass.: Harvard University Press, Belknap Press, 1975.

Green, Paul M., and Melvin G. Holli, eds. *The Mayors: The Chicago Political Tradition.* Carbondale: Southern Illinois University Press, 1987.

Hachey, Thomas E. *Britain and Irish Separatism: From Fenians to the Irish Free State, 1867–1922.* Washington, D.C.: Catholic University of America Press, 1977.

Haley, Margaret. *Battleground: The Autobiography of Margaret A. Haley.* Edited by Robert Reid. Champaign: University of Illinois Press, 1982.

Harrison, Carter H. *Stormy Years: The Autobiography of Carter H. Harrison, Five Times Mayor of Chicago.* Indianapolis: Bobbs-Merrill, 1935.

Herrick, Mary J. *The Chicago Schools: A Social and Political History.* Beverly Hills, Calif.: Sage Publications, 1971.

Holli, Melvin. *Reform in Detroit: Hazen S. Pingree and Urban Politics.* New York: Oxford University Press, 1969.

Hutchinson, William T. *Lowden of Illinois: The Life of Frank O. Lowden.* 2 vols. Chicago: University of Chicago Press, 1957.

Karl, Barry D. *Charles S. Merriam and the Study of Politics.* Chicago: University of Chicago Press, 1974.

Lasch, Christopher. *Haven in a Heartless World: The Family Besieged.* New York: Basic Books, 1977.

Lear, Linda J. *Harold L. Ickes: The Aggressive Progressive.* New York: Garland, 1981.

Leonard, John W., ed. *The Book of Chicagoans, 1905.* Chicago: A. N. Marquis, 1905.

Lind, Alan R. *Chicago Surface Lines: An Illustrated History.* Park Forest, Ill.: Transport History Press, 1974.

Link, Arthur S. *Wilson: The Road to the White House.* Princeton: Princeton University Press, 1953.

Lloyd, Caro. *Henry Demarest Lloyd, 1847–1903: A Biography.* New York: G. P. Putnam's Sons, Knickerbocker Press, 1912.

Lohr, Lenox R. *Fair Management: The Story of the Progress Exposition.* Chicago: Cuneo Press, 1952.

Merriam, Charles S. *Chicago: A More Intimate View of Urban Politics.* New York: Macmillan, 1929.

Nowland, James D., ed. *Illinois Major Party Platforms: 1900–1964.* Institute of Government and Public Affairs. Champaign: University of Illinois Press, 1966.

Oberholtzer, Ellis Parson. *The Referendum in America: Together with Some Chapters on the Initiative and Recall.* New York: Scribner's, 1912.

Pringle, Henry F. *The Life and Times of William Howard Taft.* 2 vols. New York: Farrar and Rhinehart, 1939.

Rothman, David. *Conscience and Convenience: The Asylum and Its Alternatives in Progressive America.* Boston: Little, Brown, 1980.

Schmidt, John R. *"The Mayor Who Cleaned Up Chicago": A Political Biography of*

William E. Dever. Dekalb: Northern Illinois University Press, 1989.

Staley, Eugene. *History of the Illinois Federation of Labor.* Chicago: University of Chicago Press, 1930.

Stuart, William H. *The Twenty Incredible Years.* Chicago: M. A. Donohue, 1935.

Tansill, Charles C. *America and the Fight for Irish Freedom, 1866–1922.* New York: Devin-Adair, 1957.

Tarr, Joel Arthur. *A Study in Boss Politics: William Lorimer of Chicago.* Champaign: University of Illinois Press, 1971.

Timberlake, James H. *Prohibition and the Progressive Movement, 1900–1920.* New York: Atheneum, 1970.

Townsend, Walter. *Illinois Democracy.* 2 vols. Springfield: Democratic Historical Association, 1935.

Tumulty, Joseph P. *Woodrow Wilson As I Know Him.* Garden City, N.J.: Doubleday, 1921.

Waller, Robert. *Rainey of Illinois: A Political Biography, 1903–1934.* Illinois Studies in Social Sciences, no. 60. Champaign: University of Illinois Press, 1977.

Walworth, Arthur. *Wilson and His Peacemakers: American Diplomacy at the Paris Peace Conference, 1919.* New York: W. W. Norton, 1986.

Ward, Alan J. *Ireland and Anglo-American Relations, 1899–1921.* Toronto: University of Toronto Press, 1969.

Weber, Harry P. *Outline History of Chicago Traction.* Chicago: n.p., 1936.

Wendt, Lloyd, and Herman Kogan. *Big Bill of Chicago.* Indianapolis: Bobbs-Merrill, n.d.

Zink, Harold. *City Bosses in the United States: A Study of Twenty Municipal Bosses.* Durham: N.C.: Duke University Press, 1930.

Articles

Boxman, Burton A. "Adolph Joachim Sabath in Congress: The Early Years, 1907–1932." *Journal of the Illinois State Historical Society* 66 (1973): 327–40.

Buenker, John D. "Dynamics of Chicago Ethnic Politics, 1900–1930." *Journal of the Illinois State Historical Society* 57 (1974): 175–99.

————. "Edward F. Dunne: The Urban Stock Democrat as Progressive." *Mid-America* 50 (1968): 3–21.

————. "The Illinois Legislature and Prohibition, 1907–1919." *Journal of the Illinois State Historical Society* 62 (1969): 363–84.

Candeloro, Dominic. "The School Board Crisis of 1907." *Journal of the Illinois State Historical Society* 68 (1975): 396–406.

Cheney, William L. "The Fall of a Mayor." *New Republic,* 15 May 1915, 36.

Darrow, Clarence S. "Chicago's Traction Questions." *International* 12 (October 1905): 13–22.

Dunne, Edward F. "Chicago's Fight for Municipal Ownership." *Independent* 51 (18 October 1906): 927–30.

————. "How Chicago Will Do It." *World's Work* 10 (June 1905): 6265–66.

Fairlie, John A. "The Illinois Legislation of 1913." *Journal of Political Economics* 21 (1913): 931–37.

————. "Municipal Functions in the United States." *Annals of the American Academy of Political and Social Sciences* 25 (1905): 304–8.

Fitch, George. "The Noiseless Suffragette." *Collier's*, 9 August 1913, 4–6.

————. "Politics in Illinois." *Collier's*, 24 October 1914, 21–22, 29.

Gould, Alan B. "Walter L. Fisher: Profile of an Urban Reformer." *Mid-American* 57 (1975): 151–72.

Grosser, Hugo S. "The Movement for Municipal Ownership in Chicago." *Annals of the American Academy of Political and Social Sciences* 27 (1906): 27–90.

Hale, William Bayard. "Chicago, Its Struggle and Its Dream." *World's Work* 19 (April 1910): 12792–805.

Havig, Alan R. "The Raymond Robins Case for Progressive Republicanism." *Journal of the Illinois State Historical Society* 64 (1971): 401–18.

"Immediate Municipal Ownership a Year After." *Review of the Reviews* 33 (May 1906): 549–54.

"Interview with Mr. Dalrymple." *Street Railway Journal*, 5 August 1905, 22–24.

Lindstrom, Andrew F. "Lawrence Stringer, A Wilson Democrat." *Journal of the Illinois State Historical Society* 66 (1973): 20–40.

Miller, Kristie. "Ruth Hanna McCormick and the Senatorial Election of 1930." *Illinois Historical Journal* 63 (1968): 191–210.

Morton, Richard A. "Edward F. Dunne: Illinois' Most Progressive Governor." *Illinois Historical Journal* 83 (1990): 218–34.

Murphy, Marjorie. "Taxation and Social Conflict: Teacher Unionism and Public School Finance in Chicago, 1989–1934." *Journal of the Illinois State Historical Society* 74 (1981): 242–60.

Powers, Stanley. "Chicago's Strike Ordeal." *World's Work* 10 (July 1905): 6378–84.

Roberts, Sidney I. "The Municipal Voters' League and Chicago Boodlers." *Journal of the Illinois State Historical Society* 53 (1960): 117–40.

Rogers, Walter S. "The Embarrassing Mr. Sullivan." *Harper's Weekly*, 24 October 1914, 394–95.

"Suffragette Conquest of Illinois." *Literary Digest*, 28 June 1913, 1409–11.

Tarbell, Ida. "How Chicago Is Finding Itself." Pts. 1 and 2. *American Magazine* (1908): 29–41, 124–38.

Trout, Grace Wilbur. "Side Lights on Illinois Suffrage History." *Journal of the Illinois State Historical Society* 13 (1920): 145–79.

Waller, Robert A. "The Illinois Waterway from Conception to Completion, 1908–1913." *Journal of the Illinois State Historical Society* 65 (1972): 121–41.

West, Roy O., and William C. Walton. "Charles S. Deneen, 1863–1940."*Journal of the Illinois Historical Society* 34 (1941): 12–25.

Wish, Harvey. "Governor Altgeld Pardons the Anarchists." *Journal of the Illinois State Historical Society* 31 (1938): 424–48.

Wrone, David R. "Illinois Pulls Out of the Mud." *Journal of the Illinois State Histori-cal Society* 58 (1965): 54–75.

Zventina, John A. Review of *Illinois, the Heart of the Nation*, by Edward F. Dunne. *Mid-America* 16, n.s., 5 (1934): 246.

Private Documents, Reports, and Bulletins

Anti-Saloon League of America. *The Anti-Saloon League Year-Book, 1909–1915.* Westerville, Ohio: The League, 1909–15.

Citizens Association of Chicago. *Forty-Second Annual Report.* Chicago: The Asso-ciation, 1916.

———. *Results of the Legislative Injunction Suit.* Bulletin 34. Chicago, 1916.

Civic Federation of Chicago. *Dangers of the Initiative and Referendum.* Bulletin 3. Chicago, 1911."

———. *Fifty Years on the Civic Front, 1893–1943: A Report on the Achievement of the Civic Federation, Chicago.* Chicago: The Federation, 1943.

———. *The Initiative and Referendum: A Public Danger.* Bulletin 4. Chicago, 1911.

———. *Legislative Report of the Civic Federation of Chicago, Covering the Regular Session of the Forty-Seventh General Assembly of Illinois.* Bulletin 5. Chicago, 1911.

Democratic National Convention. *Official Report of the Democratic National Con-vention, Baltimore, 1912.* Chicago: Peterson Lino-Typing, 1912.

Democratic Publishing Company, *Prominent Democrats of Illinois.* Chicago, 1899.

Dublin University Calendar. 1874, 1875.

Illinois State Automobile Association, *Illinois Highway Improvement.* Chicago: The Association, 1919.

National-American Woman Suffrage Association. *Forty-Fifth Annual Report.* New York: The Association, 1913.

Sikes, George S. "Why Edward F. Dunne Should Be Eliminated as a Candidate for Governor." Chicago: n.p., 1916.

Unpublished Manuscripts and Theses

Becker, Richard D. "Edward Dunne, Reform Mayor of Chicago, 1905–1907." Ph.D. diss., University of Chicago, 1971.

Beldon, Gertrude M. "A History of the Woman Suffrage Movement in Illinois." Master's thesis, University of Chicago, 1913.

Callendar, Richard W. "Walter L. Fisher, 1862–1935: The Regulation of Public utili-ties." Master's thesis, University of Illinois, 1963.

Eisenstein, Sophie J. "The Elections of 1912 in Chicago." Master's thesis, Univer-sity of Chicago, 1947.

Fisher, Walter L. "Autobiographic Sketch." [1932?] Illinois Historical Survey, Uni-versity of Illinois Library, Urbana-Champaign.

Green, Paul M. "The Chicago Democratic Party, 1840–1920: From Factionalism to Political Organization." Ph.D. diss., University of Chicago, 1975.

Lilly, Samuel A. "The Political Career of Roger Sullivan." Master's thesis, Eastern Illinois University, 1964.

McCarthy, Michael. "Businessmen and Professionals in Municipal Reform: The Chicago Experience, 1867–1920." Ph.D. diss., Northwestern University, 1970.

Morton, Richard A. "Descent into History: Chicago, Ideologies, and Repression, 1917–1918." Master's thesis, Eastern Illinois University, 1975.

Philip, William B. "Chicago and the Downstate: A Story of Their Conflict, 1870–1934." Ph.D. diss., University of Chicago. 1940.

Post, Louis F. "Living a Long Life Over Again." Louis Freeland Post Papers, Manuscript Division, Library of Congress, Washington, D.C.

Straetz, Ralph Arthur. "The Progressive Movement in Illinois, 1910–1916." Ph.D. diss., University of Illinois, 1958.

Thurner, Arthur W. "The Impact of Ethnic Groups on the Democratic Party in Chicago, 1920–1928." Ph.D. diss., University of Chicago, 1966.

Tingley, Ralph R. "From Carter Harrison II to Fred Busse: A Study of Chicago Political Parties and Personages from 1896 to 1907." Ph.D. diss., University of Chicago, 1950.

Warner, Mildred C. "The History of the Deep Waterway in the State of Illinois." Master's thesis, University of Illinois, 1947.

INDEX

RICHARD ALLEN MORTON received his doctorate in history from the University of Illinois at Urbana-Champaign. He is currently an associate professor of history at Clark Atlanta University in Atlanta, Georgia, where he specializes in American political history.